Solzhenitsyn

GIOVANNI GRAZZINI

Translated from the Italian by Eric Mosbacher

SPHERE BOOKS LIMITED
30/32 Gray's Inn Road, London WC1X 8JL

First published in Italy as *Solzenicyn*
Copyright © Longanesi & C., Milan 1971

This edition first published in Great Britain
by Michael Joseph Ltd 1973

Translation copyright © Michael Joseph Ltd and
Dell Publishing Co. Inc. 1973

First Sphere Books edition 1974

Set in Intertype Lectura

Printed in Great Britain by
Hazell Watson & Viney Ltd
Aylesbury, Bucks

ISBN 0 7221 3997 7

Giovanni Grazzini is a leading critic in Italy and works on the *Corriere della Sera*. He has won two Saint-Vincent prizes: in 1957 for an investigation of Soviet writers. In this book he has used Solzhenitsyn to illustrate the history of Russian literary intelligentsia since 1917, with a special emphasis on the period since 1946.

Dr. Grazzini also reveals the appalling conditions under which Soviet writers have had to work, controlled by the Kremlin's *Glavit* and the whims of carefully indoctrinated editors, ignorant of literature and subservient to every change in doctrinal wind. Solzhenitsyn's outspoken criticism of this tyranny, his defence of the writer's duty in spite of persecution and hindrance, his refusal to recant any of his comments, however distasteful to the Kremlin, his devotion to Leninism, his public scorn for the neo-Stalinists, his flat refusal to emigrate into exile, all these make of him a great and courageous man, quite regardless of his considerable literary talents.

PRINCIPAL DATES IN SOLZHENITSYN'S LIFE

1918, 11th December: Born at Kislovodsk.

1940: Marries Natalya Reshetovskaya.

1941, 18th October: Called up.

1942: Sent to the front.

1944: Reaches the rank of captain.

1945, February: Arrested and deprived of his rank by the military counter-espionage service.

1945: Sentenced by court-martial to eight years' forced labour and three years' banishment.

1945–49. In prison at Krasnaya Presnya.

1950–53: In Karlag labour camp at Dzhezkazgan.

1952, Summer: Operation for cancer of the stomach.

1953–56: Banished to Kazakhstan.

1954, Spring: Treatment in hospital at Tashkent.

1955: Begins *The First Circle*.

1956: Is released and settles at Ryazan as a teacher of physics and mathematics.

1957, 6th February: Rehabilitated by the Supreme Court.

1960: Writes *A Candle in the Wind* and *The Right Hand*.

1962: Begins *Cancer Ward*. *One Day in the Life of Ivan Denisovich* published in Moscow.

1963, January: *Matryona's Home* and *An Incident at Krechetovka Station* published in Moscow.

1963, July: *For the Good of the Cause* published in Moscow.

1964: *Stories and Prose Poems* published in Moscow.

1964, Christmas: Finishes *The First Circle*.

1965, 4th November: Article on Russian language published in Moscow.

1966, January: *Zakhar-Kalita* published in Moscow.

1966, Summer: Finishes *Cancer Ward*.

1966, November: The Writers' Union examines first part of *Cancer Ward*.

1967, May: Letter to fourth congress of the Writers' Union.

1967, September: Discussion at the secretariat of the Writers' Union.

1968: *Cancer Ward* published in Milan. *The First Circle* and *The Right Hand* published at Frankfurt.

1969: *Easter Procession, The Stag and the Camp Prostitute,* and *How They React to Ivan Denisovich* published at Frankfurt. *A Candle in the Wind* published in London.

1969, 4th November: Is expelled from the Writers' Union.

1969, 12th November: Letter of protest to the Writers' Union.

1970, 15th June: Protest against the arrest of Zhores Medvedev.

1970, 8th October: Is awarded Nobel Prize for Literature.

1970, 27th November: Letter to the Swedish Academy.

1972: *August 1914* published in the west.

Young man, make no mistake about it: your sufferings and these cruel years must not make you conclude that socialism is responsible. Whatever you may think history has rejected capitalism once and for all.

Cancer Ward, Chapter 31

CHAPTER ONE

On Tuesday 4th November, 1969 Solzhenitsyn rose early in his old wooden house in Yablochkaya Street at Ryazan. It was cold, and it was going to snow. He lit the small stove, swept outside the front door, and before she went out his wife Natalya left him a list of small domestic duties to perform. When the postman arrived, the three rooms were tidy, the country all round was silent, and he was sitting at his desk. Among the correspondence was an urgent summons to attend the local branch of the Writers' Union at three p.m. that day. 'You had better be there, things are going badly,' a colleague had warned him the day before. Never mind which way they were going, the great thing was that at last something was going to happen; for months and years he had been living in uncertainty, aggravated by having to stand up, not only to the persecutions and slanders of the neo-Stalinists, who regarded him as their country's most perfidious enemy, but also to the temptation of symbolising the blindest anti-communism, as those of his friends, not all of them disinterested, who urged him to exploit the rôle of prophet and victim, would have liked him to do. He arrived at the meeting punctually. Safonov, the branch secretary, was not present (to avoid compromising himself, he had chosen that day to have a minor operation) but, so that there should be the necessary quorum, his place was taken by Nikolai Rodin, who had been sent for urgently from a distant hospital. The meeting began promptly. Those present, apart from Solzhenitsyn and Rodin, were Sergei Baranov (in the chair), Evgeny Markin, Vasily Matushkin, the editor Povarenkin, the novelist Frantz Taurin, representing the federal secretary of the union, Alexander Sergeyevich Kozhevnikov, the propaganda secretary for the regional committee of the party, and Nikolai Levchenko, an official. The first speaker was Frantz Taurin. The meeting, he said, was one of a series organised with a view to strengthening the communist consciousness of authors. Since Kuznetsov's disgraceful flight to the west, there had been other symptoms of restlessness amongst Soviet writers. The most restless were Leo Kopelev, Lidya Chukovskaya, and Bulat Okudzhava. What was the situation at Ryazan? Let them discuss Solzhenitsyn, who was a member of the branch and was present. Who had anything to say?

The elderly Vasily Matushkin, a member of the branch, rose and spoke in tired and embittered tones. He said he was disappointed with Solzhenitsyn. 'After assuming responsibility for having had him admitted to the branch twelve years ago, I must confess that I have regretted it,' he said. 'I first had doubts about him when *One Day in the Life of Ivan Denisovich* was published. However, I was reassured by the reception given to the novel by authoritative colleagues such as Tvardovsky and Simonov, and I reverted to hopefulness that Solzhenitsyn would do honour to our branch. But in the course of time I have had to change my mind again. Solzhenitsyn has not taken part in our work, has not helped our younger colleagues, has not attended meetings. As for his latest works, all we know is that they go in a direction opposite to our own.'

Nikolai Rodin, a member of the Kasimov branch of the Writers' Union, agreed. 'Solzhenitsyn has not respected the rules, has taken no account of our association, has refused to read the manuscript of a young beginner.' Sergei Baranov, also of Ryazan, was even more severe. 'What is membership for if not to help the young?' he said. 'Also, let us have another look at *One Day* and *Matryona's Home*. The former does nothing but paint the world black, and the principal character in the latter is totally unreal; who in our country ever heard of a woman being abandoned completely to her own resources, with no-one in the world to help her? Solzhenitsyn is said to have published other books since, but where? What are they about? Here nothing it known about them.'

The fourth speaker, Evgeny Markin, also of the Ryazan branch, momentarily interrupted the flow of denunciation. 'Let us be careful not to go from one extreme to the other,' he said. 'In our country we always go too far. First we revile Yesenin, and then we laud him to the skies. Today we condemn Solzhenitsyn, and perhaps tomorrow we shall have to rehabilitate him. I don't like it, I don't want to have anything to do with it. But I agree in criticising him for not having taken part in our social life.' In spite of his reservations, Markin sided with the majority, as did his colleague Levchenko.

After a further attack on him by Povarenkin, who said: 'This man is black at heart, he soils whatever he touches,' it was Solzhenitsyn's turn to speak. 'There is no need for Comrade

Matushkin to feel any weight on his mind,' he said. 'He did not recommend me to the branch, he merely sent me a membership application form. As for young writers, when have I been asked to give an opinion of their manuscripts? I have always kept the secretary Safonov informed of the letters I wrote to the Writers' Union; I even suggested a public discussion of *Cancer Ward* here, at Ryazan. It is not I, though I live for the greater part of the year near Moscow, who have kept away from the branch, but the branch that has always refused to accept my suggestions. I have always replied to everyone, except to the *Literaturnaya Gazeta*, when it held up Kozhevnikov to me as an example of good conduct; that was in an anonymous article, which went to the extreme of throwing doubt on my rehabilitation and, among a great many other lies, stated that *The First Circle* was a slanderous work. But who said so? There are those who condemn the novel without having read it. Incidentally, how did the *Literaturnaya Gazeta* come to know about *The Feast of the Victors*, the play I wrote in the labour camp and the only typed copy of which was confiscated by the police when they ransacked my files? The situation is that generally I am denounced for works that I now repudiate, while no-one ever mentions those I fail to get published.

'Let us deal with *Cancer Ward*,' Solzhenitsyn continued, raising his voice. 'In September 1967 I informed the secretary of the union that the novel was circulating in typescript and that at any moment it might be taken abroad. To avoid that, it would be sufficient for it to appear immediately in *Novy Mir*. The secretary of the union preferred to do nothing, and thus we come to the spring of 1968, when I wrote to the *Literaturnaya Gazeta* and *Le Monde* and *Unità* to say that I denied foreign publishers the right to publish the novel. You know what happened; the letter to *Le Monde*, though registered, was not sent, and that to *Unità*, which I handed to the Italian critic Vittorio Strada, was confiscated by the customs at Moscow airport. Only later did I succeed in persuading the frontier guards to forward it (and in fact *Unità* published it in June). Meanwhile the *Literaturnaya Gazeta* did nothing. What was it waiting for? For nine weeks, from 21st April to 26th June, it concealed the letter from the public. It was waiting for *Cancer Ward* to be published in the west. Sure enough, when the book was published by Alberto Mondadori in a horrible Russian edition, the journal decided to publish my letter, accusing me of not having protested with sufficient energy. If my thoughts had been made public at the end of April, it might have been different. Evidence of this is that the American publishers Dutton and Praeger renounced publication of the book when my repudiation came to their notice.'

Solzhenitsyn had been talking for twenty minutes, and the chairman tried to interrupt him. Solzhenitsyn asked for another ten minutes, but was allowed only three. 'I asked the Ministry of Communications to stop interfering with my personal correspondence,' he went on. 'The only result was that on my fiftieth birthday, when good wishes were sent to me by way of the Writers' Union from all over the world, the secretary did not forward my mail. . . . You accuse me of blackening reality. Can you tell me according to what theory of knowledge the reflection of an object is more important than the object itself? In the philosophy of ghosts, perhaps, but certainly not in dialectical materialism. We have got to the point when what matters is not what we do, but what is said about it. . . . Our basic problem is that of truth. You will not succeed in hiding for ever the crimes against millions of people committed by Stalin. Do you have any idea at least of the type of corruption you are exercising on the young by denying the crimes of Stalin? Do you believe that the young are stupid, and that they do not understand? As for myself, I do not repudiate a single word of what I wrote in the letter to the Writers' Congress in May 1967. I am perfectly tranquil in my mind. I know that I shall do my duty as a writer in all circumstances, and perhaps with greater success dead than alive. No-one will ever succeed in blocking the path to truth. I am ready to die so that it shall triumph. Yes, I am prepared to die, not just to be expelled from the Writers' Union. Do you wish to vote? Vote then, you are the majority, but do not forget that this meeting will leave traces in the history of literature.'

After some further exchanges ('Why do you publish your books in the west?' 'You tell me why you do not publish my books in Russia.') Kozhevnikov, who in the meantime had given due instructions to the members of the party present, reiterated the charge that Solzhenitsyn ignored the directing rôle of the party that all other writers acknowledged, and Taurin delivered a summing-up. 'The conclusion is that Solzhenitsyn has not reacted against the enemy. No-one desires to humiliate him; we called this meeting in order to help him to free himself of the burdens imposed on him by the west. Fedin, the First Secretary of the Writers' Union, himself implored him, with all the authority of his age, to yield, decisively to reject the manoeuvres of the west. If he is unwilling to accept our advice, we have no alternative but to expel him from the Writers' Union.' The resolution was ready, having been typed in advance.

'This meeting,' it said, 'resolves to expel Solzhenitsyn from the Writers' Union for anti-social behaviour in conflict with the union's aims, and for grave violation of the fundamental articles of its constitution.' 'Who is in favour?' asked the chairman, addressing the six members of the Ryazan branch. Five arms were raised. Solzhenitsyn, motionless, looked at his colleagues. At heart some of them hoped he too would raise his arm, thus accepting his expulsion and admitting he was wrong, but they were disappointed. By now it was 4.30.

A telephone call to Moscow spread the news. Friends and enemies immediately appreciated the importance of what had happened. Solzhenitsyn, expelled from the Writers' Union, no longer enjoyed the benefits granted by the state to its members. He could keep his houses at Ryazan and Obninsk, but had lost the right to travel permits and facilities, and the privilege of using the union's reading room and library, the only place in Moscow where it was sometimes possible to see foreign publications unavailable in the bookshops. But these were trifling matters. The prospect of seeing his works in print in his own country had now vanished. Legally he was not forbidden to write or to be published, but no journal or publisher was likely to publish the works of such a black sheep. Deprived of his professional income, he could be accused of parasitism and banished as an enemy of the people.

By the same token the internal and external enemies of the régime would be able to hold him up as the most illustrious victim of intolerance, make him a symbol of the freedom of the arts, the freedom of the intellect that refuses to bow to any threat; his refusal to confess his guilt, to line up with the weak who in similar circumstances ate humble pie and acknowledged the party's right to silence artists, would serve as an example to the wavering who whispered to each other in editorial offices, in the houses of trusted friends or, most frequently, in the street; it would kindle other spirits, reinforce the protest front, enlarge the cracks in the communist *bloc*.

Abroad it would rouse the indignation of a public opinion that was still horrified at the military occupation of Czechoslovakia and remembered the Pasternak case. It even represented a potential threat to the whole policy of the Kremlin which, pending clarification of Soviet relations with Peking, was aimed at a truce with the west and re-establishing shattered communist unity. There were those who feared this and those who wanted it. What would be the reaction at home and abroad of the young, who continued to see in the struggle between the hawks and doves in Moscow the embarrassments of an ideology on which they had set their young hopes? What would happen in Italy and France, where the communist parties, accused of rhetorical obsequiousness to the Kremlin's word, had been overtaken on the left by new generations that had allied themselves with old champions of national communism in hatred of the bureaucratic centralism of Moscow and with the new standard-bearers of Maoism in hatred of the consumer society, peaceful co-existence and rationalism?

The name of Solzhenitsyn was now known throughout the world. To many he was the greatest living Russian writer, the only one to have picked up Pasternak's heritage. There was already talk of his name being put forward for the Nobel Prize. Only one of his books, *One Day in the Life of Ivan Denisovich*, had been published in the Soviet Union, and it had sold like hot cakes, but no-one could tell how many copies of his other works were in circulation, either in typescript or in clandestine Russian editions published in the west. There was a flourishing black market in them; one of his English translators, Nicholas Bethel, said on returning from Moscow that the price of a copy of *Cancer Ward* or *The First Circle* in 1970 was eighty roubles, the monthly wage of an unskilled worker.

To anyone of literary discrimination it was clear that here was a writer of high quality. His language was unsophisticated, he seemed totally unaffected by the experiments of the literary *avant-garde*, but even those who thought his writing old-fashioned recognised in him a moral sense, a civil courage, a narrative force, a European breath that stood out in the grey and banal landscape of contemporary Soviet literature. Among the Soviet writers who unlocked the drawers of their desks after the Twentieth Congress and denounced in prose and verse Stalin's reign of terror, the abuses of the Soviet hierarchy, the sufferings of the people, he was the only one to attain inter-

14

national stature. He had been prevented from publishing his major works, and had now been expelled from the Writers' Union. Was this not compounding the error the régime committed when it missed the opportunity of presenting itself to the world as being secure enough to permit itself the luxury of displaying this literary star in its buttonhole?

What would be the domestic reaction of those intellectuals of undoubted communist faith who regarded the liberty of artistic expression as an essential part of the Marxist-Leninist ideology and regarded the repressive action of the Stalinists as a brake on the development and export of the revolution? The popular democracies were already impatient with Soviet political and economic imperialism, and national pride was at work in them, and the process of the liberalisation of culture that was already under way in those countries, so far from threatening to undermine the system, seemed actually to be enriching and consolidating it.

What would be the reaction in those countries? Again, in comparison with practitioners of the arts, scientists and technocrats enjoyed a notable degree of freedom, because their work did not impinge directly on mass political opinion (or rather, in view of the Soviet triumphs in space and the country's increasing prosperity, seemed the most flattering reflection of the policy of the régime). What would these people make of it? Would not Solzhenitsyn's expulsion widen the gap between authors and scientists, giving the latter a position of privilege which, with the advance of technology, would encroach on wider and wider areas of the politicians' power?

Finally, was not striking at intellectual liberty through Solzhenitsyn making a desert of an area that should (however cautiously) be cultivated with a view to restoring to literature and the arts the penetrative power indispensable for the education of minds beguiled by the hope of a less dreary life?

All these were questions that crowded into the minds of intellectuals and bureaucrats, party members, the lukewarm, and all those who rubbed their hands with glee whenever the régime dropped the shovel on its own toes – questions implicit in which were all the tragic unknowns about the country's destiny, the doubts about the road embarked upon by the men who used art, culture, perhaps life itself, as pawns in a sinister struggle for power inside the Kremlin. But was the news really true? What were the reasons behind it? Decisions of the Ryazan branch of the Writers' Union had to be ratified by the federal secretariat in Moscow. Might there yet be second thoughts?

Next morning foreign and Soviet journalists, curious Muscovites, friends of Solzhenitsyn, went to the Writers' Union to find out what they could. They did not use the Vorovskova Street entrance to the rather forbidding building, with its dark and heavy door, where the atmosphere of the high bureaucracy prevailed; instead they used the other entrance, in Gerchen Street, where the Writers' Club was. Here the door was always open, there was an atmosphere of animation and bustle, and it was generally easy to find familiar faces and to pick up information. Today, however, everyone was reticent and in a hurry, a sure sign that the news was out, but that it was much too hot a potato for anyone to be willing to comment on it in public. So the journalists formally approached one of the union officials. The man was tired and irritable. 'Nothing is known here,' he replied. 'Read the newspapers.' In reality of course he knew everything, but had orders to say nothing. The anniversary of the revolution was due in three days' time, on 7th November, and to avoid disturbing the celebrations it had been decided to postpone for a week the announcement of the Ryazan decision, which in any case had to be ratified by the council of heads of branches, which was to meet in Moscow on 6th November. In the circumstances the outcome was not difficult to foresee but, after all, you never could tell; some totally unexpected turn of events was not beyond the bounds of possibility, somebody might be organising a *coup* behind the scenes. The stakes were high, and it was better to be on the safe side. If Solzhenitsyn appeared and defended himself in person he would raise his voice; caution and prudence were indicated.

But would Solzhenitsyn have appeared? Did they want him to or not? Did they send him a formal invitation, making sure it would arrive too late? All these are questions that it will be possible to answer only when we know the complete facts. For the time being the versions are conflicting; according to some, Solzhenitsyn received no written invitation; according to others, he said he received a telegram at Ryazan at 11.30 on 6th November, barely two hours before the meeting began, i.e., too late to make the four-hour train journey to Moscow. If the latter version is accepted, there are at least two possibilities: that the telegram was sent from Moscow in good time but was delivered late by order of the police (in the spirit of the 'postal pillage' previously denounced by Solzhenitsyn) or as the result of negligence in the postal service; or that, to fulfil a formal obligation, it was sent from Moscow at the last moment in full awareness that by the time it arrived Solzhenitsyn would have missed the train. There seems less foundation for a third possibility, namely that Solzhenitsyn, having been informed that the telegram was coming, deliberately went out and found it waiting for him on his return, when it was too late to leave for Moscow. He had more to gain from another verbal encounter with his accusers than from any further evidence of their bad faith. Unlike his enemies, most of whom were officials with a taste for deviousness, he had hitherto conducted his battles openly. We should not be surprised if one day the 'Solzhenitsyn telegram mystery', were cleared up and responsibility were attributed equally to the malice of the senders and the inefficiency of the Soviet postal service.

But let us stick to the hard facts. After a private meeting on 5th November, the union executive met officially on 6th November, on the eve of the fifty-second anniversary of the October Revolution, and Solzhenitsyn was not present. Frantz Taurin reported the decision reached at Ryazan, and the discussion that followed was less lively than might have been feared or hoped; reopening the whole case, going into all its aspects, would have involved the risk of putting new arguments into the hands of Solzhenitsyn's friends. Tvardovsky, the editor of *Novy Mir*, was allowed the time necessary to restate the arguments that the opposition with pathetic insistence had been reiterating for years, after which the majority readily agreed that this was a case for the application of Article III of the union's constitution, which provides for a member's expulsion if his actions conflict with the construction of socialism or he has committed actions of an anti-Soviet and anti-social nature. The resolution expelling him was duly confirmed, Solzhenitsyn was duly informed on 10th November, and the news was officially published two days later in the *Literaturnaya Gazeta* (in fifty-four lines under a double-column heading at the bottom of page three). It said:

'A meeting has been held at the Ryazan Union on the problem of the intensification of ideological work. Those who took part in the discussion emphasised that in present-day conditions the ideological struggle has grown more acute all over the world and that every Soviet writer must be more responsible in his actions and writings. In this connection those present raised the case of their colleague Solzhenitsyn. It was unanimously noted that Solzhenitsyn's behaviour was of an anti-social nature and conflicted radically with the principles of the constitution of the Writers' Union of the Soviet Union. As is known, in recent years the name and works of Alexander Solzhenitsyn have been actively exploited by hostile bourgeois propaganda to stage a campaign of calumnies against our country. In spite of this, Solzhenitsyn has not only taken a public stand but, notwithstanding the criticism made of him by Soviet public opinion and the repeated recommendations of the Writers' Union, has by certain of his actions and statements contributed to fanning the flames of anti-Soviet sensationalism that has been built up round his name.'

Solzhenitsyn counter-attacked on the same day in a letter copies of which were passed from hand to hand two days later. 'It is disgraceful,' he wrote to the Writers' Union, 'that you should have trampled on your constitution in this way. You expelled me in a violent hurry in my absence, without even summoning me by telegram, without even allowing me the four hours necessary to travel from Ryazan to attend the meeting. You thus clearly demonstrated that decision preceded discussion. Was it easier to invent new charges in my absence? Were you afraid of having to grant me ten minutes in which to reply? Thus I am compelled to substitute this letter for my reply. Blow the dust off the clocks. Your watches are behind the times. Draw aside the heavy curtains that are so dear to you. You do not even suspect that outside the day has dawned. These are no longer the sombre, gloomy and hopeless times in which you were able to expel Akhmatova, nor are they the timid and weakly times when you threw out Pasternak, showering him with abuse. Was not that disgrace sufficient for you? Do you wish to aggravate it? The time is near when each of you will try to erase his signature from the report of today's deliberations. Blind leading the blind as you are, you do not even realise that you are going in the direction opposite to that which you announced. In these times of crisis you are incapable of offering our gravely sick society anything constructive, anything good, anything but your hatred, your suspicious vigilance, your "standing firm without weakening".

'Your pompous articles fall apart, your stupidity shows some signs of life, but you have no arguments; all you have is your votes and your administrative measures. That is why neither Sholokhov nor any of you dared reply to the letter from Lidya Chukovskaya, who is the pride of Russian committed literature. But the administrative pincers will soon close on her. How could she dare to allow a book that has not been legally published to be read? When the authorities have once decided not to publish you, stifle yourself, choke yourself, cease to exist, do not allow anyone to read you.

'The expulsion is also being prepared of Leo Kopelev, a former front-line combatant who spent ten years in labour camps though he was innocent. But now he is guilty, because he intervened in favour of a man who was persecuted and revealed the hallowed secrets of a conversation he had with an important personage. But why do you have these conversations which you hide from the people? Was it not promised fifty years ago that there would be no more secret diplomacy, no more secret treaties, no more secret and incomprehensible appointments and dismissals? And that the masses would be enabled to discuss everything openly?

'Your excuse is that the enemy is listening. Eternal, omnipresent "enemies" provide a facile excuse for your functions and your very existence. As if there were no enemies at the time when we were promised that the truth would be spoken always and at once. But what would you do without enemies? You could not even live without them. Hatred, a kind of hatred that in no way falls short of racial hatred, has become the sterile atmosphere in which you live. That is the way in which the sense of a single common humanity is lost and its end is hastened. If tomorrow the Antarctic ice melted, the whole of humanity would be drowned, and in whose face would you then fling your ideas of the class struggle? To say nothing of what would happen if a few surviving bipeds were left wandering and dying on an earth that had become radioactive. It is time to remember that we belong in the first place to humanity, that men are distinguished from the animal kingdom by thought and speech. And that they must naturally be free. And that, if men are put in chains, we return to the animal state. Openness, honest and complete openness, is the first condition for the health of every society, including our own. Those who do not want it care nothing for the fate of their country and think only for their own account. Those who do not want it do not wish even to heal their country's wounds, but only to let them fester.'

This put the fat in the fire. Typewritten accounts of the Ryazan meeting and copies of Solzhenitsyn's letter were passed from hand to hand, spread to the minor cities of the Soviet Union, crossed the frontiers and reached the west. The unanimous impression was that the Kremlin hawks had caused the union officials to take a step that once more illustrated the inferiority complex of men who, still feeling themselves to be under siege and fearing having to surrender, tried to exorcise the danger by burning Cassandra. Only the hardened Stalinists, who had always refused to attribute the tyrant's crimes to the system itself, applauded Solzhenitsyn's expulsion and smiled at the prophecies of doom contained in his letter. Most people shuddered, measuring in their dismay the gap that separated them from the free and just society for which their doctrine stood. Some writers not yet silenced by revulsion and fear (Bulat Okudzhava, Boris Mozhaev, Sergei Antonov, Georgy Vladimov, Anatoly Gradilin) called for an immediate meeting of the union to discuss the case. Others, about forty of them, sent a letter of protest to the union (but only some weeks later, on 19th December), pointing out that the excommunication of a writer who was not a member of the party, and for opinions that were not concerned with the party, was a new and alarming sign of Stalinism. Abroad the most restless communist parties, the Italian and the French, showed signs of indocility.

In Rome the communist *Unità* showed concern as early as 11th November. 'There have been reports for several days past that Solzhenitsyn has been expelled,' it said. 'We are not in a position either to confirm or deny them. We still hope they will be denied, or in any case that the central council of the union will consider the significance they would have to men of culture, including those outside the USSR. What we are sure of, since we have had the opportunity of reading his books, is that Solzhenitsyn is a genuine writer. The Writers' Union will certainly not be able to deprive him of his talent and this qualification of his, even if it is able to exercise its formal right to remove him from its ranks. What we consider graver is that this right that the union possesses may be accompanied by the much more substantial one of not permitting him to publish his works. The fact that we do not share *en bloc* every

20

opinion and position adopted by him does not influence our position in this matter.'

On 18th November *The Times* of London published a letter signed by thirty writers, including Arthur Miller, Rolf Hochhuth, Graham Greene, Julian Huxley, Philip Toynbee, Muriel Spark, Pierre Emmanuel, Günter Grass, Mary McCarthy and William Sansom. 'The treatment of Soviet writers in their own country has become an international scandal,' it said. 'We now learn with dismay of the expulsion from the Soviet Writers' Union of Alexander Solzhenitsyn, the one writer in Russia who in the words of Arthur Miller, "is unanimously regarded as a classic". The two great poets who were previously so expelled were Anna Akhmatova and Boris Pasternak. One understands Solzhenitsyn's bitter exclamation: "Was this not enough for you!" The silencing of a writer of Solzhenitsyn's stature is in itself a crime against civilisation. We do not know whether any other steps are contemplated in this new witch-hunt. We can only hope that there is no repetition of the Sinyavsky-Daniel trial. Judging by experience, verbal protests do not sufficiently impress the Soviet authorities. We appeal to them, however, to stop persecuting Solzhenitsyn. Should this appeal fail, we shall see no other way but to call upon the writers of the world to conduct an international cultural boycott of a country which chooses to put itself beyond the pale of civilisation until such time as it abandons the barbaric treatment of its writers and artists.'

Next day it was the French turn. A statement by the National Committee of French Writers, an organisation closely linked to the Communist Party, published a statement in *Les Lettres Françaises* signed among others by Louis Aragon, Elsa Triolet, Jean-Paul Sartre, Michel Butor, Vladimir Pozner, Vercors, Artur Adamov, Christiane Rochefort and Jean-Louis Bory. 'The expulsion of Solzhenitsyn', it said, 'constitutes in the eyes of the whole world a gross error that is not limited to damaging the Soviet Union but contributes to confirming the idea of socialism that is propagated by its enemies. We believe we are in a position to state that in the past the most reasonable men at the highest levels of power deeply regretted the similar error committed in relation to Pasternak. Is it really necessary that the great writers of the USSR should be treated as dangerous elements? That would be incomprehensible, were it not obvious that through them and certain of their colleagues it is desired to strike, not only at all writers, but at intellectuals in general, to force them into being soldiers marching in parade step. Who would have believed that today, in the fatherland of triumphant socialism, a step that even a Nicholas II would not have considered taking against Chekhov has been taken against the writer who is most characteristic of the great Russian tradition, who has already once been a victim of Stalinist oppression, and whose essential crime is that of having survived it? Is it necessary to remind our Soviet colleagues that the signatures appended by certain of their predecessors to similar expulsions opened the way to the hangman? We still wish to believe that, as at the time of the fury unleashed by a committee that dared to crown the greatest poet then living, Pasternak, there still exist today among the high councils of the nation to which we owe the October dawn and the defeat of Hitlerian Fascism individuals capable of realising the mistake that has been committed and of preventing its effects.'

Official reactions to internal and external protests were extremely violent. In a telegram of 25th November Konstantin Fedin, simulating total incomprehension of the real terms of the problem, of the impact of the Solzhenitsyn case on the writer's position in contemporary society, replied to David Carver, the International Secretary of the Pen Club, that the Writers' Union could not tolerate unwarrantable interference in its domestic affairs. He informed the press that the resolutions and appeals signed in the west were shameful provocations by enemies of the people and stupid attempts to produce cracks in the solidity of the Soviet front. *Literaturnaya Gazeta* followed this up next day by publishing a statement by the union intended to stifle further discussion and gag those who were showing concern at the expulsion, whether in good faith or bad. Taking Solzhenitsyn's unpublished letter of 12th November as read, it said that the step had been taken in full accordance with the union's rules; and it added that, though a telegram had been sent summoning him to the meeting on 6th November, he had deliberately absented himself. 'Anything to the contrary that Solzhenitsyn may say is a lie,' the statement went on, and it added that 'by his actions and statements he has in fact joined forces with those of the enemies of the Soviet social system. . . . His letter of 12th November is evidence of his complete lack of respect for the civil powers, of his having passed over to positions hostile to the cause of socialism. . . . It is presumptuous, full of insults, threats, pseudo-theoretical claptrap already used in the ideological struggle against socialism. . . . It confirms that the expulsion was necessary, right and inevitable.'

Thus the appeals by western communists were rejected as irrelevant, the result of an error in political outlook, a trap set by the capitalist world; and the allegation that Solzhenitsyn had allied himself with Moscow's enemies laid the basis for bringing him to trial, should it be so decided, on charges that might put him back in a labour camp, while the Italian and French communist parties were charged with adopting the arguments of their enemies. Loyally adhering to an ideological standpoint now fossilised in time and space, the union refused to discuss the arguments of Solzhenitsyn and his supporters; the liberty of culture, respect for democratic forms, tolerance of minorities, were bourgeois myths for which revisionists in the guise of western communists were willing to sacrifice the glory of the Soviet empire. Nevertheless, this time Moscow did not, could not, go beyond the bounds set by public opinion. Why did Solzhenitsyn not go abroad? 'No-one is detaining him or preventing him from going,' the statement said, 'even if he desires to go where his anti-Soviet works and letters are invariably received with so much satisfaction.'

There was nothing new about this hint (Pasternak and Valery Tarsis had similarly been invited to take their departure, and the latter had accepted the suggestion, with the result that he was deprived of Soviet citizenship); but this time it was above all a cry of alarm at not being strong enough to take legal proceedings that might have ended disastrously for the prosecution. If Solzhenitsyn went abroad the west would receive him as a martyr, would build him golden bridges. That would suit Moscow's book, providing confirmation of his 'treachery' and ridding it of a pest that, from the point of view of Kremlin absolutism, was less harmful to the Soviet organism than the anti-Soviet germs he would spread in other countries. That being the course that the Soviet authorities would have preferred, he refused to take it; the humiliations and risks of life in Russia were worth more to him than life in gilded exile.

It is true, however, that western protests at the Soviet suppression of the liberty of the arts (on 3rd December solidarity with Solzhenitsyn was expressed by another sixteen well known intellectuals, including Updike, Capote, Fuentes, Mishima,

23

Dürrenmatt, Böll, Vonnegut and Stravinsky) have very different effects depending on the stature of the individuals being persecuted by the régime. In the case of relatively unknown authors, whose value the international public has no means of judging and whom, therefore, it is easier to pass off as mythomaniacs in search of publicity, if not actually *agents-provocateurs*, foreign appeals can be actually counter-productive; the authorities' attitude hardens, the judge is irritated, and the sentences are heavier. But in the case of Solzhenitsyn, whose fame was now world-wide, the boot was on the other foot. The chorus of denunciation raised in the west, combined with the protests at home, caused such a stir that a trial, resulting in the inevitable sentence to a labour camp, would have had domestic political repercussions that the ruling group in the Kremlin might have had difficulty in keeping under control.

The whole context in which the Solzhenitsyn case is embedded is much more complicated than might appear at first sight. Those who greet the action taken in Moscow against writers with satisfaction, because they see in it the self-condemnation of the communist régime, often forget that, like the measures taken against liberals in eighteenth-century Italy, it is the outcome of a desire to repress that would not be so violent if the signs of rebellion at the base were not so vigorous and so frequent. Soviet communism, particularly among those too young to have undergone the brain-washing of the Stalin years, has produced from within itself a kind of liberal conscience, centred on the problem of the liberty of expression and civil rights; and the progress of this development is exactly proportionate to the extent to which each member of Soviet society has been virtually cured of the persecution mania from which the groups in power who grew up under the Stalin influence still suffer. The inability to tolerate writers who do not follow the directives imposed from above derives from inability to tolerate criticism, fear of its introducing the germs of reformism into the system. The cultural level, the ideological sclerosis, of the governing oligarchy are such that any suggested liberal change, any suggestion that the base might contribute to the working out of a new political line, any polemical utterance about the errors committed by Stalin, is greeted, not as a spontaneous impulse towards the renovation of structures that need to be brought into line with a public consciousness in which an irreversible process of democratic development is taking place, but as a highly suspect pheno-menon that must be ruthlessly crushed as a threat to the power of the people.

Decentralisation of cultural opinion, with the resulting multiplicity of initiatives, is regarded as a threat to the leading rôle of the party, whose interests have to be identified with what the governing *élite* decides are the interests of the state, and minorities are silenced on the ground that opposing the hierarchy is equivalent to playing the game of the country's enemies. Concern for preserving the unity of an empire in which national impulses are very much alive means that literary 'cases' rouse alarm to an extent proportionate to their capacity for making an impact on the system of controls inherited from Stalin and reimposed by the joint leadership after Khrushchev's crude, incautious but effective shake-up. That explains why the Kremlin's cultural policy raises a kind of rubber wall round Solzhenitsyn off which protests, described as inspired by anti-Soviet hatred, bounce ineffectually; and for the same reason it minimises the damaging repercussions on the communist parties in the west. Having abandoned hope of exporting the revolution in Marxist-Leninist forms, the fac-tions that face each other in the Kremlin expend their energies in a struggle for power in which the contempt for the intelli-gentsia felt by the traditional politician is left far behind.

Any kind of international cooperation that can be exploited for prestige purposes, simulating a paternal tolerance for the contacts of harmless groups of specialists, for instance, is acceptable so long as it does not claim to adapt to Soviet realities certain principles such as that of the free circulation of works of talent. Moscow has interpreted these principles once and for all, identifying liberty with the prohibition of opposi-tion to the decisions made, whether in good faith or in bad, by the régime's controllers and denying to the producers of certain works, not just talent, but that minimum of rationality sufficient to protect them from the risk of being sent to a mental hospital.

The relations between the Soviet Union and the European Writers' Community (Comes) should be regarded in this light. The first president of this organisation was the Italian poet Ungaretti and, with more than 2,000 members all over the world, it seemed that it would be able to do a useful job of *rapprochement* in bringing together cultural producers of different ideological origins in the years of relaxation of tension, and in fact to an extent it did such a job.

All its activities were suspended at the time of the Soviet occupation of Czechoslovakia, because of the impossibility of securing the agreement of east European writers to a statement expressing solidarity with their Czech colleagues. At the end of 1969 the organisation tried to resume a dialogue with the Soviet Union that seemed to it to be the more necessary 'inasmuch as in every country of the world social, political, ideological, religious, cultural and artistic problems are becoming more insistent and more disquieting, but also the more fertile for that reason'. Whether the moment for this was well chosen or not, and how much value Moscow attached to a dialogue based on supra-national respect for the dignity and authority of writers, was shown by Solzhenitsyn's expulsion. 'Unfortunately,' Comes declared in a statement published on 30th November, 'Solzhenitsyn's expulsion from the Soviet Writers' Union, with all the grave dangers that consequently threaten him as a writer and a man, to the point of making him an exile in his own country, not only makes a return to the hoped-for cooperation remote but perhaps, alas, makes it impossible. On the other hand, Comes would with its own hands be wiping out ten years' concrete work, would be betraying the cause of literature itself (which, as Solzhenitsyn has taught, is not a form of "cosmetics"), and would be insulting the conscience of all the writers of Europe as well as that of Soviet writers themselves, if it did not loudly protest, in spite of its enforced formal inactivity, against the persecution of Solzhenitsyn, even though it is well aware that this, like all other protests, will be vain and that the various bureaucrats of the Writers' Union will redouble their accusations against Solzhenitsyn the more deeply felt is our total solidarity with him, his person, his work and the example of his courage.'

The statement paid tribute to the Soviet writers (more than 300 of them) who defied Solzhenitsyn's persecutors and pointed out that in several European countries, from Greece to Portugal, from Czechoslovakia to Spain, writers were living under ever greater threats and were subjected to greater and greater coercion, and that this also applied to Jewish intellectuals in Poland; and it concluded by expressing the hope that the persecution of Solzhenitsyn would cease or at any rate diminish. Otherwise the organisation would suspend all collaboration with Soviet writers, though it declared itself ready to do everything in its power to preserve and renew cultural dialogue in Europe, 'comforted by the fact that in the USSR writers not unworthy of the name have honourably dissociated themselves from the disgraceful manoeuvres of the official apparatus of a Writers' Union that has expelled the most worthy and greatest Soviet writer of recent years.'

This statement by Comes naturally embittered the struggle inside the Writers' Union. The secretariat, in a hothouse atmosphere made stifling by its mistrust of foreigners and its habit of regarding its own less submissive members as an enemy fifth column, felt assailed on every side, particularly as Peking had seized the opportunity to hail Solzhenitsyn as a victim of bureaucratic centralism. It shifted its tactics, and began acknowledging the quality of his writing, which of course made his guilt the greater. On 3rd December the secretariat of the Moscow branch, with Sobolyev in the chair, unanimously declared that 'a writer who by his activity contributes to reinforcing anti-Soviet propaganda sides with the enemies of the country'. At a meeting of the House of Trade Unions on December 3, Mikhalkov, one of the secretaries of the union, said: 'It is deplorable that this professionally gifted man of letters should have failed to acknowledge his wretched rôle as special envoy of many western organisations and institutions and should have voluntarily excluded himself from the union's ranks.'

In an interview in the *Toronto Telegram* at the beginning of January 1970 this same Mikhalkov justified the Soviet treatment of holders of minority views in unequivocal terms. He said that Solzhenitsyn's standpoint, based on personal opinions, clashed with that of the majority of the members of the Writers' Union. That was the reason why he was no longer a member. If an artist's opinions were in total conflict with the opinions and ideals of the majority, a clash was inevitable, and that was the situation in his case. A writer who was not ideologically mature was one who had not attained the level of the *avant-garde* social conscience. The freedom of the creative arts was a bourgeois idea; it did not exist even in the west, where the artist was subjected to the pressures of a system with which he might be in disagreement, but on which he was completely dependent. As for bourgeois art, it was well known that it was characterised by scepticism, pessimism, cynicism,

CHAPTER TWO

The preamble to the conditions of service imposed on Soviet writers remains the obligation to smile that was imposed on them about forty years ago. Notions such as this generally form part of the propaganda that uses irony to make up for misinformation and conceals in anti-communist insults the remorse felt for the damage produced in the west by the literature of negation and the commercialisation of culture. The fact remains, however, that the key to the drama of the human and professional condition of Soviet writers lies in this optimistic imperative, which runs right through the whole story of contemporary Soviet art, puts a brake on its development, and prevents it from fulfilling the function of bringing about a modernisation of the cultural structures, themes and tastes from which it would have to draw nourishment to meet the expectations of a progressive régime. To enable us to understand the experience of a writer such as Solzhenitsyn in its true dimensions, and see its roots in a tragically grotesque process of regression, a rapid survey is essential of the relations between the Communist Party, the Soviet state and the intelligentsia from the revolution to the present day. This will enable us to see in the Solzhenitsyn case, and the furore that has accompanied it at home and abroad, a quarrel that has remained unchanged, fossilised in its terms and arguments, throughout the years. The implications may have widened and the ingredients changed, but it has remained unaltered through three generations. In the seventies it may at last perhaps extend from the cultural field into that of civil rights (more because of pressure from the base and the international political game than because of any weakening of the convictions of those on either side); on the other hand, it may also go on festering in its present state, accompanied by an ever more melancholy decline of the Soviet intelligence, forced to languish in self-destructive solitude.

In the beginning, of course, there was Lenin, the leader of a proletarian revolution that in 1917 regarded the intelligentsia as a bastion of the Tsarist régime, the natural bulwark of the bourgeoisie that produced it and a sink of every sort of iniquity, inclined by its very nature to treachery and cowardice. This was the view of many leaders of the revolution, who themselves came from the fringe of the bourgeois intelligentsia and believed in popular education, were imbued with a spirit of Utopianism, and as early as October 1917 in Petrograd laid the foundations of Proletkult, the organisation for proletarian culture that reflected nineteenth-century Russian populist trends that by that time had to a large extent crystallised into the myth of the well-educated peasant capable of rejecting the whims and caprices of authority with the clear, simple voice of one accustomed to hard physical labour. It was from Proletkult, with its arrogant self-righteousness in preaching the necessity of abolishing the traditional idea of culture, with its trail of universal lyricism and moralising principles deriving from the inside of the system, that there arose the spark of a controversy that accompanied the earliest phase of the revolution and divided writers into three broad groups.

The largest of these regarded Bolshevism as a criminal form of Utopianism, destructive of a system of values that should be purged of its authoritarian blemishes by appropriate gradual reforms but was basically in harmony with natural morality (Gorky at the time belonged to this group). The second group consisted of visionaries and enthusiasts for folk customs, who regarded the revolution as the triumph of the Messianic spirit of Holy Russia, which was called on to save the world by the sublime violence of the Christ of the muzhiks (this was the group of mystics and symbolists); and finally there was the group of unpolished workers of little or no education, induced by intellectual poverty to dream of a landscape of ploughs and factory chimneys and a culture, totally devoted to the eulogy of labour, muscles and steel, which in the name of the triumphant revolution would silence the butterfly chasers.

The struggle, intensified by the atmosphere of class mistrust, was hard, and from the outset the dividing line was the notion of realism, which the traditionalists conceived of, if not always in the Dostoevsky manner, as imbued with magical elements, or at any rate purified of all residues of naturalism, while the innovators wanted to impose a pure and simple representation of the visible, in which the exhilarating nature of the subject, pulsating like a blast furnace, would redeem all dullness. Lenin in his 1905 essay on 'Party organisation and party literature' adopted an ambiguous position. 'It is indisputable,' he wrote, 'that literary work is less susceptible than anything else to mechanical levelling . . . that it is essential in this field to assure the greatest liberty of personal initiative, individual trends, the greatest liberty of thought and imagination.' But he added that 'every free association (and hence also the party) is free to expel those members who make use of the party label to conduct propaganda opposite to the party ideas' – as if to say that there was a limit to liberty of expression in the national interests, and that it was the business of the party to decide what might harm or help it. 'Your talk about absolute liberty, individualist gentlemen of the bourgeoisie,' Lenin also said in 1905, 'is nothing but hypocrisy. Are you free of your bourgeois editor, Mr. Writer? Are you free of your bourgeois public?'

Once in power, Lenin was faced with more complex problems. On the one hand, his revolutionism stopped short of the experimentalism of the futurists and the search for new forms of the nihilists, realists, imagists and cosmists; and his taste remained tied to the age of Tolstoy, Chekhov and Zola (he regarded Mayakovsky as one who 'bawls, invents meaningless words, is phoney and useless'). On the other hand, persuaded to some extent by Gorky, who in the meantime had been converted to the new faith, and Lunacharsky, to whom he referred for advice on all literary matters (though he solemnly rebuked him for causing 5,000 copies of Mayakovsky's *One Hundred and Fifty Millions* to be printed, as he thought that 1,500 for bibliophiles and eccentrics would have been enough), he saw the insidious danger to his theory of the abolition of classes implicit in the Proletkult approach. 'Culture is one,' he said in March 1919. 'One cannot construct a culture; one can only reconstruct the culture that results from the development of the whole of humanity.' Projecting into the future the magnificent certainty expressed by Blok in the *Collapse of Humanism* about the masses taking over the heritage of humanism, he looked forward to the critical assimilation of the bourgeois heritage, and said that the whole store of art and science transmitted by capitalism should be worked over in a completely new light; 'Otherwise,' he said, 'it will be impossible to build a communist society.'

This was very different from the crude, Manichaean ideas of Proletkult, but was not so imperative as to prevent proletarian writers, strong in the prestige of being in the front rank of the revolution, from holding high the banner of proletarianism *à outrance* and opposing the various literary trends of 1920 and thereabouts with the workers' clenched fist.

The experimental fervour existing at that time was illustrated by the daily public readings of poetry in the cafés of Moscow and Leningrad (the formalists, who believed that art existed apart from all ideological content, published their manifesto in 1919), and there was a general reawakening of enthusiasm for the things of the mind to which the prevailing hunger added a mystical touch. However, as private publishing had been abolished in 1918, things grew difficult for writers at an early stage. The civil war, with its trail of horrors, presented them with dramatic dilemmas, inasmuch as the victors tended to treat those opposed to 'popular culture' as White Guardists and traitors. Hence on the one hand the rapid, spontaneous lining up with the party of poets such as Yesenin, who through the fumes of their drugs saw the revolution as the midwife of the golden age, and on the other a process of intimidation in relation to the tepid that was violent only up to a point and involved expulsion from the country.

In the face of the success of the revolution, the fear of being left out of history began to insinuate itself among intellectuals; this was the fear that was to act, and still acts, as a brake on any assumption of responsibility that involves swimming against the stream. 'The intelligentsia is hostile to us,' Lenin said to Gorky. 'It does not understand the needs of the time, that it is impotent if we are not with it, that without us it will never have the confidence of the masses.' In fact, however, it was perfectly aware of this, and was ready to integrate itself into the new system wherever it saw a chance of ploughing its furrow with tools more varied than those that the most obtuse realists were willing to grant it.

This was the situation between 1921 (the year of the New Economic Policy) and 1925, a period characterised by memorable disputes; the controversy between the moderate wing of the party, represented first by Trotsky and then by Voronsky, and the left extremists acted as background and stimulus and to a flourishing of schools, to alliances between formalists and futurists, to linguistic experiments, to a publishing revival, and a duel between Moscow and Leningrad in an atmosphere of rare vitality. The Serapion Brothers were established in 1922, the LEF, the left-wing front given that name by Mayakovsky, was founded in 1923, and 1924 saw the dawn of constructivism; and the whole of this process seemed to be given official sanction on 18th June, 1925, when the party issued a resolution encouraging the 'free emulation of various groups and trends'. 'As any other solution to the problem would be a bureaucratic pseudo-solution,' the resolution declared, 'the monopoly of any single group or literary organisation in publishing and literary activity is unacceptable.' Thus the course seemed to be firmly set for a policy of cultural tolerance that had to some extent been foreseen by Lenin twenty years before. Instead, the struggle between the partisans of propaganda literature (whose organisation was RAPP, the Russian Association of Proletarian Poets) and the merely progressive writers, among whom 'fellow-travellers' came to occupy an important position, was intensified.

By now the issue was not so much the question of how literature could best help the development and consolidation of the revolution; behind the façade of theoretical debate, the writers of RAPP were moving to the assault on the centres of power and party control which, some of them claimed, had succumbed to revisionist myths. The followers of Averbach, the brother-in-law of Yagoda, the head of the secret police, believed that the New Economic Policy had weakened the Bolshevik front and opened the path to the class enemy, and under the banner of patriotism they demanded that art should be included in the five-year plan and that, under the new centralised structure made necessary by economic planning, they should be granted the rôle of custodian of ideological orthodoxy.

Their campaign of intimidation spiced with terrorism yielded disastrous fruits. Writers were persuaded to visit factories, collective farms, dams, power stations, saw-mills and mines to draw inspiration from the glory of labour and promote the country's productive effort by kindling the enthusiasm of workers and peasants. Those who tried to evade the duty of glorifying kolkhozes or increased steel production were accused of connivance with the enemy by surreptitious sabotage of the five-year plan. It was in this atmosphere that the obligation to smile, to see only the positive side of things, to sing the praises of socialist competition, developed into a dogma, implying the label of heretic and condemnation to the stake for all who had doubts or reservations and questioned the extraordinary

33

constructive capacities of the new man generated by the party, the prophet and motive force of industrialisation and the collective farm, the weapons that would enable the country to compete with capitalism. Any work that delved into the psychology of the individual and lingered over its complexities was condemned as impious, and the dogmatism with which this was done was a crude reflection of Lenin's illusion about wiping suffering from the face of the earth and the Marxist belief that man had the power to change his natural environment, and that he therefore must not be distracted from that task by effeminate whinings about his weaknesses; and also it seemed to be grafted on the old tradition of Russian progressive literature that exalted the writer's social responsibility (if Tolstoy had not preached non-violence, it would have been easy to include his theory of literature among the tools for the moral education of the masses). Thus various factors combined to make edification the writer's sacred duty.

The chief characteristic of the campaign, however, was the arrogance with which the proletarian writers, emboldened by the defeat of Trotsky (who in 1923 had sharply reminded them that the proletariat had taken power in order to finish with class culture once and for all), set about imposing it as an article of faith, the 'communist conceit', as Lenin himself would have said, with which they believed that party decrees were sufficient for the construction of socialism. Their oppressive methods spread an atmosphere of terror throughout the intelligentsia, and the result was such an appallingly low level of literary production (among the few exceptions were *Quiet Flows the Don* and Fadeyev's *The Defeat*), that the party, of which Stalin was now the 'great leader and master', decided on a change of course. Still with the purpose of directing all energy into a single channel, the central committee on 23rd April, 1932 dissolved the VOAPP (the Pan-Union Association of Associations of Proletarian Writers) and assumed direct control of all literary matters through the Soviet Writers' Union which was to be set up, of which all writers 'favourable to the Soviet régime' were to be members.

In the eyes of the fellow-travellers this seemed to be a defeat for the proletarian writers, who were apparently forced to give way to the party; in reality Stalin, who coined the phrase 'socialist realism' between the summer and autumn of 1932 and described writers as 'engineers of the mind', adopted

34

many RAPP principles as his own and put the authority of the party behind the idea of literature as social service. The right of 'fellow-travellers' to sing the praises of the revolution by relatively heterodox methods was formally recognised, though it was made clear that it would be possible to stake a claim to a share in the construction of socialist culture only by harmonising these with the official chorus. The setting up of a communist section inside the Writers' Union thus put part of the membership in a privileged position from the outset, the communist ideology being in control, it was obvious that the fellow-travellers would at first be regarded as a field for missionary work and later as unnecessary ballast to be dumped.

The first congress of Soviet writers took place in Moscow from 17th August to 1st September, 1934 in a much tenser atmosphere than Gorky, its chief instigator, expected, and it was only in appearance that there was any genuine discussion. Zhdanov's speech had all the characteristics of an official edict, the contributions by Ehrenburg, Pasternak and other undisciplined writers amounted to no more than pin-pricks, and it remains to the present day the régime's most discussed pronouncement on literary matters. The disintegration and decay of the capitalist system, Zhdanov said, had led to the triumph of mysticism and clericism and infatuation with pornography, the rotten fruits of bourgeois culture. 'The most sensitive spokesman of the bourgeoisie', he continued, 'have fallen a prey to pessimism, uncertainty about tomorrow, and exalt the shadows of the night. . . . With us, however, the writer draws his material, his themes, his images, his language, from life and from the experience of the men of Dneprostroy and Magnitogorsk [the hydro-electric station on the Dnepr and the steelworks in the Urals]. Our writers draw their material from the experience of our kolkhozes, the creative activity seething in every corner of our country.' The characters in bourgeois literature were thieves, private detectives, prostitutes and hooligans, while in Soviet literary works they were working men and women, the men and women of the kolkhozes, party officials, organisers of the economy, engineers, young people of the Komsomol, pioneers. 'Our literature overflows with enthusiasm and heroism, it is optimistic . . . by its very essence, as the literature of a class in the ascendant, the proletariat, the only class that is progressive and in the vanguard.' What were the obligations imposed by the definition of writers as 'engineers of the human mind?' Zhdanov asked. His answer, which was taken over verbatim into the constitution of the Writers' Union, was: 'It means knowing life in order to be able to describe it truthfully in one's work, not in a dead, academic manner, not simply as objective reality, but as reality caught in its revolutionary development. The truthfulness and the historical concreteness of the artistic representation must further be accompanied by the ideological transformation and education of the workers in the spirit of socialism. It is this method of applying oneself to literature and literary criticism that we describe as the method of socialist realism.' Later in his speech he said: 'Being engineers of the mind means breaking with romanticism of the old type, which represented a non-existent kind of life and non-existent heroes, removing the reader from the contradictions and oppression of life into an irrealisable world, a world of Utopias. Our literature, anchored in the materialist conception of the world, can accept romanticism, but a romanticism of a new, revolutionary type.'

Zhdanov also said that the literary heritage of the past must be critically assimilated and that 'many kinds' of weapons (genres, styles, forms and methods of literary creation) must be used in order to improve the language and quality of writing and thus wipe out the existing difference in level between literature and economic development. But what did this amount to in the light of what had gone before? Socialist realism having been declared to be the only method capable of expressing and realising the achievements of the revolution, it seemed obvious that anyone who departed from it deserved punishment similar to that laid down for workers who carried out sabotage in the factories. This was pointed out at the congress by Ehrenburg. 'If a steel foundryman loses his daughter,' he said, 'twenty pages cannot be devoted to the description of the foundry and only two lines to the girl's death. . . . Artistic creation does not resemble the construction of a steelworks. . . . Under the pretext of the necessity of the struggle against formalism we have seen frequent examples of the cult of the most reactionary artistic forms. This leads to a return to the aesthetics of the pre-revolutionary petty bourgeoisie.'

The same thing was felt by Koltsov, the editor of *Krokodil*, who perhaps had a presentiment of what was to come (in 1942 he was executed by order of Stalin) and rose and spoke in defence of satire, 'a literary genre whose voice should be raised more often'. But heaven forbid. The humour and ridicule now exercised at the expense of petty bourgeois elements that had insinuated themselves into the party might one day give the whole working class a taste for self-criticism, and it must be held in check, almost as firmly as the poets who wanted to soften up the Red Guard hearts of the young with the 'poison of the poetry of intimate feelings', or those sympathisers with individualism who put forward reservations about socialist realism in the name of the literary genius of Proust and Joyce. 'In Proust,' said Radek, who was also to be purged by Stalin, 'the old world, like a scabby old dog now incapable of moving, lies outstretched in the sun, incapable of anything but licking its wounds. . . . A manure heap teeming with worms photographed through a microscope – that is Joyce.'

Bukharin's declaration that the Soviet Union must catch up and overtake Europe and America in literature as well as in other fields, and Pasternak's warning to his colleagues not to sacrifice themselves and their creative individuality to the ambition of becoming literary dignitaries, fell on stony ground. For the tone of the congress was set by alarmed outcries against the elements of unreason, the spies of decadent fascism, that threatened to force a breach in the healthy, robust socialist front, and by dramatic appeals to unite against the capitalist world which, though on its last legs, seemed determined to strangle the Soviet Union. The resolutions passed at the congress and, indeed, the whole of Soviet cultural life seemed dominated by the idea that they were faced with a bourgeoisie armed to the teeth, preparing a new holocaust and organising the mass destruction of proletarians all over the world. Thus there was nothing strange in its concluding its labours with the cry of 'Long live the Red Army of men of letters'.

The establishment of a monolithic writers' association was inspired by the consideration that during a siege everything without exception must be mobilised for the common cause. The defences were perhaps less solid than Zhdanov wished to convey when he announced that the obstacles in the path of socialist construction had now been overcome. The USSR had laid the foundations of a socialist economy and liquidated the parasite classes, but it was not yet true that men's consciousness had been radically changed. 'To eliminate the survivals of capitalism in the human consciousness,' he said, 'it is necessary to struggle against every relic of bourgeois influence on the proletariat, against all slackness and idleness, all forms of petty bourgeois individualism and anarchy, all dishonest attitudes in relation to social property.' This amounted to saying that it was necessary to combat every idea, every book, every author that, under the pretext of using the formal liberty granted by the party, smuggled in principles and trends condemned as bourgeois by that party, which was the voice of the working class that had performed the service of 'assuring exceptional opportunities of development to literature, art, science, cultural progress'. This sort of warning was included in the constitution of the Writers' Union, and was addressed to those who still clung to the myth of literature isolated from its political context and were not convinced that they owed their survival to the proletariat.

According to Article I, 'the indispensable condition for the progress of literature, its high artistic level, its ideal-political wealth and its practical activity, is the close and direct link between the literary movement and the actual problems of party policy and the Soviet power, the dovetailing of writers into the construction of socialism, deep and careful study of concrete reality.' The intelligentsia must renounce the individual yardstick; the criterion was the horizontal response roused by a piece of writing among those to whom it was addressed, the people, and its utility as a simulus to communal construction. 'Social realism, the fundamental method of Soviet literature and literary criticism, requires of the writer truthful, historically concrete, representation of reality seen in its revolutionary development, and the historical truthfulness and concreteness of the artistic representation of reality must be accompanied by the task of ideological transformation and education of the workers in the spirit of socialism.' The constitution of the Writers' Union continued: 'Socialist realism assures artistic creation of extraordinary possibilities of creative initiatives and of choice between a great variety of forms, styles and genres' – a very ambiguous assurance, as we have pointed out, for socialist realism is at most consistent with a variety of forms, but certainly does not guarantee them.

Article II of the constitution was more specific. It said that the varied development of forms and styles must take place *on the basis* of socialist realism. Moreover, again according to the constitution, the Writers' Union must aim at the 'creation of works of high artistic level permeated by the heroic struggle of the proletariat, the pathos of the victory of socialism, capable of reflecting the great wisdom and heroism of the Communist Party'. This wisdom and heroism being taken for granted, it is hard to see how any writer could run the risk of casting doubt on them by works remote from the spirit of socialist realism or expose himself to the likelihood of expulsion from the union by putting his signature to books liable to be considered anti-Soviet. On the other hand, the union immediately after its establishment was allotted rest homes, clubs, canteens, libraries, summer and winter holiday homes, as well as a fund to provide for writers' needs, and undertook the protection of their rights in the Soviet union and abroad. Soviet writers, humiliated by the party, which lost no opportunity of pointing out that they played second fiddle to the workers and peasants, to whom they owed their redemption from a parasitic calling, were ready to forget their squabbles with each other and conceal their courtier's rôle behind the mask of the front-line soldier.

CHAPTER THREE

The iron age of Soviet literature began in 1934 and lasted until the war. Western critics generally regard it with horror, all the greater in that the twenties, which were so rich in experiment, seemed to western eyes to exemplify, against a background of a mingling of classes and great economic tensions, the fertile clash of ideas that can start up the mechanism of literary renewal. Regretting the developments of Soviet literature that might have taken place in the thirties is in reality the consequence of living under a pluralist system. In a political contest dominated by a single ideology that had established and defended itself by force, literary production was bound to crystallise out into forms that to us are lifeless, but are functional to the extent that the 'engineers of the mind' were presenting models of virtuous citizens and heroes of labour and prolific rural housewives instead of readers intent on existential ideas and the pleasures of style. No totalitarian system welcomes a variegated cultural landscape; what to us seems a pleasing bustle of fertile activity is from the dictator's point of view an uncontrollable chaos in which the seeds of revolt are likely to germinate. The Stalin régime, whose sights were set by definition on the mass consciousness, which was regarded as the cement indispensable for the manufacture of the new man, considered itself fortunate in having been able on 23rd April, 1932 to destroy a querulous ant-heap at a single stroke and put in its place a rigid reinforced concrete wall to be covered by standardised panelling to be provided by zealous workers with the pen.

The situation of the country, however, offered little inducement to smile or engage in literary polemics. Mayakovsky committed suicide in 1930 (Gumilev had been shot in 1920 and Yesenin had committed suicide in 1925), and perplexed or recalcitrant writers found insuperable obstacles in the publishing houses and periodicals controlled by the party, as well as the censorship. A few years later those who failed to escape persecution by going into exile, as Zamyatin, the inspirer of the Serapion Brothers did, were sent to labour camps, unless they were executed after a trial on trumped up charges in which there were no legal guarantees for the accused. 'Comrade Stalin has concentrated immense power in his hands, and I am not sure that he knows how to use it with sufficient wisdom.' If writers had been aware of the testament dictated by Lenin on Christmas Day 1922, perhaps they might have convinced themselves that the great purges to which many of them fell victim were the tragic outcome of a process cut short by a brutal hand. In the climate of suspicion, the siege mentality that prevailed, haunted by the threat of Trotskyism and the new barbarians who appeared on the western frontiers, a threat which the party deliberately magnified, it is not surprising that in some cases they went to their death without wavering in their communist faith or sacrificed their condemnation to forced labour on the altar of patriotism.

The Leninist critical conscience having been stifled by the myth of socialism in a single country and the necessity of competing in productivity with the west, the obsequiousness to authority that had been fostered by the Tsarist régime reasserted its oppressive rôle among the intelligentsia, affecting not only individual vitality, to which Slav fatalism represented a perpetual threat, but artistic invention also. The Soviet writers of the thirties who managed to survive had at their disposal the obligatory keyboard of socialist realism as interpreted by the officials of the party. They were advised to avoid evocation of the past, except to picture it as a realm of darkness; to avoid searching for new forms other than those aimed at a more immediate approach to the reader; to choose themes rooted in native folk customs, which were so much healthier than cosmopolitan models; to beware of passivity or Bohemianism, which were cesspools of every kind of moral iniquity and the ante-chamber of suicide.

Human perfectibility being a mandatory assumption, the writer was delegated by the régime to situate man in the dynamic framework of a social reality in which every gesture, every feeling, had value only for its edifying, positive content, measurable by the yardstick of economic productivity and a unidirectional political consciousness. Hence the consecration of the utilitarian theory of art, of the interpretation of literature as the product of a collective consciousness that rejected delving into the individual unconscious, in which animal nature tried to quench the light of reason. Hence the 'varnishing of reality' denounced by many ex-varnishers after Stalin's death.

Hence the novels, stories, poems, plays and films in which no-one ever committed a dishonourable action without duly paying the penalty (often in the form of remorse for having betrayed his comrades); in which women, children and the old were never allowed to be neglected, the young were set firmly on the path of virtue, and fathers of families were always shown in a favourable light because of their force of character and muscular strength.

In every manual of Soviet literary history the chapter on the Stalin period contains long lists of works full of noble sentiments, battles for the wheat harvest, factory chimneys rising into the blue of heaven. Digressions into intimacy or irony having been abolished, together with unhappy love affairs, poverty and the sense of guilt, emotional conflicts being for the most part restricted to the clash between the good that is inevitably destined ultimately to triumph and the evil that is condemned to inevitable failure, the recalcitrant poets having been cast into the outer darkness (between 1933 and 1943 Pasternak published nothing but translations of Shakespeare), Soviet literature during those years was the hand-maiden of a master who tried to persuade the world and himself that evil was on the point of vanishing from the Soviet landscape, thus demonstrating the correctness of the Marxist theory of the relationship between happiness and the socio-economic environment. 'Life is becoming more beautiful, life is becoming more joyous,' Stalin said, after sacrificing ten million kulaks and peasants between 1936 and 1939 and imprisoning or executing on charges of Trotskyist conspiracy or connivance with the enemy all those suspected of standing in the way of his absolutism; and among them were hundreds of artists and writers – Babel, Mandelstam, Pilnyak, Meyerhold, Oreshin, Vasilev, Vesely, Tretyakov, etc., etc.

All these things are too familiar for there to be any need to linger over them. Nevertheless it should be borne in mind that it was in those years, behind the triumphal façade imposed on a bloodthirsty reality, that the monumental literary model of the New Hero, spurred to action by unshakable faith in communism, took shape and consolidated itself. It continued to set the standard for Soviet prose and poetry even after Stalin's death, giving them a moral force that has been rightly described as Victorian. Henceforward there was a constant point of reference in the literary battle between the writers who stayed at home and those who went into exile, between the orthodox and those suspected of heresy. This was not so much the universal values expressed in a work of art, the humanity and truth of its lights and shades, as its interpretation of socialist realism in the national context. To one side it involved the idealisation of characters, generalising their feelings and sublimating their psychological peculiarities into a positive portrait (this postulated the sanctity of the family, the formal beauty of the dam and the tractor, the high aesthetic value of the scientific agriculturist); to the other side it meant equating forms of expression and content to the development of a human consciousness enriched, not flattened, by the dynamic Soviet political experience. In other words, to the latter the Puritanism of the former was a sign, not of aesthetic advance, but of a bourgeois development expressing itself in the didactic forms of edifying literature. They wanted certain elements derived from naturalism to be recovered and employed as dialectical factors, and to use introspection to examine the motivation of individual behaviour in the social context, and in works such as *Quiet Flows the Don* and *The Young Guard* they succeeded.

It should not, however, be supposed that during the Stalin years a debate of this sort took place in the absence of personal intimidation. A permanent factor in cultural polemics in the Soviet Union is the pressure exercised by the authorities on the always very limited number of persons belonging to the base who adopt the most mildly critical attitude towards them. As soon as doubts or reservations of any kind make their appearance, the authorities raise the spectre of counter-revolution and pronounce condemnations in the name of orthodoxy, and thus the more firmly orthodoxy imposes the labour camp or shooting as an alternative to the complete acceptance of dogma, the more concealed dissent has to be. The situation was substantially modified in Khrushchev's time, as we shall see, but under Stalin a writer who wanted to survive had to resign himself to the rôle of court poet, illustrator, and pedagogue; his only consolation being the illusion of bringing new grist to the mill of an ancient literary genre – if it is true, as Lukács maintained in the middle thirties, that the substance of the socialist realist novel lies in the epic trend inherent in the proletarian struggle.

Trotsky said that the art of the Stalin period would enter

history as the most striking illustration of the deep decline of the proletarian revolution. If this judgment is regarded as of suspect origin, it is sufficient to refer to the views expressed with the consent of the party during the Khrushchev period. A disastrous picture emerges of the years during which the Russian writer, after a century and a half of denunciation of social conditions and rebellion against authority, was forced, partly by his own Messianic trends, to turn himself into a champion of the established order. The transformation was accepted without excessive difficulty by the popular reader who wanted to escape from the burdens of everyday life with the aid of a novel with a happy ending, but it had grave long-term consequences.

The suspicion with which a section of Russian public opinion follows debates between writers at the present time derives from the contempt that it feels for an intelligentsia that dares to discuss orders from above with a view to acquiring the right to paint the world black and delve into the 'filth' of the unconscious, thus betraying the hopes of the 'new humanism' and socialist realism, which wants man to be healthy and long-lived. This suspicion and mistrust which has spread through Soviet society and has been passed on from generation to generation can be traced back to its origin in the grimmest years, of the nature of which there is endless evidence. Among this evidence is the letter written to Stalin on 17th August, 1939 by the ex-Stalinist Raskolnikov, then an *émigré* in France.

'After hypocritically proclaiming that the intelligentsia was the salt of the earth,' he said, 'you deprived writers, scientists and painters of the slightest degree of personal freedom in their work. You pushed the artistic movement into a pond in which it suffocates, fades away and dies. The raging of the censorship and the understandable servility of editors (of periodicals and publishing houses) whose heads are at stake have led Soviet literature into sclerosis and paralysis. The writer has no-one to print him, the dramatist has no-one to produce him, the critic cannot express his opinions if he has not received official blessing. . . . You foster an artistic pseudo-movement that with tedious monotony exalts your famous "genius" *ad nauseam*. Untalented scribblers exalt you to the skies like a demigod descended to the earth from the sun or the moon, and you, like an oriental despot, intoxicate yourself with the incense scattered in the course of this vile adulation. Where is Boris Pilnyak? Where is Sergei Tretyakov? And Alexander Arosev? And Mikhail Koltsov? And Tarasov-Rodionov? Where is Serebryakova, whose only guilt was that of having been Sokolnikov's wife? Stalin, you put them in prison. Following Hitler's example, you have revived the burnings of books, as in the Middle Ages. . . .

'Sooner or later,' Raskolnikov's letter concluded, 'the Soviet people will bring you to book as the betrayer of socialism and the revolution, the principal saboteur, the real enemy of the people, the apostle of famine and of phoney trials.' That day did not come until after Stalin's death. Meanwhile the hour of war had come, and the Soviet writer was more than ever obliged to go to the aid of the socialist fatherland.

CHAPTER FOUR

The historians have given us ample information about the condition of Soviet writers during the four years of war. The USSR, in alliance with the capitalist great powers, confronted a monstrous aggressive force that threatened to strike a fatal blow at what seemed to be the noblest myth of the twentieth century – the redemption of the masses that were to change the destiny of the world. The Soviet Union was not only defending itself against a long-expected assault – an assault that was almost desired, so that the strength achieved by socialism might be measured by the destructive hatred shown by the enemy; it was also an ideology facing the test of arms against what it regarded as the blackest form of bourgeois reaction. Many years had still to pass before the criminal price paid by Stalin for the construction of modern Russia was appreciated and the man in the street came to regard the clash between two totalitarianisms as the peak of irrationality reached by our scientific century.

Meanwhile Mother Russia rose to defend all the griefs and terrors suffered in the hope of achieving a juster society in which men would be liberated from suffering and enabled to realise their potentialities thanks to the triumphs of labour. Writers were in the front rank. Party discipline no longer had to be enforced; in the hour of peril it was spontaneous, silencing dissent and causing everyone to line up behind the soldiers. Writers, already habituated to their subordinate rôle, adapted themselves to the new task of stimulating the morale of the troops in the back areas. Hundreds of them were exempted from military service; in the rôle of war correspondents or glorifiers of the indomitable, struggle-hardened Russian soul, they saw new prestige accruing to their mission of interpreting the national virtues.

In a way the war confirmed and consecrated the function that Stalin entrusted to the 'engineers of the mind'. After co-operating in the construction of the new Russia, now, when the people were making the greatest effort in their history, it was their duty to supervise and inspect, to prevent any diminution or breakdown of morale. The better the people stood up to the test, the greater its triumphs over the enemy, the greater the writer's share of glory, for collective victory would free him of the suspicion of having continued to cultivate his garden of private poetry.

One consequence, naturally enough, was a huge output of novels, poems and plays, all inspired by the heroic struggle and the consciousness of defending in the name of the father-land and the family the human values the perfidious Nazis wanted to destroy. Another consequence, and in certain respects it was an important innovation in Soviet literature, was the greater attention paid to human suffering. To illus-trate the courage of the troops and of starving civilians, the horrors of war had to be portrayed with pitiless realism (it was sufficient to look around one and reproduce the appalling truth; this time the photographic mechanism functioned in reverse). The idyllic picture of the world painted by official literature having been destroyed by the horrors of reality, the ordinary human being, whose deepest and most primitive feelings were played on by the war lords, returned to the centre of atten-tion; his crises of despair, the surge of his feelings, varying from selfishness to the most complete self-abnegation, in short, the whole moral life of the individual that had hitherto been looked at only in a radiant light, was now seen in the light and shade of suffering. The consequence was that in some authors the analysis of feelings was refined and charged with pity, the novel and poetry dug deeper, and under the stress of events recovered some of the psychological realism of the old Russian tradition. But when victory had been won, in the eyes of the orthodox it seemed but a short step from this rejection of official emphasis and patriotic magniloquence to a revival of lyricism and psychologism of the bourgeois type; this was a risk that could not be afforded, so the authorities tightened the reins again.

All the historians, and notably Marc Slonim, who has very perceptibly explored this field and provides an admirable account for those who wish for detailed information about authors and titles, agree that the primary reason for the stop order to which Soviet literature was subjected from 1945 to 1953 was the cold war. In a country in which there is a double link between culture and politics, on the day when the régime reawakened the spirit of competition with the western world, insisting that the only defence against new aggressions was a solid military and economic bulwark in the construction of which everyone must lend a hand, the writer once more reverted to the state of vassal and loudspeaker.

The United States having been represented, in accordance with the traditional pattern, as a wild beast thirsting for proletarian blood, it was the patriotic duty of Soviet writers to present a united front, to take their stand on the positions consecrated by what had again become socialist realism, and fire point-blank at the west. It was also necessary to keep an eye on the home front, in case the custodians of dogma, in the chaos resulting from the war, had permitted the infiltration of fifth columns whose purpose was to produce cracks in the solid concrete of ideological unity.

Writers were given the choice with which Stalin presented them in the thirties, and they are still faced with it; they must either agree that, while the Soviet Union is besieged by enemies, they have no right to play with words, or they expose themselves to the charge of parasitism and must take the consequences. It was unavailingly pointed out by the more far-seeing that a defensive front is more solid if the traditional ideological concrete is manufactured with the tools of modern technology and aligned with historical necessities; the cerebral sclerosis of the dogmatists is such that observations of this kind invite an immediate charge of revisionism.

On May 26, 1947 the death penalty was abolished (it was reintroduced in 1950 for treachery, espionage and sabotage and later extended to economic crimes), but in the preceding months a series of edicts had been issued that in practice contemplated a kind of civic death for those who did not rapidly adapt themselves. At a meeting of the party central committee on 14th August, 1946 Zhdanov complained that artists had neglected 'the vital essence of the Soviet system'; this was the prelude to savage reprisals that were extended for six long years to practically every branch of the arts (resolutions by the central committee on the theatre and the cinema were issued in August and September 1946, and the turn of music came in 1948).

Once more the results were grim; newspapers and periodicals were closed, and Anna Akhmatova and Mikhail Zoshchenko were expelled from the Writers' Union (the former was found guilty of eroticism, mysticism, political apathy and 'sentiments alien to the Soviet people'; the latter was accused of slanderous satire and of Freudism, and was actually deprived of his ration cards); Prokofiev, Shostakovich and Khachaturian were denounced for formalism (it is said that Zhdanov, to show what kind of music Stalin liked, played some popular tunes on the piano). Philosophers, biologists, linguists (who were personally attacked by Stalin in an onslaught on the Marr school), and even students of comparative literature were scolded and sent to labour camps if they dared criticise Stalin's behaviour during the war, or flirted with the ideas of heretical thinkers, or showed signs of having absorbed the poisonous fumes of bourgeois culture, or displayed sympathy for cosmopolitanism or art for art's sake.

The great campaign against classical genetics conducted in August 1948 in support of Lysenko's theory of the heredity of characteristics acquired through environmental influence is well-known. Let us add that a charge of cosmopolitanism led to the death of twenty-six Jewish writers in August 1952, a few months before Stalin, speaking to members of the Presidium, issued his celebrated rebuke. 'You are as blind as newborn kittens. What would happen without me? The country would go to ruin, because you are unable to recognise your enemies.'

Being able to recognise one's enemies meant taking part in a man-hunt, having a sharper nose than others for what was in store, having an X-ray eye for the hidden thoughts, the most secret intentions of others, attributing one's own obsessions to one's enemies. Is there any need to describe the state of mind of the Soviet writer in a post-war period characterised by new intimidations, shaken by the defection of Tito, made uneasy by the ephemeral but alarming establishment of opposition student groups (in 1948 members of a movement called 'The Real Work of Lenin' were sentenced to twenty-five years' forced labour), haunted by the spectre of a warmongering America and fear of playing the game of the country's internal enemies, that is, the heirs of Trotsky who, it was believed, were ready to expose the country to the danger of collapse for the sake of revenging themselves on Stalin?

Faced with Zhdanov's menacing pronouncement ('the aim of Soviet literature is to educate youth in accordance with communist principles; it must become party literature and portray Soviet man in all his fullness'), the majority, having to live by their work, put the novels and verse published during the last years of the war on their highest bookshelves and returned in a disciplined manner to their place in the courtiers' ranks. Military victory, the fortitude and moral fibre of the defenders of Leningrad, the huge effort of reconstruction, not only offered a wide variety of subject-matter, but also provided an excellent excuse for the abandonment of the critical spirit that had timidly asserted itself during the war years while the chief concern of the censorship was the protection of military secrets.

Nevertheless the chorus was not so unanimous as the régime hoped. The war had made gaps in the smoke-screen put up by Stalin round Soviet culture. Names of western writers were bandied about, the example of American literature, often so critical of the capitalist system but nevertheless free to express itself, often with notable artistic success, did not fail to make an impact on those who saw in Stalin's absolutism an obstacle to the assumption by the writer of a more mature, responsible rôle. These were the men who, while the Zhdanov storm raged and after his death in 1948, began writing in secret in the expectation of better times, or at any rate adopted a dual personality, churning out the material required for newspapers and periodicals and locking up their real writing in their desks, thus giving rise to a usage that in the years to come waxed and waned in accordance with the loosening or tightening of the screw and the risks inherent in the circulation of the *samizdat*, the clandestine press.

Thus Stalin's death on March 5, 1953 occurred at a time when, in spite of the rigid controls aimed at preventing ideological contamination, the idea of liberty and the necessity of artistic expression were present in writers' minds, if nowhere else. An irreversible process, foreshadowed while Stalin was still alive, had begun.

In the summer of 1952 an article in *Pravda* by Nikolai Virta deplored the idealisation of reality in Soviet writing and the failure of authors to criticise the negative aspect of Soviet life, and Pudovkin's film *The Return of Vasily Bortnikov* noticeably departed from the official line. From the autumn of 1953 onwards there was tension between the base and the bureaucratic *élite* in control of artistic production.

Even before the Twentieth Congress the most alert and sensitive section of the intelligentsia had the feeling that Stalin's death would mean either an advance in the arts and in socialism or their collapse, depending on whether the new régime revived the liberty of artistic production or continued the methods of authoritarian monolithism. It was highly significant that neither the Berlin revolt of June 1953 nor, in a quite different dimension, the strikes that took place a month later among the political deportees in the uneasy region of Vorkuta (where a 'north Russian democratic movement' had been crushed in blood in 1948) acted as a deterrent, as it would have done in earlier times, or prevented *Novy Mir* from printing an article by Ehrenburg on 'The writer's work' (in which he declared 'our artistic literature' to be 'weaker and more pallid than our life' and recalled the artist to the duty of following his creative impulse); or *Soviet Music* from publishing in November an article by Khachaturian 'On creative audacity and inspiration' (in which the music hitherto demanded of Soviet composers was branded as 'second-hand goods') or *Novy Mir* from printing in December the celebrated article on 'Sincerity in literature' by the critic Vladimir Pomeranchev, which was greeted as little less than revolutionary. In reality the latter did no more than state the obvious: that it is the writer's task to pose problems and sow doubts, to say what he thinks and avoid commonplaces, because what does not come from the heart is hypocrisy, and hypocrisy leads to the betrayal of art and of the people.

The sensation caused by these articles, and by superficially minor incidents, such as the first performance for twenty years of Mayakovsky's *The Bath* (a satire on the bureaucracy), the success of Panferov's novel *Volga-Matushka* and Ovechkin's chronicle of provincial life, both of which in certain respects represented departures from the official triumphalism, pointed to the direction in which things were moving. The timid were raising their heads and unlocking the drawers of their desks, and the officials of the world of culture were pricking up their ears and putting themselves on the alert.

The first knots appeared in the comb in 1954. That was the year in which, in counterpoint, as it were, to the elimination of Beria, Yevtushenko first went abroad and the first part of Ehrenburg's *The Thaw* was published, as well as Nekrasov's *In the Native City* and Pasternak's poems, all works that would have enraged Stalin. But it was also the year in which *Literaturnaya Gazeta* and *Pravda* accused Pomeranchev of revisionism ('The nature of Soviet literature,' the former said, 'is to be partisan as against the vague notion of sincerity'); indiscipline led to expulsions from the Writers' Union (one of the victims was Virta); Tvardovsky, the editor of *Novy Mir*, who had published Pomeranchev, lost his post, which went to Simonov; Panferov was dismissed from *Oktyabr*; and the musician Makrusov was expelled from the Composers' Union.

The line of battle was now drawn up between the followers and opponents of the Zhdanov line, and the issue was clearly defined; it was concerned with the limits of the freedom of movement within the system that should be allowed communists who wished to use criticism to strengthen the system and broaden the base of popular consent.

The second congress of the Writers' Union, held from 15th to 26th December, 1954 (its membership had grown in the meantime from 1,500 to 3,700) was not, as might have been expected, the battleground on which the quarrel exploded. Stalin's body was still too warm, his followers still had too many levers of power in their hands for the scandal-makers to have the courage to aim at the heart of the establishment. The excitement of meeting in congress after twenty years, and the hope of a spontaneous increase in the pace of destalinisation (Akhmatova was readmitted to the union) combined with the fear of irritating the old guard to make caution seem advisable. Many speakers angrily condemned the banality, crudity and hollowness of contemporary fiction (Ehrenburg complained that most books described a world 'inhabited by primitives or wax model children'; and Lugovskoy said that critics praised to the skies and the state rewarded phoney books that were remote from the great problems of man). But the impression was created that dissent was only indirectly concerned with the method of application of the ideology.

The writers in congress seemed to wish above all to push their professional claims. Kaverin, a former member of the Serapion Brothers, called for a literature that would include a strong and independent critical wing, and appealed to professional solidarity in calling on editors of periodicals to put off their hateful censor's clothing and courageously defend the works of their colleagues against the outrages suffered at the hands of obtuse bureaucrats. Intellectuals were reminded of their duty of promoting culture against the short-sightedness of the mandarins (Ketlinskaya deplored the fact that the offices of the Writers' Union were just like a ministry), and this was to be regularly repeated in the years to come, and found its highest and most dramatic expression in Solzhenitsyn's letter to the fourth congress.

The soundness of the strategy adopted in 1954 seemed to be shown by the results. More important than the big reception given for the writers in the Kremlin, which was a recognition of their status, were the many rehabilitations (of Babel and Bulgakov, among others) that took place in the course of 1955; the readmission to the executive committee of the Writers' Union of Tvardovsky, Grossman, and Panova; the appearance among the *dramatis personae* of works of fiction of the innocent victim of persecution for political reasons; the stepping up of attacks on bureaucrats; and the public tribute paid to Dostoevsky on the occasion of the publication of an edition of his complete works.

This last was an event of great significance, as in 1934 Gorky, the patron of the first writers' congress, had himself put Dostoevsky in the dock. Gorky said at that time: 'The role of a searcher for the truth is attributed to Dostoevsky. If he indeed searched for it, he found it in the ferocious, animal nature of man, and he found it, not to disown, but to defend it.' There had been a real change in the USSR if in 1955 the complete works of a great writer who had hitherto been regarded as a morbid delver into the unconscious were being printed at the public expense.

The second congress also amended the constitution of the Writers' Union. It deleted the reference in Article I to the necessity that truthfulness and historical concreteness in the artistic representation of reality should be accompanied by the ideological transformation and education of the workers in the spirit of socialism.

A few months later all these whiffs of fresh air turned out to be the prelude to a storm. The secret session of the Twentieth Congress of the Communist Party at which Khrushchev made his speech on Stalin took place on 25th February, 1956, but some days previously Sholokhov denounced the degeneration of the Writers' Union, which had been transformed into a purely administrative machine by Fadeyev, 'who for fifteen years has claimed that writers should stand to attention in his presence' and (apart from making secret accusations against his colleagues) 'had betrayed himself' by making alterations by order of the Kremlin in his novel *The Young Guard*. 'The fact that the Writers' Union now has 3,773 members should not impress anyone,' Sholokhov said. 'There are a large number of dead souls among them.'

Things now started moving. So rapidly did the ice melt that in May Fadeyev committed suicide and Simonov, who had inherited Tvardovsky's indocility, published in the summer number of *Novy Mir* Dudintsev's *Not by Bread Alone*, in which the new class of bureaucrats was pilloried with unaccustomed frankness in the figure of Drozdov, a factory manager whose chief preoccupation is his own career. This was the so-called great thaw, which later, without good reason, became legendary as a sort of golden age.

The domestic effervescence provoked by the shock given to the system by Khrushchev was accompanied by greater courtesy and good manners towards the outside world, but not by any genuine desire to enter into a real dialogue with the west; such a dialogue would have involved renouncing a gramme of mistrust and trying to establish a common vocabulary as a first step.

An east-west meeting was organised in Venice by the European Society for Culture from 25th to 31st March, 1956. The Soviet delegation included two winners of the Stalin prize for literature. It consisted of Konstantin Fedin, the secretary of the Moscow Writers' Union, Boris Polevoy-Kampov, secretary of the presidium of the Soviet Writers' Union, the art historian Mikhail Alpatov, and the taciturn Victor Volodin. The Russians were lavish with their smiles and obviously ready for any strategic operation that, glossing over all differences, might procure Soviet admission to a cultural institution that promised to put them back into circulation. But when the discussion advanced from anodyne generalisation about intellectual solidarity to concrete historical analysis of the writer's responsibility, they turned a deaf ear; they said they wanted to discuss literature, not politics.

Ignazio Silone put his finger on the sensitive spot by asking what was the present position in relation to the Zhdanov doctrine and exactly what the cultural thaw consisted of. Fedin replied evasively. He began with a lecture on the writer's double responsibility, towards himself and towards the society in which he lived ('his duty is to create forms accessible to the environment that surrounds him and provides the raw material for his work'), and made a point of announcing that he was not a member of the party. But he reiterated the well-known position taken by Lenin in 1919 in his criticism of Proletkult, saying that 'socialism is the heir to the cultural riches accumulated by humanity in the course of history, including the bourgeois riches'. Without specifically referring to the Stalin era, he claimed that Soviet writers had remained faithful to the old tradition of Russian literature, according to which culture was a tool for promoting the well-being of the people. 'At this moment,' he went on, 'the task of the Soviet writer is to perfect his art, and without dogmatism; he is free in his choice of forms and literary trends, and if we talk of socialist realism it means that our culture has its roots in a society that has founded socialism. This is a historical fact, and no living culture can arbitrarily change the facts of history.'

He was echoed by Alpatov, who lauded the moral integrity of the writers of the past, who were conscious of serving 'a high and noble cause' in the form of art. Guido Piovene vainly pointed out that art also had a critical function, and that a writer's greatness was not necessarily measured by his moral virtue. Fedin denied that the 'decadent' Joyce and Proust had 'the general sense of art' possessed by authors such as Stendhal, Balzac, Dostoevsky and Thomas Mann.

Once more it was Silone's turn to deny the continuity of the service rendered to the people by Soviet writers; he accused them of having betrayed the example of Gogol, Tolstoy and Dostoevsky after the anti-conformism of the twenties. 'The Twentieth Congress,' Silone went on, 'denounced many infamies, admitted the reign of terror and the massacre of many innocents, but you, Soviet writers, must ask yourselves what you were doing in those years, what Stalin made of you, whether you really fought in defence of the oppressed and the humiliated against the arbitrary power of the state. Since Soviet literature and art of the present day do not in any way reflect the terrifying reality of the Stalin years, and since it is impossible to believe that the spring of generosity and courage that gave such drive to your predecessors in the Tsarist period suddenly dried up, the régime must take the blame for interrupting an anti-conformist literary tradition and turning literature into state-inspired propaganda. Invoking the necessity of revolutionary discipline is a piece of sophistry typical of an essentially reactionary bourgeois historicism. What help can an artist without liberty give in the creation of a new world?

. . . Writers belong to society, not to the state. The claim that the proletarian revolution leads to the identification of society with the state is stupid also from the Marxist point of view . . . To a writer there can be no greater betrayal than being outside or against society.'

Fedin took Silone's indictment without batting an eyelid. 'Russian writers have always been guided by the hope and desire of affirming the positive sides of the revolution,' he said. His greatest concession was to admit the possibility 'that illustration of those positive sides, and the necessity of accentuating their value, may have had some influence on the objectivity of their way of stating the facts.'

At the end of the meeting Merleau-Ponty correctly remarked that the Soviet representatives had been very polite, had shown full willingness to work with their western colleagues, but had in fact said nothing whatever. The illusion that the meeting had nevertheless been useful, because it took place in an atmosphere of reciprocal human sympathy, soon faded. The Hungarian rising took place, and the Russians did not attend the second east-west meeting planned for August 1958.

Meanwhile, however, in September 1956, only a few months after the Venice meeting, a meeting of editors of cultural periodicals took place at Zürich attended, among others, by the Russians Chakovsky, Anisimov and Kozhevnikov, Nadeau, Barthes, Bataille from France, Stephen Spender from England, and Silone and Chiaromonte from Italy. Here again the Russians failed to show that they had acquired any of that independence of judgment in relation to their own government by which the west hoped to assess the change that had taken place among the intelligentsia. The only progress lay in Anisimov's agreement to answer in writing five questions put to him by Silone. By the time his reply arrived three months later there had been a notable change in the situation.

On 22nd October, while the exciting news was coming in from Warsaw that the base of the Polish party had secured the dismissal of many Stalinist members of the hierarchy, the Writers' Union organised a trial of Dudintsev's novel in Moscow that turned into a sensational political demonstration, aided by the intervention of a group of students from the Lomonosov University who called for free discussion. The distinguished author Konstantin Paustovsky said: 'I do not propose to linger over the literary merits or defects of the novel. The moment has come to speak clearly. Comrades, in my opinion Dudintsev represents a highly important social phenomenon. His novel is the first battle against the Drozdovs, whom our literature must attack until they have been completely liquidated. . . . The book has a pitiless truth, the only truth of which the people has need in its difficult march towards a new social régime.'

After sarcastic references to the ignorance of certain officials (one of whom had thought that Michelangelo's *Last Judgment* was connected with the trial of Mussolini, while another had asked how it came about that the ancient Greek proletariat had consented to the construction of the Acropolis), Paustovsky denounced the 'new petty bourgeois caste' that flourished with impunity in the country. 'They are a gang of carnivores and tyrants who have nothing in common either with the revolution or with socialism. . . . Where do these profiteers, toadies and traitors come from who claim the right to speak in the name of the people, for which in reality they nourish nothing but hatred and contempt? . . . They are the consequence of the personality cult . . . survivors who regard the people as dung, whose weapons are treachery, calumny and murder. But for the Drozdovs, great men like Meyerhold, Babel, Vesely and others would be still alive. The Drozdovs killed them off. . . . If they were alive, our culture would be in full efflorescence. . . . But I am convinced that the people, when they realise the dignity of our life, will sweep away the Drozdovs very definitely and very soon. It will be a hard struggle, we are only at the beginning.'

Paustovsky's speech made a great stir. This was the first time that a writer of great reputation, speaking at a public meeting, had blamed the bureaucracy for the literary stagnation from which the Soviet Union was suffering. But this too was a seed buried beneath the snow. Barely twenty-four hours later the Budapest revolt broke out, which made it easy for the Stalinists to attribute responsibility for sabotaging the solidarity of the communist *bloc* to the intellectuals, because of their 'crazy presumption' in criticising the leading cadres. In November, when the second volume of the almanac *Literary Moscow* appeared, with more articles and stories about the harm done by the bureaucrats, Kochetov, the leader of the Stalinists, accused the authors of trying to imitate the writers of the Petőfi circle. The almanac was confiscated, and turns of the screw multiplied on the pretext that the country was again in danger.

In this atmosphere it was unthinkable that the timid dialogue between writers of east and west initiated at Zürich should leave the rails of the cold war. The replies to Silone's questions sent from Moscow at the beginning of January 1957 were evasive behind an air of frankness.

The first question was whether there had been any change after the Twentieth Congress in the directives imposed on writers by the state, the consequence of which, in Sholokhov's own words, had been a literature of 'dead souls'. Or were directives still in existence? Before answering the question Anisimov gave a Stalinist version of events in Hungary. 'Recent events have demonstrated with terrifying clarity,' he said, 'that in Zürich we were only a few steps away from the fascist horror, and that the most ferocious enemy was hidden behind the door near which we were talking.' Here again was the siege mentality, masking its insecurity behind the fear of fascism. In these circumstances, the answer to the question, though completely calm, was highly equivocal. Anisimov did not deny that the state had imposed directives on writers, but claimed that Sholokhov had never complied with them, and recalled what he had said at the second writers' congress. Moreover, he added, socialist realism by no means included the whole of Soviet literature. Nevertheless, 'with all its originality, its daring refusal ever to be satisfied, its drive towards the future, its confidence in the triumph of socialist ideals, its wise understanding of life and its ability to penetrate into the most complex traditions', it was naturally present in the great achievements of Soviet literature. Anisimov tried to run with the hare and hunt with the hounds. 'We repudiate the "formula" of socialist realism just as we repudiate any other dogma,' he concluded, after admitting the existence of works 'that do not go beyond the limits of uninspired, naïve, platitudinous naturalistic representation.'

Silone's second question was: 'What literary or artistic expression has yet been given in your literary periodicals to what has been officially denounced as abuse of the personality cult and violation of socialist legality?' The reply to this was that Soviet literature was now 'in a complex situation of creative tension', marked by the desire to free itself from dogma. It was true that 'the historical environment had for a time forced Soviet literature to live in the unfavourable conditions of the Stalin cult but, apart from the fact that in those years works such as *Quiet Flows the Don* and Alexei Tolstoy's *The Road of Torments* were written, besides excellent novels by Fadeyev, Fedin and Krymov, it should be borne in mind that to a great extent writers had been sincere and without ulterior motive in their adulation of Stalin, because to them he had been a personification of the people and of a high ideal.' However, Anisimov went on, the strength of Soviet literature should not be judged by the standard of its mediocre works, but by that of writers such as Tvardovsky, Antonov and Prishvin. He claimed that since Stalin's death Soviet literature had acquired 'new possibilities of development, its creative efforts were no longer hampered either by illusions or by the dogmas of the personality cult. . . . We contemplate its immediate and more distant prospects with great confidence.'

The third question was whether, in the atmosphere of the thaw, the time had not come to allow the Soviet public to read, not only American pamphlets and the conventional novels of certain western writers, but also the works of the independent left. The reply to this was even more evasive. What thaw? Anisimov asked. The idea of a thaw had never taken root with them. The right words to describe the great and profound changes that had taken place in the Soviet Union since the elimination of the Stalin cult were not to be sought in meteorological bulletins. 'Great events require great ideas, great images, that have not yet been provided by literature and will be provided in non-sensational form. . . . Today as never before in the history of our literature powerful advances are being made by the aspiration to understand profoundly our own great tradition, to base ourselves on it, and to develop all its inherent potentialities, so that every word of our literature may be alive, bold, authoritative and worthy of its great significance.' As for translations, there could hardly be any other country in which so much foreign-language material was translated. They were entitled to print what they liked. They were very willing to publish works by the 'independent left'; let Silone suggest names and titles. 'If the works that he suggests are good and interesting to our readers, we hope that the Soviet publishing houses will follow his advice.' Anisimov glossed over the real problem, which is that the decision which works are good and interesting is not left to the market, but is made paternalistically, by its manipulators.

The fourth question was whether the Soviet authorities would be willing to publish books by Weissberg, Czapski, Herling and Lipper, all witnesses to the crimes of Stalin. This he refused to answer, on the grounds that 'he did not know' these works.

The fifth and last question was: 'The changes that have taken place in Russia in the course of the past few months have been greeted with great pleasure in literary and artistic circles in Hungary, Poland and Yugoslavia. Can you tell us whether these repercussions have been brought to the knowledge of Soviet writers?' The answer to this contained a surprise. Anisimov not only agreed that ferment in other countries had had repercussions in the Soviet Union, but said that this was a field in which there were divergences of view. 'So far as we are concerned,' he said, though just previously he had rejected the 'label' of socialist realism, 'we have always been and remain on the side of socialist realism, since in our opinion everything new, bold and progressive that the socialist period brings to literature is concentrated in that concept.' On the other hand, he went on, searching for a formula that would override all contradictions, 'the idea of socialist realism is a universal synthesis that makes it possible to include in its rich gamut Gorky and Mayakovsky, Sholokhov and Tvardovsky, as well as Fadeyev, Prishvin and Maria Puzhmanova, Aragon and Bronevsky, Eluard and Nezval and Pablo Neruda;' in other words, the whole of the 'literature that belongs to the people and expresses its aspirations' – the people being an abstract category, the cultural and economic stratification produced by the development of Soviet society being completely ignored.

In his reply to Anisimov (who slammed the door on further exchanges in April) Silone asked why the Writers' Union had not instituted an exhaustive inquiry into the holocaust of Russian writers in the early thirties, denounced a theory of art that regarded a writer's politico-social ideas as the obligatory point of departure for judging the artistic merit of his work, and recalled that, when Simonov had asked that an end should be put to the prescribing of socialist realism as the only literary method and that the authorities should confine themselves to recommending it as an auxiliary aid, he had earned himself an official rebuke. That the transfer of power from Zhdanov to Molotov had changed nothing was demonstrated, in Silone's view, by the condemnation of Dudintsev, of Granin for his story 'His Own Opinion', of Yevtushenko for his poem 'The Others' and of Kirsanov for his poem 'The Seven days of the Week', to say nothing of the continuing persecution of Jewish intellectuals, the failure to translate the greater part of the works of Lukács and Gramsci's critical and philosophical writings, and the failure to stage Brecht. 'From my point of view,' Silone concluded, 'your "socialist realism" has no right to the term; it would be more realistic to call it "state realism". . . . What other description does an aesthetic directive deserve that forces the man of letters, and the artist, to present an optimistic image of a society in which man is more than elsewhere exposed to oppression and terror? . . . It is truly foolish to divide literature, or science and art, into two camps, one capitalist and the other proletarian. Above all, the distinction is unreal, confusing the writer's conditions of life and work with his inspiration; and, finally, it is reactionary, since it provides an excuse for the passivity and irresponsibility of weaker spirits. Instead, particularly after the events in Hungary, writers should be recalled to a sense of the nobility and responsibility of their calling.'

The Silone-Anisimov exchanges were not the only sign of a relapse towards freezing point of the political temperature that had been suddenly raised by the Twentieth Congress. But it would be a mistake to believe that the variations in temperature that ensued took place in the kind of void that characterised the Stalin years. One new feature was that in the course of 1956, when political camps were officially abolished, a number of deportees were freed (including a certain Alexander Solzhenitsyn, of whom nobody had yet heard). In 1957 the Russians were at last able to see the second part of Eisenstein's *Ivan the Terrible*, which Stalin had banned in 1946. It was also the year of Kalatozov's *When the Storks Fly*. It was above all the year in which Gagarin became the first man in space; and it was also the year in which writers reacted to this extraordinary scientific and technological achievement by a leap forward in professional pride and dignity. They established contact with each other, formed spontaneous groups, and responded to bureaucratic reprimands with a shrug of the shoulder.

The threat of physical force had receded if it had not

vanished, writers who had greeted the Twentieth Congress as the dawn of a moral and cultural revival proudly stood up to attacks such as that launched in January by the Ukraine Writers' Union (which delivered yet another monotonous denunciation of the anti-realist trends, the formalism, nationalism, cosmopolitanism, anarchical liberty and nihilism rampant among writers of poetry and prose) and a speech made in March by Shepilov, who reiterated the principle of socialist realism. Many of them believed that the criticism of Dudintsev and *Literary Moscow*, the invitations addressed to periodicals and newspapers to confess having fallen into error, the resolutions passed by outlying branches of the Writers' Union, were merely the backwash of the personality cult, blocks of ice that would melt in the spring and be compensated for by a freer kind of writing that it would now be more difficult to stifle. They believed that among the characters in novels, plays and films there would at last be robust sinners and adulterers (Chukhray's film *Ballad of a Soldier* included a wife who was unfaithful to her husband while he was fighting at the front), drinkers and gamblers, or individuals who wasted their energies in private rows (Galina Nikolayeva's novel *The Battle is On*, for instance, caused a sensation because it described the adultery of an engineer who was a member of the party with the widow of one of Stalin's victims). Also many translations of books from capitalist countries had been or were about to be published. Camus's time had not yet come, but Russians were now able to read Steinbeck and Caldwell, Zweig and Mann, Mauriac and Sartre, Moravia and Carlo Levi. An appeal by Shostakovich to Russian composers to engage at last in experimentation with new forms was actually published in *Pravda*.

In May, however, another cold douche was delivered in the form of a statement, 'For a closer relationship between literature and the people', approved by the party central committee, siding with the neo-Stalinists against the writers accused of ideological deviationism. 'I should shoot the lot,' Khrushchev himself said to a group of writers whom he received in the summer in the suburbs of Moscow, referring to the intellectuals who had inspired the Budapest revolt (this so alarmed the poetess Margarita Aliger that she fainted in his presence). This was the prelude to a tightening of the reins that disappointed innumerable hopes and led to a chain reaction of depressive neurosis that gave rise to extreme forms of anxiety in October 1958, when the Pasternak case broke.

Dr Zhivago was published in Italy by Feltrinelli on 15th November, 1957, and was awarded the Nobel Prize on 23rd October, 1958. Few in the Soviet Union had read the novel, and even *Novy Mir* had refused to print it in 1956, but hardly anyone was willing to believe that an artist of Pasternak's stature, who lived apart from but not hostile to the régime, deserved the epithets of counter-revolutionary, slanderer, Judas and pig that *Literaturnaya Gazeta* applied to him for the mere fact of having been published abroad. When it was announced on 28th October that he had been deprived of his status as a Soviet writer and expelled from the Writers' Union for treacherous action damaging to the Soviet people and the cause of socialism, peace and progress, it was not only his loyal friends who rallied to his side.

The edict forced him to renounce the prize, but roused anger and indignation because of the blow it struck through him at a national pride and love of literature that overrode the petty reasons of everyday life and linked up with the great eternal values of mother Russia. All these things converged in the wave of protest that resulted, and fury and resentment set in motion political mechanisms of incalculable and irreversible strength. Manoeuvres by dogmaticians such as Kochetov (who tried to counter Ehrenburg's *The Thaw* and Dudintsev's *Not by Bread Alone* with his novel *The Ershov Brothers*) made little impact, as did the fact that at the third writers' congress in May Khrushchev again spoke favourably of Dudintsev, comparing writers' work to the heavy artillery that opens the way for the infantry, and invited them to decide for themselves whether a book was useful and good, without 'troubling the government'.

Many realised that Tvardovsky's reappointment to the editorship of *Novy Mir*, Kochetov's appointment to the editorship of *Oktyabr* and Smirnov's to that of the *Literaturnaya Gazeta*, and Fedin's election to the secretaryship of the Writers' Union, with Tvardovsky and Panferov as vice-secretaries, were moves and feints in a game played on a chessboard much bigger than their own. Khrushchev said that he did not want to be 'troubled' by the writers, but the party central committee sent a message to the third congress reiterating that 'writers must become enthusiastic propagandists for the seven-year plan and bring gladness and vigour to men's hearts'. Thus the men in the seats of power could change their positions like gloves, pretend to believe in everything and its opposite, move from the extreme right to the extreme left, depending on the relations of strength existing at any particular moment. But writers, obliged to bring gladness and strength to men's hearts, were left with a very limited field of manoeuvre. The sense of being mere pawns in a power game the participants in which ignored and despised them, restricting them to the role of loud-speakers just as in Stalin's time, did not, however, lead merely to frustration and disgust.

Two lines of advance that were to characterise the sixties gradually became perceptible. One was aimed at acquiring sufficient freedom of movement to make it possible to defend professional pride without breaking with the established structures; the other, at the cost of clandestinity, aimed at the establishment of the right to express oneself, if necessary in a fashion contrary to the edicts of socialist realism as interpreted by the bureaucrats. Thus a group of young people who gathered round the twenty-year-old Alexander Ginzburg began publishing and distributing a few hundred copies of the type-written, underground poetry magazine *Sintaksis* in Moscow in December, 1959.

The fifty or so poems that it contained included no incite-ment to rebellion against the régime. For the time being dissent manifested itself in an elementary fashion congenial to a generation that hungered for truth. In contrast to the rosy image of Soviet society that the hierarchy insisted on project-ing, it presented a real, matter-of-fact picture of a world that did not practise what it preached, wrote 'peace' on the walls but was full of pettiness and squabbles, horror and despair, so that man's only hope was escape into dream. The poems in *Sintaksis* were of unequal merit (the best, by Bella Akhma-dulina, appeared in the second issue in February 1960). But as soon as it was discovered to be circulating outside Moscow (the third and last number, that of April 1960, was also pub-lished in Leningrad) the police pounced, and Ginzburg was sentenced to two years' imprisonment.

At the twenty-second party congress, held in the second half of October 1961, Tvardovsky was in the forefront, with a speech that re-echoed all the themes that had nourished the intellectual debate since the days of the Khrushchev report.

Sholokhov had urged writers to leave the towns and live in the country in order to share the real experiences of Soviet men; Tvardovsky replied that the problem was not topographical. 'The defect of many books,' he said, 'is primarily a lack of veracity, due to the author's cautiousness, his tendency to see only the festive days of life, the dates printed in red in the calendar, neglecting all the other days of the week, full of stress, worries and compulsion of every sort.' Once more it was the same old story – condemnation of the lack of confidence, the atmosphere of suspicion, the incomplete representation of the manifold processes of life, the mistrust of satire, all things that were damaging both to art and to society. 'One must not be taken in by lies,' Tvardovsky said, quoting Lenin. 'Here lies the principal source of our bureaucratism.'

This time it seemed as if things were going to take a turn for the better. In vain Kochetov boasted of always having been and wishing to remain a faithful helper of the party, and repeated that the Writers' Union, having lost its capacity for struggle, needed drastic reorganisation; the congress passed a resolution that allowed the optimists to hope for progress in the direction of liberalism. The resolution said: 'In the art of socialist realism, based on the principles of its popular and party nature, bold innovation in the artistic representation of life is combined with the utilisation and development of all the progressive traditions in world literature.' Carefully balanced concessions to both sides were contained in this formula, which could be interpreted at one's pleasure, depending on how one read it. But the fact that it implied more tolerance than had been expected (though always within the framework of Khrushchev's anti-Stalin line) was shown by the repercussions that the congress, which vetoed the re-election of twenty-five per cent of former leading figures, solemnly undertook to restore socialist legality, and resolved that Stalin's body should be removed from Lenin's tomb, had on Soviet intellectual life and publishing.

One of the first signs of this was the behaviour of editors of periodicals and in publishing houses. For years authors had protested against censorship by editors who constantly changed words and phrases, denouncing as socially dangerous stylistic usages the only fault of which was that they were unpalatable to bureaucratic thickheads (the misfortunes of Veresayev, who had to accept 140 corrections in a story three pages long had become proverbial, and in 1960 Lydia Chukov-skaya published in Moscow her *In the editor's office*, a vigorous indictment of the manipulators of manuscripts). The censors' claim to the right to subject everything presented to them to stylistic polishing, obviously for the purpose of reducing it to the level of the inexpressive jargon of the bureaucracy, now clashed with the writers' privilege of choosing 'progressive' forms.

The change of personnel for age reasons in the offices of some periodicals enabled a number of writers to choose more open-minded outlets (*Yunost* came to occupy a position in the advance guard). In the field of the cinema, the success of Chukray's *Clear Skies*, Romm's *Nine Days of the Year*, Alov's and Naumov's *Peace to Him who Enters*, and Tarkovsky's *Ivan's Childhood* (in 1962 Tarkovsky was to win the Golden Lion award at Venice) gave rise to hopes that wider horizons were opening in that field too, and that it would be possible to exercise the artistic imagination in an atmosphere more open to poetical impulses or the tragic interpretation of reality. For a year, in short, smiles returned to the faces of the intellectuals. There were even some who believed that Khrushchev's idea of changing the name of the MGB (the secret police) to KGB ('committee for state security') was a sign that the forces of oppression were weakening. Reiterated condemnation of the crimes of Stalin reopened the vein of re-evocation of the past, and description of acts of tyranny and the suffering they caused provided ample opportunity for exploration of the human soul, and for poetry rooted in gravity rather than the smile.

While the courts busily sentenced the producers of clandestine publications (Osipov, the editor of *Boomerang*, was sentenced to five years' forced labour), without, however, managing to stem the flow (the first number of *Phoenix 1961* appeared in November of that year) and *Inostrannaya Literatura* defended socialist realism against attacks on it made by an anonymous Soviet writer (who later turned out to be Andrei Sinyavsky) in the French periodical *l'Esprit*, Nina Kosterina's *Diary*, which recalled the trials of the Old Bolsheviks, sold like hot cakes in the bookshops, as did the republished anthology *Literaturnaya Moskva*, Bondarev's novel *The Silence*, Simonov's *The Living and the Dead* and Nekrasov's *Reportage*, the *Starred Ticket* by Vasily Aksyonov, the son of Evgenia Ginzburg, who

66

was deported with her husband and related her appalling experiences in *Into the Whirlwind*, and Rosov's *ABCDE*, which expressed the impatience of the younger generation. All these works were like a breath of fresh air. But passers-by in Mayakovsky Square in Moscow on an autumn day in 1961 felt they had been transported to another world – so much so that for a long time they could not believe the evidence of their senses – when they came across a group of young people gathered round Ginzburg, who was reading at the top of his voice Yuri Galanskov's poem 'Human Manifesto', a heart-rending *cri de coeur* by an adolescent to whom 'life is as dreadful as a prison built on bones', from which freedom was attainable only by revolt.

Film-makers, however, saw the hopes born in the past two years fading again. In August 1962 a resolution by the party central committee condemned films not directed 'to the discovery of the moral depth of Soviet man and the many-sidedness of socialist reality', criticised the Ministry of Culture for not adequately supervising the activity of film studios, and failing to influence the subject-matter, ideological trend and artistic quality of script writers, and it laid down that films should be produced that 'faithfully reconstruct the achievements of the people under the guidance of the party in the struggle for the construction of socialism, films that reflect in clear colours the heroic undertakings of Soviet men in the construction of communism'. The Ministry of Culture was called on to organise permanent courses in script writing and to set up 'artistic soviets' in all film studios. Thus it was made clear that at any rate in this field the party had no intention of loosening the reins. The cinema, the mass art *par excellence*, had to remain a principal tool of communist education of the people and had to be provided with efficient cadres. Film-makers, whose work influenced millions of people, and especially the young, could not be allowed to spend public money on films that did not teach the lesson of virtue and confidence in the future.

Nevertheless the cinema was to some extent a special case. In other sectors the ideological controls were less rigid. Whether out of weariness or political calculation, signs of greater liberalism multiplied. In August and September 1962 the economist Liberman, writing in *Pravda*, actually pleaded for the reintroduction of the profit motive and for the granting of greater independence of management to Soviet industries. Natalie Sarraute went to Moscow and Leningrad to lecture on the *nouveau roman*. The American Salinger's *The Catcher in the Rye* was translated and sold out immediately. Research into linguistics flourished, students of cybernetics, historians of formalism, theorists of structuralism, openly discussed together problems that hitherto had been confined to laboratories and seminars. In March Nekrasov took part in the congress of the European Community of Writers in Florence.

One evening in October Tvardovsky, cheered by the new mood that was spreading in the country and pleased at having contributed to the process himself, returned home with a pile of manuscripts that had been sent to *Novy Mir*. Most of them had been sent in by unknown writers who preferred *Novy Mir* to other journals because, in the light of its record, they considered it to be the most open-minded and courageous. Tvardovsky, in accordance with his usual habit, undressed, got into bed, lit a cigar, and picked a manuscript from the pile. He found himself turning the pages of *One Day in the Life of Ivan Denisovich*, which had been sent in from Ryazan, signed by one Alexander Solzhenitsyn, and his enthusiasm was fired immediately.

'I realised at once,' he said later, 'that here was something important, and that in some way I must celebrate the event. I got out of bed, got fully dressed again in every particular, and sat down at my desk. That night I read a new classic of Russian literature.' What was it that impressed him so much?

In the first place, it was the book's utterly convincing veracity; next came the warmth of the writing. *One Day in the Life of Ivan Denisovich* tells the story of a political prisoner who for eight years (the time is the beginning of 1951 and the principal character is aged forty-six) has survived the hardships and outrages of Stalin's camps. What had his crime been? Ivan Denisovich Shukhov had been called up on 23rd June, 1941 and immediately drafted to the north-western front, where in a moment of chaos resulting from Soviet military unpreparedness he was surprised by the Germans in a wood and taken prisoner. But his imprisonment did not last for long; a few days later he and a few companions slipped away and rejoined the Russian lines. 'If they had been sensible,' Solzhenitsyn writes, 'they would have said that they had lost their way in the woods, and perhaps they would have got away with it.

Instead they blurted out everything. 'We have come back from imprisonment by the Germans,' they said. 'Imprisonment? Sons of bitches, etc., etc.'

Military discipline at that time reflected Stalin's own ferocity; the propagandists claimed to have roused such hatred of the enemy that no good Soviet soldier would for one moment tolerate the idea of falling into German hands; he would rather commit suicide. Things, of course, did not always turn out as the leaders hoped; as in all wars, there were soldiers who gave themselves up of their own accord and others who let themselves be taken prisoner without turning their arms against themselves. Many lived to regret it. For years it was considered shameful to have been a prisoner of the Germans. There are still men who recall with horror the persecutions to which they were subjected when they came home, for coming back alive was considered proof of cowardice, if not of connivance with the enemy.

Solzhenitsyn's hero was still more unfortunate; he was court-martialled and sentenced to forced labour 'for allowing himself to be taken prisoner, wishing to betray his country, and for returning from imprisonment on a German espionage mission'. Solzhenitsyn did not strain reality; cases such as that of Shukhov were frequent, and it was on the ferocity of such sentences for imaginary crimes, most of them inflicted on peasants and workers whom the war had torn from their homes and whose lives were shattered by a verdict from which there was no appeal, that the popular horror of Stalin's inhumanity was based.

In dry, sharp language and with uncommon power *One Day in the Life of Ivan Denisovich* told the story of these innocent men, sent to heavy labour in camps in the far north, where the temperature was sometimes forty degrees below freezing point, where in a short time they were reduced to the state of animals wallowing in the mud or snow, incited against each other by hunger, under the eyes of guards armed with sub-machine guns and wolf-hounds. No Soviet book had yet portrayed life in Stalin's camps with the desperate sincerity Solzhenitsyn put into describing the prisoners' struggle to get hold of an extra crust of bread to hide in their straw mattress, or the stub of a cigarette, or an extra helping of millet or oatmeal broth, the struggle to protect themselves from the cold, the searches, the bullying of the gangers, the spies, and the temptation to rebel.

The camp in which Shukhov and his wretched companions were confined (one of them had been sentenced for taking milk to some Ukrainian nationalists in a wood, and another for being a Baptist) is an unvarnished symbol of Stalin's Russia, in which personal life was reduced to a minimum, crushed by an implacable machine that destroyed the individual's human dignity and reduced him to a jackal, leaving him with nothing but the choice between death and adapting himself to a law that was a mockery of Soviet power. 'Do you think Moustache [Stalin] will have any pity on you?' one prisoner says. And another: 'Prayers are like complaints. Either they don't reach their destination or they are rejected.' Those are two brief examples of the atmosphere of *One Day in the Life of Ivan Denisovich*, in which indignation and irony combine to express the stupefaction of a survivor.

The impact is made the greater by the writing, which is varied in rhythm and construction, has the vigour of common speech and yet re-echoes the feel of the classics, turning the description of a devastating historical experience into an allegory. An ordinary man, carried away by a storm that passes his comprehension, driven on in the midst of a black, hostile crowd through the frozen steppe, livid in the light of the moon, tries to save his humanity by touches of sad, self-irony, comforting himself with the thought of those still worse off and caressing the thing that is dearest to him, a spoon made with his own hands in the camp at Ust-Izma in 1944. No wonder that that night Tvardovsky felt the need to respond like Machiavelli, who put on his best clothes before reading the classics, to the high level of the work that he was reading, and decided to publish it immediately, conscious of the importance of a book that described the infamy of the Stalin camps in writing of such outstanding quality.

In the past few years there had been no lack of writing about the sufferings of the people during the years of greatest darkness, or about the camps in which many innocent people had suffered, but none of it had Solzhenitsyn's vigour. After years and years of prose flattened by the censors, he was the first to recapture all the colour and strength of the Russian language, and no other writer made an impact on the civil and moral conscience of the Soviet reader comparable with that made by this novel that represented 'a judgment on a whole historical period'. Vittorio Strada, anticipating Lukács, called it a milestone dividing the literature of the thaw into periods before and after Ivan Denisovich, or rather marking the end of the thaw and the opening of a new phase of Soviet letters.

It remained to be seen whether the new phase would have time and opportunity to develop. Meanwhile Tvardovsky was in a state of agitation. On the one hand he was convinced that he had laid his hands on a book that would do more than any of his other discoveries to strengthen his reputation as a talent-spotter; on the other, he could not help wondering whether the censorship would pass this anti-conformist work, and whether the more timorous of his colleagues on *Novy Mir* would not be the first to advise him to seek the *nihil obstat* of the party leaders and Glavlit, the organisation directly responsible to the Council of Ministers on questions of literature and art. He was sufficiently experienced to know that the blind machinery of the censorship had itself been shaken in recent years, was unsure of itself, and had been losing ground. Since 1956 the chief concern of the bureaucrats barricaded in Glavlit had been to ensure that the output of the printing presses contained no violations of military secrecy or offences against decency; so it should be possible to evade the obstacles by using the right tactics.

Tvardovsky decided to go straight to the top. He wrote to Khrushchev, pointing out the advisability of publishing a novel on which, among others, a personality as reliable as Fedin had expressed a favourable opinion, and meanwhile he sent the manuscript to the printers, intending to publish it in the next number of *Novy Mir*. These tactics worked. The manuscript put the censors into a state of high alarm, but it was sufficient for Khrushchev to glance at it to see that fortune had put a formidable weapon into his hands; it would help him both to strike a blow at the Stalin myth by this demonstration of the horrors and injustices to which it had led and to establish himself as Stalin's providential successor, an apostle of freedom of expression and historical truth.

Khrushchev was in as great a hurry at Tvardovsky. He covered himself by having the manuscript read by Sholokhov, who reported favourably, and the matter was summarily dealt with at a meeting of the Presidium. 'Isn't it a fine book?' Khrushchev asked his colleagues. No-one had the courage to say anything. 'Silence means consent,' Khrushchev remarked, and adjourned the meeting. Thus in a flash, in accordance with the logic of dictatorships, undreamt-of horizons opened up for Solzhenitsyn – not so much because of the literary merits of his book as because of the use the régime wanted to make of it.

The serialisation of *One Day in the Life of Ivan Denisovich* began in the November 1962 number of *Novy Mir*, two editions in volume form were published in January 1963, and its success was fantastic. Those who could not get a copy in the bookshops borrowed it from their luckier friends, formed long queues outside the public libraries, made typed copies. *Pravda* praised it on 23rd November. Kruzhikov in *Ogonyok* and Tityerov in *Moskovskaya Pravda* called it a work coming from the past that looked to the future. Ilyichev, the secretary of the central committee, praised it, and at the Writers' Union and among intellectuals the sensation was immense.

As the Kremlin had foreseen, Khrushchev's popularity increased at a bound. Even those not concerned with literature were moved and astonished to find in a book which was freely on sale a real picture of a state of affairs that no-one had hitherto been willing officially to admit. In thousands of humble homes Ivan Denisovich was identified with fathers, husbands or brothers who had perished of hunger and disease in the labour camps. Survivors recognised themselves in his sufferings and his loathing of Stalin. Writers who for so long had been degraded into spokesmen for the régime recovered prestige and self-confidence.

Tvardovsky wrote an outspoken preface to the book. Insistence on the truth, he said, was the guarantee of a complete and irreversible breach with the past, the age of the personality cult which the party had disowned and rejected. Solzhenitsyn's story accorded with Khrushchev's insistence at the Twenty-Second Congress that many things must be made plain and that the truth must be told to the party and the people, so that certain things should never happen again. Solzhenitsyn's testimony, which could hardly have been given until recently, was limited to the prisoners in the camps, but it could be extended to include all those who had had to face exceedingly harsh physical and moral ordeals at the front or at post-war work sites. The book, with the extraordinary truth to life of its human characters, reflected bitterness and pain, though without driving the reader to discouragement and despair;

instead it freed his mind from remorse at not having said what should have been said.

Tvardovsky did not confine himself to a moral and political assessment of the book, but pointed out that it provided confirmation of the vast number of themes open to the Soviet artist and illustrated the fact that form must be harmonised with content, and he seized the opportunity to give a quick lesson in aesthetics to that part of the intelligentsia that still identified socialist realism with varnishing reality and restricted stylistic experiment to ringing the changes on *clichés*.

One Day in the Life of Ivan Denisovich presented with striking clarity the crux of the literary and political debate. Its publication not only represented as Tvardovsky said, the entry into Soviet literature of 'an original and fully mature artist' to whom gratitude was due. Here the intellectual identified himself with the popular conviction that art is based on sincerity and loyalty to real feelings, and that no ideology can justify human suffering or stifle indignation at injustice and tyranny. *One Day in the Life of Ivan Denisovich* is a monument to the living reality of suffering as against the débris of the class struggle and endless squabbling about the correct interpretation of Marxism-Leninism.

This appears most plainly in the collection of letters sent to Solzhenitsyn after the book's publication ('I think they should be looked through,' he wrote. 'From the reception given to the first novel about the camps, which tells only part of the truth, toning down the colours, one can imagine what will happen when everything comes out'). These letters were confiscated by the police, but were published in *Possev* in May 1969. In the introduction to them that he wrote he remarked bitterly that 'our compatriots, greatly deceived, believed that the age of truth was about to begin, and that they too would be able to write something. And a single, unanimous cry arose (but naturally they were disappointed again).'

Many ex-deportees believed they recognised their own portrait in Shukhov, and now boasted of having lived in the same hut as Solzhenitsyn and suffered ordeals similar to his. 'I read, and my hands shook,' one Voychenko wrote. Another, named Kravchenko, said: 'Now I read and weep, but when I was at Ukhta I had no tears to weep.' Some ex-camp inmates whose experience dated from more recent times compared Solzhenitsyn's experiences with their own and maintained that since

73

Stalin's death nothing had altered; the guards had changed from wolf's into sheep's clothing, but still carried out their duties oppressively in the penal settlements.

For their part, guards wrote to Solzhenitsyn denouncing Shukhov as a 'toady', 'all belly and no brain', a coward who had had himself court-martialled to avoid going back to the front, a traitor for whom ten years were not enough, he should have been given forty. 'Since when has *Novy Mir* started defending bourgeois nationalists who have killed thousands and thousands of activists?' asked a reader from Uzhgorod. 'This novel is an insult to the officers, non-commissioned officers and men of the Defence Ministry,' another said. 'We supervisors work with the refuse of society, putting up with a hard life for the benefit of the whole people; why should we be depicted like this?' 'We do our duty, and do not want to be insulted.' 'The novel would have a positive value if it did justice to the tasks entrusted to the penal institutions,' a certain Grigorich wrote, and Solzhenitsyn ironically noted that such were the 'great tasks' entrusted to literature in the USSR.

Nearly all the charges made by the slanderers and persecutors who later held up Solzhenitsyn to popular ignominy were anticipated. 'You trample honest Soviet citizens in the mud . . . you have a bad conscience. . . . Was it by smearing someone's palm that you regained your freedom?' 'You whine, comrade, you have no confidence in the new life.' 'This Solzhenitsyn's eyes are blinded by perfidy. . . . He is incapable of understanding real greatness.' 'History has never needed the past, and the history of socialist culture needs it even less.' 'We need neither compassion nor pity.' There were even some who blamed the 1937 purges on remnants of the former privileged classes who had insinuated themselves into the police and in 1941 became *agents-provocateurs*. 'That makes everything clear,' was Solzhenitsyn's comment. 'The class enemy ruined the party, lured Hitler to Stalingrad, and then handed over to experienced generals and the wise Generalissimo. The terrible thing is that that is how history is written.'

So much for the reactions of the general public. Solzhenitsyn's chief cause for anxiety was the line taken by some moderates, who acknowledged the book's truth, but considered it inexpedient to expose it to public view and to put it in the hands of the reactionary press. It was written specifically to promote awareness, particularly among the young, of a blot on the national life, and the principle that dirty linen should not be washed in public has always been the refuge of hypocrites who by spreading the seeds of public alarm and anxiety ensure that the dirt remains. However, the expressions of sympathy and gratitude that Solzhenitsyn received definitely outweighed the insults of those who rebuked him for digging up a past that should be forgotten. Solzhenitsyn noted that 'our compatriots too seldom have the opportunity of expressing their views on matters of public interest'. Now that they had such a chance, now that the *détente* seemed to favour confidences, it was not surprising that a people that in the last resort had always equated life with suffering should welcome the advent of this writer with the admiration due to one who swept away the false trophies of a mystificatory art without raising his voice, merely by depicting a single day in a man's life.

Nor was what followed his début as a writer surprising – the way in which he was fêted and exalted beyond objective limits, the way in which newspapers, e.g. *Sovietskaya Rossiya* on 28th November, referred to him as a victim of unjust political accusations, and his experiences and example were used for the purposes of the anti-Stalinist campaign ordered from above. In a country in which the mechanism of public praise makes use of the same channels and systems as the slander factory, the new element in the situation was the participation of public opinion in the harmony existing between the Kremlin and the democratic intelligentsia and the spontaneity with which the reading public tried to find out who this Solzhenitsyn was and what his experiences had been, almost as if seeking an assurance in the obscurity of his life that they were not once more confronted with a hero mythicised in the struggle of factions.

This brings us to the period between November 1962 and February 1963. While the Stalinists, who had been caught on the wrong foot by Khrushchev's move, were preparing their counter-offensive, and writers such as Simonov (in *Izvestya* on 18th November) praised *One Day in the Life of Ivan Denisovich* to the skies, Soviet man discovered in Solzhenitsyn's life-story a kind of self-portrait.

CHAPTER FIVE

Solzhenitsyn enjoyed the favour of the authorities and the Soviet press too briefly for the propaganda machine of the USSR and the cultural industry of the west to be able to point the searchlight of publicity at his life and reveal all its details. The Soviet people know much less about him than they would like to know, and that little has to do with his experiences in Stalin's labour camps and his relations with the Writers' Union rather than with the central biographical facts, the family and cultural background of his literary talent.

Alexander Isayevich Solzhenitsyn was born on 11th December, 1918, at Kislovodsk, in the south of the Russian Federal Republic, where the Stavropol region borders on the two autonomous republics of Kabardino-Balkaria and Karachayevo-Cherkesk. Kislovodsk, which now has 100,000 inhabitants, lies about 2,500 feet above sea-level on the slopes of the Caucasus range, forty miles as the crow flies from the summit of Mount Elbruz. It is well-known as a spa, but it also has a place in Russian literature, for it was here that Lermontov situated one of the stories in *A Hero of Our Own Times*. 'The people who live here,' he wrote, 'say that the air of Kislovodsk is propitious to love, and that all the idylls that begin on the slopes of the Mashuk reach their fulfilment here. In fact everything here is solitude and mystery. The lime-trees along the avenues cast a dense shade, and down below the stream splashes noisily between the green hillsides. Ravines, full of mist and silence, open up in every direction. The scent of tall southern grasses and white acacia pervades the brisk and fragrant air. You are continually lulled by the gentle murmur of cold rivulets that converge towards the end of the valley and amiably compete with each other until they flow into the Podkumok.'

Solzhenitsyn's father, a state employee, had been a student of literature at Moscow University, volunteered for military service in 1914 and served as an artillery officer on the German front. He was killed in an accident six months before Alexander was born, and at the age of six his mother, who was a typist, took him to Rostov-on-the-Don. His childhood

76

and adolescence cannot have been easy, troubled as they were by frequent disturbances of the respiratory system that later prevented him from going on the stage, an ambition inspired by his admiration for the actor and producer Yuri Zavadsky, who was exiled to Rostov. In those early years he wrote three plays (which were never produced). He studied mathematics and physics at Rostov University, and simultaneously took a correspondence course in history, philosophy and literature conducted by the Institute of History in Moscow. In 1940 he married a fellow-student, the chemistry graduate Natalya Reshetovskaya. After graduating with distinction in mathematics in 1941, he taught mathematics at a secondary school at Morozovka, in the Rostov region.

He had not yet discovered his vocation; his first attempts at writing were rejected by the periodical *Znamya*, Fedin and Lavienev, which seems not to have encouraged him in the literary direction. 'I found mathematics easy,' he said later in an interview with Pavel Ličko, a Slovak journalist who was to be arrested at Bratislava in September 1970, 'and they offered me an academic career in that field; but I did not want to devote the whole of my life to mathematics. I was chiefly attracted to literature, but I realised that mathematics offered me a livelihood.'

The war saved him from having to choose, however, and on 18th October, 1941 he was called up. For a time he was a transport driver, then spent a year as an officer cadet at the artillery training school at Saransk. He was then transferred to Gorky (the experience is reflected in his story *An Incident at Krechetovka Station*), and then, in 1942, he was sent to the front, first in command of an acoustic range-finding section and then as a battery commander. In 1944 – during which his mother died of tuberculosis – he reached the rank of captain and was awarded the Order of the Patriotic War, Second Class, and the Order of the Red Star. After fighting at Leningrad and taking part in the campaign right through White Russia and Poland, in February 1945 he was in East Prussia at the beginning of the Soviet offensive in the Königsberg area.

One day General Travkin, his divisional commander, sent for him, ordered him to surrender his pistol, and handed him over to two agents of SMERSH (the army counter-espionage organisation) who arrested him for treachery and removed his decorations and emblems of rank. Before they took him away

77

General Travkin shook hands with him as a token of his personal esteem. 'They arrested me because of my naïveté,' Solzhenitsyn later said. 'I knew it was forbidden to mention military secrets in letters from the front, but I thought that thinking was legitimate.' He was accused of having criticised Stalin's strategic ability, and even his grammar (though without mentioning him by name) in letters to a friend in 1944 and 1945 and of having stated that Stalin had betrayed Lenin's ideas and had committed blunders that had led to the disasters of the opening stages of the war. Notes for stories and other jottings found in his haversack were also included in the indictment.

He was taken to the Lubyanka prison in Moscow, made to confess his guilt, and on 7th July 1945, after a brief court-martial in which he had no defending counsel (it was not even thought necessary that he should be present), he was sentenced to eight years' forced labour plus three years' banishment. The court found that he 'had conducted anti-Soviet propaganda among his acquaintances since 1940', and found him guilty under Article 58, No. 10, second paragraph, of the penal code, which provided severe penalties (in war-time including shooting) for disseminating, compiling or keeping writings tending to subvert or weaken the Soviet power. The court also found him guilty under Article 58, No. 11, which provided penalties for participation in an organisation created for the purpose of carrying out counter-revolutionary activity (Solzhenitsyn's friend Vitkevich, to whom the letters were addressed, was sentenced to ten years). 'I did not consider the verdict unjust,' Solzhenitsyn admitted later. 'I had expressed opinions which were then forbidden.'

His prison years can be divided into three periods. In the first, that lasted from July 1945 to 1949, he was kept in the Krasnaya Presnya prison in Moscow and worked on a building site in the Kaluga district in the neighbourhood of the capital. His degree in mathematics was not of much use to him; the work consisted of helping to lay parquet flooring in buildings intended for the Ministry of the Interior, including a towered mansion on the Leningradsky Prospekt.

Soon, however, in 1946 he was transferred to an establishment at Mavrinka, where the secret service used prisoners for scientific research purposes. This experience is reflected in his novel *The First Circle*, and this was also the time of his

78

first notes on the crimes of Stalin, for whom he was compelled to work on the development of a secret telephone-tapping system. His verse drama *The Feast of the Victors* (in which Stalin is compared to Hitler and Russian deserters who went over to General Vlasov are not denounced as traitors to their country) dates from this period, i.e. 1949–50; this work was later confiscated by the police and used as evidence of his anti-patriotism, though he had several times declared that he repudiated it. Up to this point prison had been relatively supportable; prisoners were allowed visits by members of their families and to read books. It was now that Solzhenitsyn, with the aid of dictionaries, plunged into the study of the Russian language.

In 1950, however, his situation changed for the worse; after spending time in various transit prisons he was sent to northern Kazakhstan, to the Karlag camp at Dzhezkazgan (in the province of Karaganda), where he worked in the quarries, partly as a bricklayer and partly as a foundry worker (he was prisoner No. SH.232). This was the worst period, the most immediate inspiration of his future works. It was here that the idea of *One Day in the Life of Ivan Denisovich* was born; and his situation was aggravated by the development of a stomach tumour, for which he underwent an operation in the camp infirmary in the summer of 1952.

And so we come to the beginning of spring, 1953 ('the most agitated and the most beautiful in my life'). He was discharged from the camp in February, and on the morning of 5th March he was awakened by an old woman and told to go down into the street to listen to the loudspeakers announcing the news of Stalin's death. He was sent for by the political police, who failed to make him countersign a certificate of permanent deportation, and was then sent to Dzhambul, in southern Kazakhstan, and from there to Berlik, in the district of Kok-Terek, a Tartar village near Lake Balkash, where he spent three years of banishment, teaching mathematics and having to report to the police twice a week. Here he was rejoined by his wife (who in the meantime had thought of divorce to escape the persecutions to which the wives of political prisoners were subjected).

In the autumn of 1953 his cancer returned and he was taken to the hospital at Tashkent, but recovered after lengthy treatment (the tumour was stopped by X-rays). Meanwhile, he had made up his mind to be a writer, while continuing to earn his living as a mathematics teacher. In 1954 he wrote poetry (including the poem 'Prussian Nights', which he subsequently repudiated), and the play *The Stag and the Camp Prostitute*. In 1955 he began *The First Circle* and in 1956 began thinking about *Cancer Ward*. This year was that of his release. After serving his term in full, he at last became a free man again. He lived for a time in the province of Vladimir, where he wrote *Matryona's Home*, and then settled at Ryazan, in central Russia, south-east of Moscow. (Ryazan has its place in history because of the defeat of the Russian princes there by the Mongols in 1237.) His wife had a house there that he himself put back into habitable condition. She taught chemistry at the local agricultural institute, and helped him to obtain a post teaching physics and mathematics at the local secondary school. He taught, wrote (later he also conducted a course for amateur photographers), and followed the struggle in the Kremlin with intelligible trepidation, without for the time being intervening in literary polemics.

At the beginning of 1957 he was summoned to appear before the military division of the Supreme Court, which had begun reviewing the cases of individuals sentenced under the Stalin régime (the outcome was 600 rehabilitations among writers alone, of which 180 were posthumous). Solzhenitsyn replied to the questions of the court by reading passages from *One Day in the Life of Ivan Denisovich*. The three judges, Borisoglabsky, Dolochev and Konev, looked at each other in perplexity but, in view of their orders, had no difficulty in agreeing that he had been the victim of a miscarriage of justice. After hearing some witnesses, including his wife, all of whom denied that he had ever engaged in anti-Soviet activity, they decided that Article IV, Section 5, of the Penal Code applied to his case. On 16th February, 1957 the Supreme Court published a decree of rehabilitation (No. 4N 083/57), stating among other things that from 1942 to the time of his arrest Solzhenitsyn 'had fought bravely for his country' and 'had several times shown genuine heroism and inspired by his example the unit of which he was in command'. The charges against him were unfounded. 'It is clear,' the decree said, 'that when Solzhenitsyn in his diary and the letters to his friend discussed the problem of the correct interpretation of Marxism-Leninism, the progressive content of the socialist revolution in our country and the inevitability of its victory throughout the world, he was opposing the cult of the personality of Stalin and was referring to the artistic and ideological inadequacy of many works by Soviet authors and their sense of unreality.'

During the same year Solzhenitsyn was admitted to the Ryazan branch of the Writers' Union and acquired the halo of a persecuted innocent; he had been banished from the world for eleven years, from the age of twenty-seven to thirty-eight, stricken in body and spirit by cruelties compounded by the horror of cancer. Meanwhile he had also written other things, including a film script, *The Tanks Know the Truth*, but when he sent the typescript of *One Day* to *Novy Mir* in 1962, after several rejections elsewhere, it was natural enough that he should not only be hoping for literary fame but also seeking some recompense for the loathing of Stalin and the world that he embodied that he had nourished for so long. The roots of the whole of his future work, and of all the public attitudes that he was henceforward to adopt, literary, psychological and ideological, lay in the ordeals he suffered between 1945 and 1956, and in the belief, forged in suffering and indignation, that no political decisions should be taken by his country that ignored the price paid in individual suffering.

In the winter of 1962–63 he decided to devote himself principally to writing and reduced his teaching to nine hours a week, with the result that his income fell to fifty roubles a week; he was motivated by a sense of mission, the sense that he must bear witness in his books to a personal experience that might make an impact on a growing body of opinion and turn into a human and civil lesson of high value to socialism itself.

The success of *One Day in the Life of Ivan Denisovich* at the end of 1962 (94,000 copies of *Novy Mir* were sold out in two days, and it was translated into fifteen languages) enabled him to buy a car, a Moskvich that he called Denis Ivanovich; later, with the proceeds of reprints by the *Roman Gazeta* and the *Sovietsky Piatyel* in 1963, he acquired a small *dacha* in the woods at Obninsk, fifty miles south of Moscow. The sense of relief at Khrushchev's liberalising measures, felt in circles wider than those of the Moscow writers, seemed to justify his decision to reduce his teaching commitments. Optimism was by no means unjustified. True, reactionary or merely conservative novels continued to be published (Kochetov's *The Secretary of the Regional Committee*, Dolmatovsky's *Our Years*), the Tarsis case was settled for the time being by that author's internment, and at party meetings ex-soldiers, reactionaries and firemen continued to issue warnings against pushing criticism of Stalin beyond the limits of political expediency.

Nevertheless the literary climate as a whole was marked by enthusiasm for the works of the 'progressive' writers, poetry in particular (in October Yevtushenko's poem 'The Heirs of Stalin' appeared in *Pravda*, followed by *Babi Yar*), as well as for a type of fiction represented by Nekrasov's *The Two Sides of the Ocean*, published in *Novy Mir*, that was in line with Khrushchev's policy of co-existence, broadening the sources of inspiration and rejecting dogmatic aggressivity against other cultural traditions. The fruitful idea seemed to be gaining ground, among the general public also, that Soviet and western literature should not be judged by a rigid yardstick which contrasted the rationalism and optimism deduced from the belief that Marxism was the explanation of absolutely everything, with the pessimism, nihilism, triviality and pornography of the west, but by the efficacy of the formal tools chosen for the exploration of the recesses of the human mind, the roots of a human condition that was aware, not only of the joys of construction, but also of the fear of death. In other words, the suspicion began to spread that Soviet literature, conditioned by socialist realism and turning the human condition into a fossilised smile instead of offering some consolation for the harshness of life by virtue of style and freedom of the imagination, had rendered less service than had western literature to contemporary man.

At the congress for disarmament and peace held in Moscow in July, Sartre proclaimed the necessity of 'demilitarising culture' and quoted with indignation the case of Kafka, who was still banned in the countries of eastern Europe. There was talk of a film version of *One Day in the Life of Ivan Denisovich* (mentioned in a despatch to the *Literaturnaya Rossya* from Bukanov, its special correspondent sent to Ryazan), and the Sovremennik Theatre in Moscow had on its list of forthcoming productions for the spring *The Stag and the Camp Prostitute*, which Solzhenitsyn himself read to the actors on New Year's Eve (it was published in England in 1969 under the less indelicate title *The Love-Girl and the Innocent*). This play, which was written almost contemporaneously with *One*

Day in the Life of Ivan Denisovich and contains the same motifs of alienation and horror, is infused with powerful dramatic tension.

The action takes place in the autumn of 1945. A 'stag' in camp jargon is an ex-front-line soldier, in this case the former officer Rodion Nemov, who has been given a ten-year sentence and, being new to the camp, has not yet absorbed the poisons of a world in which all moral values are turned upside down, and he engages in a sad idyll with the unhappy Lyuba, a kulak's daughter, who has to sell herself to remain alive. Their love affair, a feeble gleam of light in a grim world (the background is the bare, wind-swept steppe) lasts for barely a week, because the woman cannot refuse to become the mistress of the camp medical officer; another agonising picture of human beings wounded in their most tender feelings, victims of a moment in history and a symbolical place, the Stalin camps, that behind a cheerful curtain representing a busy industrial landscape destroy all sense of justice and turn men into wolves.

The scene is set in the seething mass of humanity in a camp in which political prisoners and common criminals work in a foundry or at other forms of heavy labour, all forced to exceed their norm for the sake of an extra ration or some female companionship. In Solzhenitsyn's typical fashion, individuals emerge from the chorus, expressing the tragic essence of a collective condition with human simplicity and without any ideological supercharging, and then just as swiftly fall back into the chorus again. When the curtains fall the spectator feels he has been looking at a painting in reds and greys of a horrible reality in a barbed wire frame that can nevertheless be coped with and mastered with the aid of the moral conscience. For, as Nemov says, 'the most important thing that we have is not our skin, but our conscience.'

Another reminder of the conscience and morality is provided by *A Candle in the Wind* (also known under the biblical title *The Light that is within Thee* – Luke, XI, 35), but this time, unusually for Solzhenitsyn, the dramatic conflict does not arise directly out of Soviet reality in the Stalin period. The play, which was written in 1960, is situated on the shores of an ocean in an unknown country at an unspecified time. The characters have international names. Solzhenitsyn explained to his Slovak interviewer Pavel Ličko that the object of this was not to hide anything. 'I wanted to present the moral problems of society in the developed countries, independently of whether they are socialist or capitalist,' he said. Against this generalised background, which, however, contains hints of a socialist form of organisation, Solzhenitsyn tackles one of the most crucial contemporary questions – the motives, limitations and nature of scientific research, and the rôle of spiritual values in a world that scientific achievements and technological developments threaten to dehumanise. Another way in which this play differs from nearly all Solzhenitsyn's other works is that it consists in the confrontation of two characters, two attitudes to life.

Philip Radagais and Alex Koriel, both in their forties and friends from their university days, have a scientific background and experience of prison, though not for political reasons. Philip wants to forget prison. He is the head of a bio-cybernetics laboratory; he believes that human progress depends on science, success in life is all he cares for, and he is driven on by a furious urge to make up for the time he has lost. Alex, on the other hand, looks back to his years in prison without resentment; in fact he actually comes to regard them as a blessing in disguise (this is a recurrent theme in Solzhenitsyn's great novels), since they refined his sensibility and led him to reflect on the absurd efforts men make to achieve a material prosperity accompanied by progressive spiritual impoverishment. But he does not have the strength to refuse his friend's offer of a job in his laboratory; he is tempted by the material comforts that Philip has rapidly acquired and by the hope that science may really be able to wipe out grief and pain; and he brings Philip his neurotic cousin Alda, who suffers from anxieties and phobias, so that he may try an experiment on her with a view to 'stabilising' her nervous system. The woman is cured of her phobias and anxieties, and of all other kinds of emotion as well; to such an extent that when she is again afflicted with grief at her father's death she chooses once more to submit to Philip's methods, degrading herself to the state of a human cabbage in order to avoid suffering. Alex is horrified at the success of the experiment (a general immediately sees its potentialities when applied on a large scale) and at the materialist principles of Philip and his assistants, and he abandons bio-cybernetics to devote himself to the study of social cybernetics in the hope of contributing to diminishing the chaos and injustice of the world.

Solzhenitsyn did not regard this play as a success, and in fact it is less convincing than his other works, mainly because its very artificial initial assumption is ambiguously developed in the character of Alex; it is not clear to what extent he is really presented as a moralist or criticised as an involuntary accomplice of violence. His decision to devote himself to social cybernetics is justified by his recognition that science must have a conscience, but Solzhenitsyn does not seem to have very much confidence in him; in contrasting his Christian maxims about the need of suffering with his illuministic search for Utopian mechanical devices that will produce models of social reform he was probably expressing the ideological difficulties arising from those long years of imprisonment that sometimes seemed to him to have been a valuable exercising ground for the conscience.

Nevertheless the play has its effective moments, particularly in connection with the subsidiary figures; e.g., Alex's aged uncle, a distinguished musicologist who has spent his whole life in pursuit of material happiness, but on his death-bed sings the praises of the simple life; Tilya, his young wife, who has been corrupted by the consumer society; Kabimba, an African physicist, who is led by remorse to give up the laboratory and return to his country; and Sinbar and Annie, Alex's scientific aides, who put Alda's soul in cold storage.

The play as a whole is of questionable merit, because of its wavering between psychological analysis and a lesson in moral principles, but it is unquestionably a cry of alarm at the danger of science being put in the service of tyranny. This may have been one reason why, in the euphoric atmosphere produced by Gagarin's and Titov's feats in space, the Vakhtangov and Leninsky Komsomol theatres were prevented from producing it. *The Stag and the Camp Prostitute* never got beyond the proof stage in the edition for the Sovremennik Theatre supervised by the producer Oleg Efremov, and the plans to make a film of *One Day in the Life of Ivan Denisovich* were shipwrecked immediately. (Eight years were to pass before a film was made of it by Caspar Wreder, with Tom Courtenay in the title rôle; in October 1970 Alexander Ford began filming *The First Circle* in Israel and Denmark; a radio version of the latter was made in France.)

The reasons for the bans imposed on Solzhenitsyn's work at the beginning of 1963 are readily intelligible when one recalls the events of the previous year. In October Khrushchev emerged from the Cuban crisis with badly ruffled feathers, and his opponents were already manoeuvring to persuade him to move to the right, i.e., water down his attacks on Stalin and take a strong line in relation to the intelligentsia who, as the conservatives had foreseen, were now threatening to take advantage of the liberty they had been granted to strike insidious blows at ideological orthodoxy.

The opportunity of making Khrushchev face up to his responsibilities in the matter was provided by a Moscow art exhibition at which a whole room was reserved for abstract painters. When Khrushchev visited it on 1st December there was no difficulty in whispering into his ear that it was the policy of liberalisation that had led to this degenerate art being brought out of the cellars, involving the risk of spreading the infection among healthy Soviet youth. The fact remains that, whether because of an obscure sense of guilt or a revulsion resulting from his natural incomprehension of artistic experiment, Khrushchev listened to his conservative escort (especially Serov, the secretary of the Artists' Union) and was very rude about the abstract canvases.

Henceforward Khrushchev's attitude to the intelligentsia underwent a change that became the more ominous the more his attitude to the figure of Stalin changed. The hard-liners were by no means resigned to the besmirching of the memory of one who in their eyes symbolised Soviet military power and prestige in the world and the internal solidarity of the régime. The face he had lost in Cuba, the ideological deviations to which writers seemed inclined as soon as they were allowed a little rope, the absurd hopes they nourished of a régime in which everyone could express himself freely, were in conservative eyes so many aspects of a disgraceful situation that must be remedied while there was still time, beginning with a restoration of the supremacy of the party and the vindication of Stalin. In the face of the massive counter-attack by the dogmatists Khrushchev felt ill at ease, and to meet it he made a series of moves and counter-moves.

Addressing the Supreme Soviet on 12th December, he admitted that, though Stalin had made many mistakes, he deserved well of the communist movement. But five days later, at a meeting of four hundred intellectuals at which Ilyichev, the director of propaganda services for the central committee, attacked painters and musicians, he solicitously introduced Solzhenitsyn to guests who did not know him. Solzhenitsyn still enjoyed his favour, and it was only because he felt himself strong in Khrushchev's support that Tvardovsky published in the January 1963 number of *Novy Mir* two new stories by him, *Matryona's Home* and *An Incident at Krechetovka Station*.

Matryona's Home is again inspired by a real experience of Solzhenitsyn's, dating from the time immediately after his release from the labour camp. At a village called Torfoprodukt (which he renamed Ignatich), sixty-five miles from Moscow, he lodged with an old woman who lived alone in a humble *isba*. She treated the young mathematics teacher with a great deal of human sympathy and looked after him until she and one of her grandsons were killed in an accident at a level crossing. Solzhenitsyn turned this episode into one of his finest stories. Matryona is poor and ill, but is content with her lot; and her portrait is painted with admiring tenderness against the briefly but effectively sketched-in background of a village – once more a symbol of the social context – dominated by greed and malice.

Matryona, who is always so willing to help others, has had an unhappy life. She was married before the revolution to the brother of the man she loved; during the war her husband was reported missing, believed killed, and all her six sons are dead. Now she has had to give up part of her *isba* to some relatives who have come to rob her before her very eyes; she is actually helping them, pushing a cart across a level crossing, when she is killed by a train. Detached from material possessions, uninterested in accumulating money, things or clothes, she cares only for a nanny-goat, her cat, and her plants. Ettore Lo Gatto calls her 'perhaps the most human feminine character in the whole of Soviet Russian literature'. Solzhenitsyn intones a kind of severe psalm in her memory, with clarity and a striken heart.

The story, written at Kok-Terek in 1956, has passages of great bitterness, particularly when the trials and tribulations that the woman patiently suffers are contrasted with the rapacity of her relatives and the petty hierarchs of the kolkhoz in the background; and sometimes a note of horror creeps in, particularly in the descriptions of life in the *isba*, which is infested with rats and cockroaches. Like *One Day in the Life of Ivan Denisovich*, the story is a parable on the real meaning of life as a fleeting journey through evil in which purity of heart is the only consolation.

An Incident at Krechetovka Station was suggested to Solzhenitsyn by his military experience in 1941–42, when the tide of war seemed to be flowing in the German favour. It is a more complex story, in which psychological penetration combined with the closely painted in background brilliantly reproduce the atmosphere of the time. The principal character is the young Second-Lieutenant Vasya Zotov, a recent engineering graduate, now employed as railway transport officer at a station busy with train-loads of men and war materials passing through on the way to the front. The back areas are teeming with troops and evacuees, most of them hungry and ill-clad; there is a great deal of confusion, increased by the rigours of an early winter, the fear of enemy air raids, alarming news about the retreating army and the panic that seems to be in the air in Moscow. It is a dramatic moment, but Zotov fights hard to prevent himself from giving in to despondency and alarm. He is a convinced communist, utterly loyal to Stalin, and hitherto his conduct has been exemplary. He has not succeeded in getting himself sent to the front, but carries out his wearing duties at Krechetovka with a strict sense of military duty and complete devotion to the cause of his endangered country. He is faithful to the wife from whom the war has parted him and rejects with contempt the temptations of other female society, preferring to spend his spare time reading Marx's *Das Kapital*.

Zotov is no caricature of the positive hero. Solzhenitsyn presents us with the portrait of a Soviet young man genuinely concerned for his country's fate and ready to sacrifice his life for the revolution; he shows a certain sympathy with him, but sees in his behaviour the virtues and failings of a generation to whom the war was the most tragic moment in their lives; fear of defeat brings ignoble instincts to the surface under cover of love of country.

The crux of the story, the incident referred to in the title, is Zotov's encounter with a middle-aged stranger who, having missed his train, duly applies to him to find out how to continue his journey. Zotov has just returned to his office after carrying out a humanitarian action, involving a breach of military regulations, in relation to four hungry soldiers, and he is immediately captivated by the stranger's courteous and dignified appearance; his name turns out to be Tveretinov, and he is an actor by profession. His voice and manner rouse spontaneous sympathy and, in contrast to the rough and ill-clad men by whom he is continually surrounded, he is fascinated by this man of sensitivity and intelligence who comes from a cultivated and refined environment. Initial suspicions about his true identity vanish after a short conversation, in the course of which he shows him family photographs and tells him he enlisted as a volunteer. Zotov returns confidence for confidence, and tells him how in his youth he applied to fight in the Spanish civil war; he gives him cigarettes, and advice about continuing his journey; his only concern seems to be to help the man. Then, talking about his destination, Tveretinov asks what Stalingrad was called before its name was changed. To Zotov this is a cold douche. How could a Soviet citizen possibly not know all about Stalingrad? The mechanism of distrust has been set in motion; the man must be a spy, perhaps a counter-revolutionary *émigré*, a White officer in disguise. The principle on which Stalin educated a whole generation, the defence of communism against enemies everlastingly ready to pounce, changes the cordial atmosphere of the conversation into a dramatic game that the timid Zotov tries to play with cunning. He pretends to accompany Tveretinov to the food store to find him something to eat, but hands him over to the political police. 'What have you done? Oh, what have you done? For this there is no remedy,' the poor devil explains; and the desperation on his face remains indelibly imprinted in Zotov's mind, tormenting him for the rest of his life with doubt whether or not he has committed a crime.

Thus this is another condemnation by Solzhenitsyn of the ideology that caused a whole country to grow up in an atmosphere of suspicion, and led to agonising crises of conscience that projected the shadow of neurosis over a whole society. It is also one of the most successful examples of the way in which Solzhenitsyn conceals and sublimates his polemics in the cloak of a broad and colourful symphonic poem, with characters taken from life itself; the power and strength of the narrative absorb even the most powerfully charged themes into a picture of universal validity.

The two stories were published at a time when the wind

seemed to be changing. Such was the confusion in Moscow that no-one could guess what turn the relations between the intelligentsia and the authorities would take next. At Christmas Ilyichev attacked Okudzhava and Nagibin, but praised Voznesensky (who, however, was denounced by *Izvestya* a month later) and Yevtushenko, who was about to leave on a semi-official trip to Germany and France. At the beginning of January 1963 *Pravda* and *Trud* scolded Ehrenburg and *Izvestya* chided Nekrasov (for his *The Two Sides of the Ocean*), but Simonov's *The Living and the Dead*, followed by *Soldiers are not Born*, both novels that frankly recalled the disasters suffered by the army in 1941–42 and the arbitrary behaviour of the military police at the front and in the back areas, were received without much fuss. But in April the Academy of Agricultural Sciences reverted to praising Lysenko's theories.

One thing was certain, however, and that was that Solzhenitsyn would soon feel the crack of the whip. Khrushchev's campaign against the personality cult worked like a boomerang. Though power in the Kremlin was still in his hands, there were those who could not deprive themselves of the pleasure of criticising his literary tastes.

Hostilities were opened by a woman, Lydia Fomenko, who in *Literaturnaya Rossya* of 11th January criticised *One Day in the Life of Ivan Denisovich* for culpable tendentiousness. She did not deny the disagreeable living conditions in the camps, but complained that Solzhenitsyn had not also shown the positive aspects of the Stalin era. As the purpose of the novel was certainly not to provide an exhaustive account of a period in the country's history, but was intended merely to throw light on one of its black pages, this was a curious complaint, but henceforward it was the continual refrain of Solzhenitsyn's enemies.

Lydia Fomenko was soon echoed in *Oktyabr* by Sergovanchev, who criticised Shukhov, the chief character in the novel, for being too remote from the model of the active and enthusiastic combatant typical of Soviet literature. 'Yes, Ivan Denisovich is dehumanised by the terrible conditions in which he is forced to live, but the fault is his own,' Sergovanchev said. 'The author tries to turn him into an example of moral firmness, but what sort of firmness is it if he is solely concerned with surreptitiously scrounging things and satisfying his physical needs?' According to *Oktyabr*, Shukhov should have protested, studied the causes that led to his difficult situation, at least tried to obtain information from qualified persons. But by adapting himself to his condition he showed he was an ordinary type.

In short, the attitude of the press towards Solzhenitsyn was veering rapidly. *Literaturnaya Rossya*, perhaps bowing to the protests roused by Lydia Fomenko's article, sent a special correspondent, Victor Bukanov, to Ryazan to interview Solzhenitsyn and, though he succeeded in exchanging only a few words with him, he described him on 25th January, 1963 as a teacher who was esteemed by his colleagues and pupils, and as a reserved and upright man. This was the only personal report on Solzhenitsyn to appear in the Soviet press. In the March *Literaturnaya Gazeta*, which up to the middle of February had printed letters favourable to him, found fault with *Matryona's Home*, and was immediately followed by *Komsomolskaya Pravda*. In April Mikhail Sholokhov referred to Solzhenitsyn's stories as tending to ideological confusion.

All these criticisms were certainly not motivated by purely literary considerations. What happened was simply that, as Khrushchev's position weakened, the Stalinists began to raise their heads in every sector of Soviet life; strong in the support of Khrushchev's rivals in the Kremlin, they turned into defects the characteristics of Solzhenitsyn's work that had seemed valuable to their enemies. Literature and politics are so closely linked in a country such as the Soviet Union, where opinions are conditioned by propaganda and ideological considerations take precedence over literary taste, that such judgments are not so much determined by the intelligence and sensitivity of reviewers as by the use that it is intended to make of a piece of writing within the social context, to influence or encourage a certain type of political consciousness.

The factors in the struggle for power in the Soviet Union have been too thoroughly analysed by political observers (above all by Michel Tatu, to whom the west is indebted for invaluable information) for it to be necessary to summarise it here. It is sufficient to recall that Khrushchev, feeling the ground vanishing from under his feet, in the course of a few weeks accelerated his march to the right to such an extent that Ilyichev was able to ridicule the Trojan horse of ideological co-existence and personally to inveigh against the intelligentsia that he had so recently been calling on to reform itself.

Khrushchev's celebrated speech of 8th March, 1963 was a crushing blow to the writers and young progressives who had regarded him as an enlightened dictator. It put weight behind the cries of alarm at the 'pernicious trends in literature and art', and brought the whole cultural debate back under party control. Khrushchev reiterated that literature and art were 'powerful means of communist education' and that nothing could give greater satisfaction to the artist than the knowledge that 'his talent is entirely devoted to the popular struggle for the construction of communism and that his works have been accepted and appreciated by the people'; he recalled that 'Soviet literature and art have been called on to recreate in vivid artistic depictions the great heroic period of the construction of communism and truthfully to reflect the affirmation and triumph of new communist relations in our life', and he added that 'artists should be able to discern the positive element that constitutes the essence of our reality'. True, writers were again invited not to neglect negative phenomena, but that this was empty rhetoric was shown by the rest of the speech, which went on to hold up to public contempt those artists who 'judge reality solely by the smell of latrines, present people only under a deliberately ugly aspect, use gloomy colours than can give rise only to depression, anxiety and despair among the people'. Such artists, Khrushchev implied, were in reality traitors to the régime, since they tended to cause a disastrous vision of the human condition to be attributed, not to the abuse of the personality cult, which the party had denounced, but to the Soviet system itself.

He included *One Day in the Life of Ivan Denisovich* among the works in which the Soviet reality of the Stalin era was reflected 'in a veracious manner from the party point of view', but evidently did so chiefly out of personal pique. Torn between inconsistencies as he was, he acrobatically walked the tightrope of distinguishing between positive and negative works of art, reiterated a large number of commonplaces, and attacked Yevtushenko with arguments that the dogmatists were shortly to use against his beloved Solzhenitsyn. 'You must clearly understand,' he said, 'that when we criticise you for deviation from orthodox positions, our enemies praise you. If the enemies of our cause start praising you for works that please them, the people will rightly criticise you. So you must choose which you prefer.'

This speech of Khrushchev's was in fact a milestone on the road to re-Stalinisation, the most explicit prelude to a process of repression that, in spite of pauses that seemed to show an opposite trend, was to continue remorselessly on its way, restoring high drama to the life of the Soviet intellectual. The most striking characteristic of the speech was its overriding nature, its application to practically every sector of cultural life, literature and art, music and the cinema, recalling them to order and shattering the illusion that the party had relaxed control. There were rebukes and threats all round – for the 'disgusting daubs' of the painter Neistvestny; for the film director Marlen Kuchev, who had made *The Ilyich Bastion*, subsequently renamed *I am Twenty Years Old*, and committed the crime of telling the story of three discontented youths and a father who was unable to answer his son's questions; for satirical writers ('he who does not possess the necessary skill should not enter this field, because he damages others and cuts off his own hands'); for the poet Rozhdestvensky, the devotees of abstract art and formalism ('one of the forms of bourgeois ideology'), progressive architects and musicians 'who give one the stomach-ache'; for 'obscene' contemporary dancers, and for Nekrasov, Paustovsky, Voznesensky and Katayev. 'We are far from meaning,' he said, 'that today, after the condemnation of the personality cult, the time of *laissez faire* has come, that the reins of government have been loosened, that the navigation of the public ship is left to the caprice of the waves, and that everyone can behave as he chooses. No. The party has followed, and will continue consistently and firmly to follow, the Leninist course that it has marked out for itself, implacably opposing all ideological uncertainty and all attempts to violate the norms of life of our society.' Thus the intelligentsia were warned to toe the line; as in the blackest days of the past, henceforward it was sufficient for anyone in the party to cast doubt on the political expediency of mentioning any of the negative aspects of life, or to depart from the canonical forms of socialist realism, to expose him to the suspicion of ideological deviation. Khrushchev, Solzhenitsyn's patron so long as his work was useful to him, thus handed him over into the hands of his enemies.

'Nowadays madmen are put in straitjackets, depriving them of the possibility of harming others and themselves,' Khrushchev said, and for the rest of 1963 and the first ten months of 1964 the progressive intelligentsia underwent a series of alternating hot and cold douches, either intimidated or terrified, depending on their moral fibre, by the threat of the straitjacket or encouraged by unexpected signs of tolerance (with which the departure from the scene of Kozlov, Khrushchev's most obdurate opponent, cannot have been unconnected).

These difficulties were reflected at the Italo-Soviet round-table conference for representatives of the film industry held in Moscow in April 1963. The veteran director Grigory Alexandrov reiterated that the chief task of socialist realism was to demonstrate the good works of which man was capable, but the representatives of the younger generation of Soviet filmmakers, Tarkovsky, Kuchev, Talankin, Daneliya and even Mikhail Romm, did not open their mouths. Chukhray, who spoke, well described the condition of the greater part of the intelligentsia. 'We lived through the times of the personality cult,' he said, 'and it is impossible that we should not have preserved the imprint of it in our brains and hearts. Try to understand that inside us there is a struggle between dogmatism and creative communism. It is a process, like others, that requires time to develop; and, like every process, it has its ups and downs. In the struggle about culture that the party is engaged in at the present time dogmaticians of the purest water make their appearance every now and then and try to drag us all back.'

In the summer of 1963 the prize given to Fellini's $8\frac{1}{2}$ at the Moscow film festival, in spite of the opposition of those who condemned it for pessimism, subjectivism and psychologism, seemed to be a sign of a return of relaxation of tension though the film was not distributed on the Soviet market; and this was followed in September by a round-table conference on the problems of the novel at Leningrad, organised by Giancarlo Vigorelli on the initiative of the European Community of Writers.

Writers of various ideological trends were able on this occasion to conceal divergences of view behind courteous expressions of reciprocal cordiality, and some were actually ready to believe that Soviet writers, who were by no means unanimous in identifying themselves with socialist realism, might feel encouraged to embark on a variety of experiments. In fact the only Soviet representative who defended the writer's right to choose his own public, though he did so with the usual ambiguity, was Ehrenburg. Nearly all the others echoed Sholokhov's introductory remarks and repeated in general terms that art must serve man and the cause of peace. 'I am proud to belong to a literature committed to the service of the people,' Simonov said, and Fedin recalled that in 1917 an edict had been issued enabling literary works to be declared part of the state heritage.

The most lively speaker on the western side was Robbe-Grillet. 'A writer cannot know what purpose he serves,' he said. 'Literature is not a means to be put in the service of a cause, of whatever kind it may be. The form of a novel is much more important than its contents, even if these are anti-fascist. Why do I write? I write to try and find out why I want to write.' The more astute of the Soviet representatives tried to reply to these shocking remarks by quoting Solzhenitsyn (who was not in Leningrad) as evidence of the liberty of expression enjoyed by Soviet fiction in recent years. First Boris Ryurikov, then Aksyonov, and then Tvardovsky claimed that Solzhenitsyn was a demonstration of the healthy, fertile dialectics of Soviet culture. 'Soviet novels of recent times,' Ryurikov said, 'express the two aspects of a unique, regular process in our life; on the one hand, the exaltation of the creative activity of the individual, his increasing consciousness and sense of dignity, and on the other denunciation and criticism of everything that hampers the advance of the new.' Aksyonov said that new splendour had been given by Solzhenitsyn to the old and still very valid method of indirect/direct discourse, in which the voice of the author and those of his characters were fused. Once more the highest praise for Solzhenitsyn came of course from Tvardovsky, who said that henceforward it would not be possible to examine any new literary phenomenon without reference to him. Since no-one would have the hardihood to deny that this artist, though loaded with the chains of socialist realism, was not free in his dialogue with the reader, he was a living example of an author who was free 'in his total emotional commitment in relation to man, his ideas, plans and hopes', and the creator of a spiritual world of such quality 'as to enable us to talk to Matryona as to an Anna Karenina'.

The conference ended with many smiles (Khrushchev himself received the delegates at his summer residence on the Black Sea) and hopes of an early resumption of discussions. No agreement had been reached on any matter of substance, apart from the self-evident proposition that the problem of the relationship between the novel and reality existed, and most of the participants' previous opinions remained unchanged. Nevertheless the meeting was not unfruitful, because it helped to establish personal relations, and some Soviet writers were given the feeling that there was a prospect of their emerging from their long isolation. To many Solzhenitsyn was still a vital link in the chain that connected Soviet fiction to the great Russian tradition and might help to secure its admission to the system of European values.

In the wake of the admiration of Solzhenitsyn shown in the west and his success at home, and encouraged by the *Novy Mir* group – a long essay in the January 1964 number of that journal was to reject the charges of sensationalism levelled at *One Day in the Life of Ivan Denisovich*, which 'could look forward to a long life' – sensitive readers welcomed the publication of a new story by him in the July 1963 number of that journal (Tvardovsky, in an interview with the Italian Ripellino, after Tolstoy's name had been mentioned, did not hesitate to compare his protégé with Gogol).

The new story was called *For the Good of the Cause*, set in the early sixties in an unnamed provincial town that could well have been the Ryazan in which Solzhenitsyn lived and taught in a technical college of the type round which it centred. This time the mood is cheerful, at any rate at the outset, full of happy voices and singing. To do away with double shifts and increase the efficiency of the place, the students, nearly a thousand of them, have themselves built two new buildings that will enable it to expand and have more spacious lecture rooms, laboratories and accommodation. They have done everything with their own hands, inspired by a woman teacher who is universally popular because of her honesty and decency, and is encouraged by Mikheich, the principal. When the work has been completed, the students impatiently await official approval and authorisation for the transfer to the new premises. Instead, like a clap of thunder from a clear sky, a committee arrives, headed by one Shabalygin, the head of a factory at which relaying equipment is produced. After briefly inspecting the old premises and pretending not to see how inadequate they are, he informs Mikheich of the official decision to assign the new buildings to a scientific research institution covered by military secrecy. This sacrifice, he says, must be made for the good of the cause. Mikheich indignantly appeals to the local party secretary, who in turn appeals to the regional secretary, and the outcome is that the young people have to content themselves with one new building only, because the other goes to Shabalygin. As a result of his exploitation of the young people's labour, a successful career opens up for him as the head of a much more important institution (the last page of the story sees him cheating in demarcating the land allocated to him from that which is to go to the school), but there is no hope of persuading the students that they have not been defrauded and victimised. 'If it happened once, it can happen again.' In other words, a compromise is reached at the expense of these young people's enthusiasm and the credibility of a system that on the one hand exalts to the skies the creativity of the people, the spontaneous resourcefulness of 'collectives', and on the other humiliates them, leaving a free hand to bureaucrats and careerists.

For the Good of the Cause is written with sober realism and is one of Solzhenitsyn's best stories, animated by a sympathy for the young that is the greater for his indignation at seeing their enthusiasm betrayed. Above all, he sympathises with Lydia Georgevna, the popular teacher, whose chief bogey is moral indifference among the young, whom she encourages to prefer books to films and television. The tears of rage and disappointment with which she greets the news of the authorities' abuse of power express his own reaction to injustice, aggravated in this case by the fact that it is not just the school that suffers as a result, but the whole community, because if the greatest need of Soviet industry is specialists, the blow to the development of technical education is a blow to the whole country. Thus in *For the Good of the Cause* individual morality once more goes hand in hand with social morality. Not only are the young sacrificed to the selfish interests of a rogue, but this arbitrary act amounts to a self-inflicted wound committed by a public administration that lacks the strength to oppose the personal manoeuvres of those who assume the mask of patriotism.

The story was of course subjected to bitter attacks as soon as it was published. Yuri Barabash, a well-known conservative critic, severely criticised it in *Literaturnaya Gazeta* of August 1963 (three old members of the party replied to this attack in *Novy Mir* in October) and *Oktyabr* took the opportunity to accuse Solzhenitsyn of constructing his world on an idealistic concept of good and evil, as if Soviet life consisted of nothing but the conflict between bureaucracy and socialism. *Novy Mir* later announced that of 508 letters it received from its readers 505 were favourable to Solzhenitsyn, while two commented on his style and only one was thoroughly offensive about him. In proportion to the circulation of *Novy Mir*, the number of letters was certainly small, but the figures confirmed the extent of his following. In view of this, the ban that was now imposed on republication in a single volume of *One Day in the Life of Ivan Denisovich*, *Matryona's Home* and *An Incident at Krechetovka Station* was the more surprising.

In reality, whichever way things were going in the Kremlin, Solzhenitsyn was now out of favour, and his difficulties were increased by the praise lavished on his first works when they appeared in the west and aggravated by the furore roused in his own country (two English editions of *One Day in the Life of Ivan Denisovich* appeared in Moscow itself). A campaign of slander was being worked up that was soon to bear fruit. He was alleged to have formed a defeatist group during the war and to have handed himself over to the Germans in order to collaborate with them, and he was soon banned from reading his works in public or on the radio.

The arrest in Leningrad in November 1963 of the young Yosif Brodsky (author, among other things, of a poem called 'Let us erect a monument to lies') and his sentence to five years' forced labour on a charge of parasitism (though he was released in 1965) was certainly not compensated for by *Novy Mir's* continuing to publish writing less conformist than that which appeared in other journals (including General Gorbatov's memoirs of the 1937 purges), or by the fact that permission was at last given for the publication of a Russian version of a work of Kafka's (*In the Penal Colony*), or that *Pravda* published a favourable review of *For the Good of the Cause*.

Less than three months later, in April 1964, *Pravda* published an unsigned letter opposing the idea, put forward by *Novy Mir* in December 1963, that the Lenin Prize for Literature for 1964 should be awarded to *One Day in the Life of Ivan Denisovich*; it urged, persuasively enough, that awarding it to such a book would encourage the dangerous 'liberal' tendencies of Soviet writers. (Meanwhile in Italy the communist Vittorio

Strada, motivated by the spirit that caused Togliatti to write the Yalta memorandum, announced that such an award 'would be an excellent augury for Soviet literature in the eyes of all and a reason for cheer to all who love it.')

Khrushchev fell on 14th October, 1964, and the last praise of Solzhenitsyn to appear in the Soviet press was contained in the January 1965 number of *Novy Mir*, in which Tvardovsky, on the occasion of that periodical's fortieth anniversary, stated that each of Solzhenitsyn's works so far published 'testifies to the many-sided development of the talent of an author who is at the height of his powers and has a long and promising career ahead of him'. Another piece by Solzhenitsyn was to appear in *Novy Mir* in 1966, but from 1965 onwards, *pari passu* with the progress made in the rehabilitation of Stalin's memory, and in spite of some sporadic breaks in the smoke-screen (we shall see that the most surprising of these took place in November of that year), so far as he was concerned the skies of Moscow darkened.

Even his *Studies and Miniature Tales*, fifteen short pieces of prose, half way between the lyrical and the gnomic, were restricted to clandestine publication. They were published in *Grani* in Frankfurt in 1964. They praise the beauties of nature, the good old days, respect for the religiousness and the virtuous ways of the old; above all, they express his nostalgias and his rejection of all the vulgar aspects of contemporary Soviet society which, driven by pride to believe itself perfect and immortal, forgets that the spirit of life and the sense of liberty are man's only permanent values, and is populated by blasphemous and arrogant louts ('but some day they will revolt and trample on us all, even those who have encouraged them,' he prophesies in a longer story, 'Easter Procession', published in *Possev* in 1969).

But for their stylistic quality, for appreciation of which recourse to the original is probably necessary, these *Miniature Tales* would seem to be of only marginal significance in Solzhenitsyn's work. Lament for the past often turns into a mannered moralism. 'So long as one can breathe under an apple tree after the rain, one can go on living,' he writes in 'Breathing'; and in 'The Duckling' he says: 'In spite of all our nuclear power, we shall never succeed in making a duckling in a test-tube.' Nevertheless they point to the cultural affinity between Solzhenitsyn and the spiritual trend peculiar to

Russian mystical Christianity that stands by the ancient liturgy of the Church, swathed in incense and sacred hymns, and the right of rural civilisation to remain faithful to its ancestral traditions, and exalts *pietas* as an antidote to a society that has substituted gymnastics for prayer. Solzhenitsyn's religiosity is also confirmed by a real 'Prayer to the Lord', attributed to him in *émigré* circles and distributed by the *samizdat*, the underground press, in which the existence of God is held up as an assurance that the 'gates of good' are not closed and that beyond the uncertainties of the present there is a world of hope. 'Having reached the edge of earthly glory,' the prayer says, 'I am astonished at the path I have travelled. Alone, desperate as I was, I should never have found it. It led me to a place from where I was able to transmit to humanity a reflection of Your rays. Continue to allow me to transmit them in the ways that will be necessary, and if I do not have the time you will give the task to others.'

To Solzhenitsyn the skies of Moscow were threatening storm, but meanwhile in other socialist countries they were opening up. In China and Albania his works had immediately been condemned as scandalous, but George Lukács, the most outstanding Marxist philosopher, in 1964 published an essay praising him for having made a real breach in the ideological defences of the Stalinist tradition and describing *One Day in the Life of Ivan Denisovich* as a 'notable step towards literary self-discovery in the socialist present'. If the central problem of socialist realism was to discover the road to the representation of contemporary man, Lukács said in effect, Solzhenitsyn provided the model for a kind of writing that, while providing a faithful description of the Stalin era, with all its inhuman aspects, contributed to a critical understanding and decipherment of the present situation by clarifying its background and anticipated 'the great literature of the future'. Solzhenitsyn's style was remote both from symbolism and from naturalism, and Lukács claimed that socialist realism was capable of reviving a classical nobility. Solzhenitsyn was 'a milestone in the process of transformation and regeneration of socialist literature, directed to the feeling of a sense of artistic responsibility in the face of the great problems of its present'; and Lukács declared him to be a champion of the critical realism that could be called socialist only to the extent to which the seeds of the Twentieth Congress bore fruit. If this did not occur, and the authorities persecuted Solzhenitsyn as an 'enemy of the people', socialist realism would remain that of the Stalinist illustrators, and there could not be said to be any link between Solzhenitsyn and them.

Whatever Lukács might have to say about it, however, *One Day in the Life of Ivan Denisovich* was disappearing from the bookshops in the Soviet Union. The Solzhenitsyn case was passing out of the hands of the literary critics and into those of the police, who were preparing to do everything in their power to boycott his new novels, *The First Circle* and *Cancer Ward*. From their point of view, they had every reason to do so.

The First Circle, which Solzhenitsyn began in 1955, when he was banished at Kok-Terek, and finished on Christmas Eve 1964, carries much further the process of deflation begun with *One Day in the Life of Ivan Denisovich*. The latter, based on the tragic experience of the labour camps, laid bare only one aspect of Stalinist perfidy, while the new novel amounted to a denunciation of the whole of Soviet life during the post-war years, condensing its caprices and convulsions into the four days from Christmas Eve to 27th December, 1949. It begins with an episode reminiscent of a thriller.

Innokenty Volodin is a colonel in the diplomatic service. Without revealing his identity, he rings up a doctor-friend from a public call box in Moscow; the latter has recently been to Paris with a scientific delegation, and has promised to send a certain preparation to his French colleagues. The cold war is at its height, and Volodin tries to dissuade his friend from doing something that might be interpreted as an act of espionage in favour of the west. The opening chapter fills barely three pages, but this is sufficient to plunge us into the atmosphere of suspicion and fear that prevailed in the Soviet Union during those years, when generous human impulses, even those arising from long-standing personal friendships, were subjected to a kind of self-censorship, made necessary by the fear of committing an act of imprudence harmful to the country's interests. Volodin himself hesitates a great deal before making his telephone call, but in the end two considerations turn the scales – the impossibility of retaining his sense of manhood if he allows himself perpetually to be governed by fear, and his belief that, in spite of the existence of telephone-tapping devices, it is impossible to identify by his voice alone, particularly if he changes it, an individual who telephones from

101

a public call box and leaves it immediately afterwards. But Volodin is naïve. Just at this time, as the result of an order of Stalin's, a number of physicists from the labour camps have been assembled in a lonely building in a village in the Mavrino district (near Moscow) and in great secrecy have been carrying out experiments with a view to the development of a device that will enable voices to be classified, and will thus make it possible, by comparing recordings of telephone tappings with those of suspects, to identify 'enemies of the people'. Volodin then vanishes from the story, to reappear in Chapter 55, which tells us how he developed a moral conscience from reading old books and his mother's letters, but is nevertheless more frightened than ever of being arrested, and then again in Chapter 78, when he finds comfort in Epicurus.

The story moves to Mavrino, to the first circle, the highest and least terrible of a Dantesque inferno symbolising the condition of Soviet citizens condemned for crimes against the State (it is implied that the last and deepest circle harbours the wretches condemned to forced labour in distant areas). The population of Mavrino (221 prisoners and fifty guards) constitute a picture gallery of unforgettable types, depicted in such a way as to put their physical and psychological characteristics in relief. But two of them stand out. One is the Jew, Lev Grigorevich Rubin, a student of German language and literature who during the war rose to the rank of major in the Red Army and was given the task of enlisting spies from among German prisoners and saved whole Soviet battalions as a result. This did not prevent him from being arrested by his own side on a charge of carrying out propaganda against the order 'blood for blood, a death for a death'. The other is Gleb Vikenty Nerzhin (in whom it is easy to recognise Solzhenitsyn himself, who in 1949 was the same age as this character of his). Nerzhin has a degree in mathematics, but is not ignorant of linguistics, and was arrested at the front, where he had the rank of captain, and was given a ten-year sentence. Rubin is still a convinced communist, tragically loyal to the Leninism for which he fought and to the party in whose service he denounced a relative to the GPU and shot peasants hostile to collectivisation. Nerzhin, however, five years of whose sentence have still to run, has since boyhood doubted the legality of the political trials, and the purges filled him with horror; he rebelled against the dogmas preached by the party propagandists and has always tried to understand what was happening in Russia behind the triumphalist façade. Such is his contempt for Stalin that he calls him the butcher, and even in prison writes fiery pages denouncing him and the historians and novelists who are his cringing flatterers.

Rubin and Nerzhin have frequent arguments, which often end in bitter quarrels. To the former, in his certainty of being in possession of the absolute, crystal-clear truth, the communist ideology explains and justifies the whole of history, and he regards men's errors as dialectical elements in progress. Nerzhin has used the years he spent in labour camps before being transferred to Mavrino to persuade himself of the need of associating love of mankind with a virile scepticism, the surest way of freeing oneself from the dogmatic mentality. His own sufferings and those of others have convinced him that the reality of life, the fatigue of labour, the bite of hunger and cold, are preferable to any mythicising ideology. To him pain is a constant factor in history and its key, but by tempering one's spirit any misfortune can be faced and man's frail nature overcome with dignity.

The clash between Rubin and Nerzhin, which is given bitter overtones by their common experience as prisoners and their feeble hope of liberty, provides the double track that the story of life at Mavrino follows, running parallel with the increasingly more frantic efforts to perfect the voice-identifying device. But there is also a dense traffic of other characters: prisoners, police, supervisors, officials and bureaucrats; the portrait of each includes aspects of Soviet history.

The moral standpoint is also Dantesque. Pity for the victims sometimes extends to their taskmasters, caught in the grip of a tyrannical system that causes the weakest to sell their souls; but generally the condemnation of the cowardly and the perverse, and even more of the cultivated who try to justify their baseness, is total. Solzhenitsyn's ultimate purpose is to rise above complaint at the havoc wrought by Stalinism, the diabolical detonator of the vices sown in individuals by nature, to the glorification of man, who is capable of conquering fear and remorse, provided he has preserved a single seed of love and a gleam of intelligence sufficient to enable him to discern the crude fraudulence of those in power.

Thus the portrait gallery of *The First Circle* is crowded with terrible and wretched figures, tremendous in their grief and pride, sometimes destructive in their visionary plans, all moving against the background of the experiments being conducted for the purpose of making language visible. These experiments seem to belong to the realm of science fiction, but take place within a framework of searches, interrogations, and threats to send back the recalcitrant to their labour camps, and they are the technologically most advanced product of the inquisitorial system operated by the régime to extract men's most secret thoughts and degrade life to a man-hunt.

Apart from Nerzhin and Rubin, there are the engineers Valentulya Martynyts, Mamurin and Pryanchikov and Bobynin, and Sologdin, Potapov and Khotobrov, Gerasimov and Kondratyev-Ivanov, Adamson and Dyrsin; all dressed in blue overalls, with years of prison behind them, Old Bolsheviks who have fallen into disgrace or soldiers who had the misfortune to be taken prisoner by the Germans, degraded members of the hierarchy or party officials convicted of treason, forgers and artists, embezzlers and philosophers, sharing rooms and work-benches, thanks to the good fortune that has temporarily delivered them from the degradation of the camps. Normally, unless one of them has hopes of being prematurely released, they present a united front against the tyranny of the guards and the traps set by the spies put among them.

Among them there is also the timorous figure of Serafina Vitalevna, commonly known as Simochka, a plain, compassionate girl, to whom Nerzhin, the man whom it is her task to watch, gives her first kiss – she is prepared to have a child by him; and there is also the aged Spiridon, formerly commissar of a kolkhoz and now forced to act as supervisor of his fellow-prisoners, who, having seen the beastliness of a way of life in which men prey on their fellow-men, in his peasant simplicity sums up the whole drama of his generation in a phrase: 'The wolf-hound is right, the cannibal is not.' Also there is Klara, the 'free employee' of the institution – sister-in-law of Volodin, the diplomatist with whom the novel begins, who in her love for Ruska, a prisoner who hopes to save himself by playing a double game (he agrees to play the spy, but warns his comrades of the fact), is working towards a new moral conscience, in profound disagreement with her family.

On the other side, the security service chiefs, the prison bureaucrats, the guards, who live in a state of perpetual suspicion and rivalry because of fear of their respective superiors and the blots on their own past, agree only in spying on each other, inventing new ways of keeping the prisoners under control, and zealously obeying orders from above. There is the engineer Anton Nikolayevich Yakonov, the police colonel in charge of Mavrino, himself an ex-prisoner, now in the service of Abakumov (a minister who enriched himself during the war by preying on the Germans), but tormented by a perpetual recurrence of religious fears, which flare up when he remembers the Christian woman who dropped him when he sold himself to the régime. His deputy, Adam Roytman, a Jew, at night, when he does not feel himself protected by his major's epaulettes and the award of the Stalin Prize, follows with increasing apprehension the régime's latest campaign against the Jews. There is Major Sikin, who on the pretext of preserving security finds ways and means of censoring even the prisoners' thoughts and threatens to shoot those who fail to carry out the patriotic duty of spying. Finally, high above them all and unreachable in his demoniacal solitude, but omnipresent as a terrifying nightmare, there is Stalin himself, with his yellow, tiger's eyes, old and run down in health (he is now in his seventies). Solzhenitsyn imagines him sleepless in his room in the Kremlin, busy writing his essay on linguistics and telling Abakumov (who comes to inform him of a forthcoming attempt on Tito's life) that he must be more severe towards political prisoners, while he raves about becoming emperor of the world. Solzhenitsyn coins the most ridiculous epithets for Stalin, whom he calls the Leader of All Progressive Humanity, the Telephonists' Best Friend, the Most Brilliant of Generals, the Great Generalissimo, the Best Friend of Counter-Espionage Agents, the Coryphaeus of Science, the Greatest of the Great, the Sailor's Best Friend, the Dearest and Most Beloved.

These are the principal characters of *The First Circle*, many of them taken from life, who summon up in the reader's mind a historical and psychological landscape of uncommon breadth and terrifying substance. The great fascination of the novel, however, lies in its brilliantly articulated structure, the way in which episodes of fear and cruelty lead harmoniously into elegiac moments, and in the painful truthfulness with which the author penetrates into the minds of his characters. He skilfully uses the pattern of the detective novel (the suspense about the fate of Innokenty Volodin is resolved in the last chapter with his arrest by the secret police, who have been able to make use of the apparatus developed at Mavrino, and the terrifying destruction of his personality in the Lubyanka prison, while Nerzhin is put in a Black Maria and sent off to an unknown camp).

Solzhenitsyn explores with unexceeded brilliance the psychological and political situation of Soviet man at the beginning of the fifties (and not only on the prisoners' side), covering the whole gamut from the most bereft and disillusioned who are motivated by loathing of the Stalin régime to those who still preserve faith in communism and hope of redemption. Even outside the Mavrino establishment, in the office of the minister Abakumov, in the streets of Moscow through which the pensive Yakonov walks, at the reception given by the public prosecutor Makarygin – it is attended by a writer who has adapted himself to the requirements of the régime's propaganda and has won the Stalin Prize, and the host quarrels with a Serbian Leninist – all Solzhenitsyn's characters bear the scars, often the still bleeding scars, of a debate solidly rooted in the drama of the Russian people, presented as a sample of the universal human destiny. The elements of the great debate between Christian humanism and Stalinist communism are brought down from the ideological skies and seen in terms of living men and women who torment and abuse each other, and become elements in a moral and intellectual clash of universal proportions.

The First Circle reflects the Russian taste for interminable disputes about general principles; but above all it is the application of a microscope to various levels of opinion for the purpose of evaluating the meaning of life and the impact of the party on private life. The talk, and even the quarrels, in which the prisoners of Mavrino spend their leisure (most of them are intellectuals – physicists, mathematicians, writers and philosophers) amounts almost to a catalogue of the ideas current in those years, and it expresses them with a freedom, an ability to link them with the major trends of contemporary thought and the Russian tradition, which were non-existent outside prison in the universities and research institutions separated from the living body of culture by adherence to dogma. The sarcasms at the expense of the educational system, that takes precious time from studies to devote it to political work, Nerzhin's and Rubin's long discussions about the idea of happiness, the charges laid at the door of the régime, the comments on the anti-Jewish campaign, the stupidity of the bureaucracy, the rebirth of privileges, all the subjects of dispute and reflection scattered through the novel, whether political, cultural or moral, are not ornamental extras, touches of local colour added to give actuality to the book. They are the real connective tissue of an allegory of Soviet life expressed in terms of the conflict between nature and ideology, right and wrong.

This is especially clear in the case of the women charcters – Serafina, a lieutenant employed by the Ministry of Security, who bursts into tears because of love; Klara, the public prosecutor's daughter, tormented by the suspicion that she is taking part in an act of injustice (her father may even have sent innocents to gaol); Mura, who is compelled to act as spy in the students' hostel; and above all Nadya, Nerzhin's wife, who comes to Moscow to see him after years of agonising separation and may perhaps be forced to seek a divorce to escape from the perpetual suspicion by which the wife of a state criminal is surrounded. The whole of Chapters 33 to 38, which are devoted to the portrait of Nadya and the wives' visits to the prisoners, is perhaps the part of the book most exposed to the risk of relapse into melodrama and sentiment. If Solzhenitsyn avoids this pitfall, it is by virtue of the sobriety of tone, the balance between pathos and irony, the insistence on concrete, human truth that governs the whole of the book, in which grotesque flashes (Borodin's trial in Chapter 50, the fable about the smile of the Buddha in Chapter 54) and the atmosphere of affliction ('life as grey cotton-wool') merge into a hymn of praise to the martyred victims of the law of large numbers that provides an excuse to the perverted consciences of those who comfort themselves with the thought that 'the greater the scale on which an historical event takes place, the greater, of course, is the probability of errors in individual cases, judicial, tactical, ideological and economic'. It is here, in fact, that Solzhenitsyn's battle-front in defence of man is drawn up, along the line that separates the standard-bearers of reasons of state, who in the best of cases camouflage themselves as historicists, from those who judge a civilisation by the suffering it inflicts. That is why we said that the police, from its own point of view, could hardly be blamed for being infuriated by *The First Circle*.

No Soviet novel has ever stated with so much vigour and

CHAPTER SIX

The spring of 1965 was a memorable one in the annals of the Soviet police. More was required of them than merely keeping an eye on an unruly writer who embodied certain popular aspirations that were considered dangerous; for this it was sufficient to trail him in the street, intercept and read his correspondence, tap his telephone calls. If need be, they could (and soon did) ransack the house of a friend of his and search his papers or even give a confidential agent the task of sending his most compromising works to the west without his knowledge in order to be able to accuse him of anti-Soviet activity. The machinery of the KGB, which had been run in for nearly half a century, and that of Glavlit, whose former functions of ideological control had been restored, would have worked perfectly if Solzhenitsyn had been merely a crazy hothead or an isolated counter-revolutionary, a festering growth that merely needed the surgeon's knife.

The fact of the matter was that Khrushchev had left behind more than mere weeds that required eradication. Whether he intended to or not, he sowed hopes and doubts that many were not resigned to dismissing as illusions or giving up again. The seeds of revolt against the principle of authority, which had been encouraged in relation to Stalin, had sprouted rapidly and spread at various social levels; a new awareness of personal rights had developed among intellectuals and technocrats and sections of the young. Moreover, police repression was made more difficult by the fact that the new masters of the Kremlin found it necessary to secure the allegiance of the younger generations which, not having passed through the revolution, were ideologically tepid, and of the literary and scientific intelligentsia, to whom the country's rigid political superstructures were much more restrictive than they were to the technocrats. At the same time a brake had to be put on the democratic development of certain areas of public opinion, to prevent a disorderly growth of sectional claims at the expense of the interests of the community, resulting in the creation of islands of privilege, small but insidious centres of power. Control of public affairs and of individual thought must remain in the party's hands; every request put forward from the base outside the orthodox channels was therefore regarded as an outburst of anarchical subjectivism or a revival of Trotskyism – in any case, a threat to public order. The fact that the orthodox channels had grown rusty and unserviceable because the bureaucratic apparatus had transformed them into a threadbare, one-way transmission belt counted for less than the need to establish respect for the governing apparatus, the sole authorised repository of power and truth.

If that was the only point on which the rival factions in the Kremlin agreed, the party of dissent was in turn divided and split; the range of opinion extended from basic anti-communism to opposition to Stalinist terrorism, from forms of nationalist revanchism to forms of religious or intellectual protest. But the dissenters were united in calling for two things, the right to express themselves publicly and the right to see that the law was appplied. As we shall see, most of the protesters justified their claims by appealing to the Soviet constitution. Their protests almost invariably took the form of appeals to the law violated by those who had the levers of power in their hands. Things were at the phase at which an *élite*, having overcome its fears, sounds the alarm signal, hoping that, though the slope is steep and the drivers drunk, the train may nevertheless be stopped in time, even though at the edge of the abyss.

The first, and in many ways very surprising, public demonstration indicating a desire to intervene from the base originated in university circles. A procession (initially of about 200 persons, though it grew to about 1,000) formed in Mayakovsky Square on the late afternoon of 14th April, 1965, applauded the manifesto of the SMOG group and, in spite of police intervention, marched through the streets of Moscow carrying placards calling for the freedom of artistic creation and the release from prison of Brodsky, Osipov, Bukovsky, Naritsa and others. It took up the cry of a young man: 'Those who are not cowards, those who love Russian art, follow me', and marched towards the Writers' Club in Gerchen Street, where a resolution was handed in to the secretary, Ilyin, calling for the recognition of SMOG, for freedom of propaganda, and for SMOG to be given permission to publish an organ of its own. The police naturally had the better of the *mêlée* that followed in Gerchen

Street. (One of the demonstrators, after being beaten until the blood flowed, shouted to his companions: 'Those who love art, help me', while the police were putting him into a car.)

The impact made by the demonstration was disproportionate to its size. Dissent, having gone out into the streets, publicly raised the question of an alternative, not to the régime, but to its absolutist methods. This was the first that ordinary Russians heard of young rebels in their midst, but they realised almost at once that the official attempt to identify them with hooligans did not detract from the validity of a type of appeal with which a large body of opinion agreed. The only reservations felt by the more cautious arose when they heard that the procession had been instigated by a clandestine organisation that appealed to the 'free world' to intervene to prevent 'young forces from being crushed by the nailed boot'.

The automatism that led the authorities to identify themselves with the country functioned once more, and the spring and summer of 1965 passed in a state of renewed nervousness, aggravated by the belief (following Brezhnev's speech in May) that the process of rehabilitating Stalin was now irreversible. The intelligentsia were disconcerted by the ambiguous position adopted by *Izvestya* on the eve of the congress of the Writers' Union of the Russian Federal Republic ('It is senseless and harmful to impose dogmatic restrictions,' it said, though 'artistic creation cannot take place independently of society'), and they were divided and split. There was some who, like the painters Korin and Konenkov and the writer Leonid Leonov, approached the problem by calling for protection of the monuments of the past, especially the sacred treasures of the churches, as a repository of moral and aesthetic values that were also inherent in socialist society; and there were also those who, rather than associate themselves with a campaign that had a flavour of aestheticism and spiritualism about it, preferred direct intervention on the level of cultural policy and sought to take advantage of opportunities to extend and rationalise the basis of underground protest.

The SMOG group that organised the procession and produced the clandestine journal *Sfinsky* ('Sphinxes') edited by Valery Tarsis, in the following July was characterised by a generous but ambiguous impulsiveness. The word SMOG consisted of the initial letters of the words *samoye molodoye obshchestvo geniev* ('the youngest association of genii'), and it chose as its motto four words having the same initials (*smelost, mysl, obraz, glubina,* 'courage, thought, form, and depth'), and it distributed a manifesto saying: 'We are the new force of the future. We are reviving and continuing the traditions of our immortal art: Rublev, Dostoevsky, Pasternak, Bayan, Radishchev, Tsvetaeva, Berdyaev, Tarsis, have entered our veins like fresh blood and living water. We struggle against all, from the Komsomol to the petty bourgeoisie, from the Chekists to the philistines. . . . All are against us, but our people are for us and with us. . . .' A similar publication was called *ARI,* standing for *avangard russkogo iskusstva,* 'advance-guard of Russian art'.

For its part *Sfinsky,* of which about fifty typewritten copies were produced, plainly declared itself on the cover, on which its place of publication was stated to be 'Russia' rather than the USSR, and one contribution was date-lined Petrograd instead of Leningrad. It stood for a clear distinction between art and ideology, the rejection of socialist realism, contempt for the bandmasters of cultural politics.

The introductory editorial in the first number recalled the sister publications *Syntax, Boomerang* and *Phoenix,* and declared that *Sfinsky* too wished to contribute to 'raising the veil of silence brought down on Russian literature by politicising illiterates and their henchmen', and apologised to the authors of contributions for not having informed them in advance that works of theirs were going to be included. 'It is possible, friends, that this may cause you trouble. But we hope that this will not be so tragic as to make you cease to be artists ready to answer for every line and every word, even at the sacrifice of life.'

As for the contents, the verse was very eclectic in nature (among the poets published were Alexander Vayutkov, Julia Vishnevskaya, P. Vladimirov, Alexander Galich, Evgeny Golovin, Leonid Gubanov, Vladimir Kovshin, Alexander Mironov, Artemy Mikhailov, Sergei Morozov, Yuri Stefanov, and Boris Sluchky). It ranged from meditative poems full of nostalgia for old Russia, and melancholy inspired by the memory of friends who had vanished who knows where, to angry attacks on a society in which it was necessary to put a gag on one's mouth in order to become '*grands seigneurs,* controllers and butchers'; from poems slashing the profiteers and swindlers who got away with their crimes under cover of the party to denunciations of the horrors of the Stalinist camps and the suspicion, cowardice and fear in which Soviet people continued to drag out their lives. The quality of the verse was generally mediocre, but the driving force behind it was plain enough: a love of country so disillusioned as to produce a kind of disgust with life in most, and in others a furious determination to use poetry to rouse sleeping consciences.

It seems clear that the SMOG group was not homogeneous, but included both solitary poets who offered themselves as witnesses to Russia's everlastingly painful destiny as well as young people with a political vocation who attributed the evils of the times to the moral sickness of the system and wished to redeem it. What united them (and to an extent other clandestine groups as well, such as the Leningrad 'Young Communards' who took the name of their clandestine paper *Kolokol*, 'The Bell', from Herzen, the 'Ryleyev circle', and the 'Democratic Socialists', who published *Notebooks*) was a kind of conscientious objection that had the most varied motivations but a constant model of behaviour, i.e., rejection of everything imposed by the state machine that prevented human beings from making their own choices. It is hazardous to suggest that this form of dissent, in spite of its element of violent protest, could serve as a focal point for political opposition; mostly it was the expression of a youthful intolerance, an iconoclastic enthusiasm, that the police had no difficulty in tracking down and stamping out. Nevertheless groups of the SMOG type had a rousing and stimulating effect at a time when the whole cultural establishment, in spite of the tightening of the reins that followed Khrushchev's downfall, was undergoing a series of shocks that produced fresh disarray.

Barely two months before the demonstration in Mayakovsky Square *Pravda* published an article by the critic Rumyanchev again calling for a multiplicity of schools and trends; and in the same month it also attacked *Oktyabr*, the bastion of the conservatives. In a scene so full of contradictions overestimation of the significance of the protesters was inevitable, both on the part of the orthodox, who tended to see in an unauthorised procession the threat of an insurrection, and on the part of the young, who felt encouraged to put pressure from the left on the 'liberals' of *Novy Mir* and soon – after another demonstration on 16th August – were able to claim the credit for having contributed to Brodsky's premature release.

As for Solzhenitsyn, manoeuvres by the authorities with a view to minimising the impact of his work and keeping him under control were in full swing. This was shown, among other things, in June and July by the obstacles put in the way of his moving from Ryazan to Obninsk, where the local radiological institute offered his wife a chemical research post. As Medvedev was later to relate, the appointment was approved by eighteen votes to two by the executive committee of the institute, and there were no difficulties in regard to accommodation, for Solzhenitsyn and his wife would have been able to live in one of the flats reserved for the staff. The project came to nothing, however. The authorities were alarmed at the prospect of Solzhenitsyn's coming into close contact with the scientists at Obninsk, for his movements would be more difficult to check than they were at Ryazan, where he lived practically in isolation, and they succeeded in having the appointment cancelled. A little over two months later, in September, the police raided the house of Teush, a friend to whom Solzhenitsyn had entrusted many of his papers, and confiscated documents and manuscripts, including three copies of *Cancer Ward* and the old play *The Feast of the Victors*.

It was in this nervous atmosphere that the Sinyavsky-Daniel affair broke. From the point of view of the hawks, this was intended to make a clean sweep of the intellectuals' pretensions and finally recall them to order and discipline. Instead it provided new grist to the mill of dissent, which it widened and reinforced. The case became a definite parting of the ways between those who, whether they belonged to the intelligentsia or not, aspired to a democratic interpretation of Soviet law and those who concealed their obscurantism behind reasons of state.

The affair began on 8th September, 1965, when Andrei Donatovich Sinyavsky was arrested in the street in Moscow by two agents of the political police. Sinyavsky was no turbulent student, hooligan or hothead. He was in his forties, a collector of icons and old manuscripts, and taught literature at the Nemirovich-Danchenko school of drama. He was not a member of the party, but was a member of the Writers' Union, and since 1959 he had been a contributor to *Novy Mir* (Tvardovsky had given him an honourable mention in the January

1965 number). He had written an excellent introduction to Pasternak's poems, published in Moscow in 1965, and worked at the Institute of World Literature of the Academy of Sciences of the USSR, where he enjoyed a high reputation. Among his more important works were essays on Gorky and Bagritsky, a monograph on Picasso, and a book on the poetry of the first years of the revolution, published in 1964. What everyone did not know was that he also wrote fiction under the pen-name of Abraham Terz, and that his novels (*Lyubimov* and *The Trial Begins*, as well as a book on realism that was very reserved about the official doctrine) had since 1959 attracted the attention of western critics by the vividness with which he substituted the grotesque for a realistic description of everyday life, postulating a 'phantasmagorial art' that attained the truth by way of the absurd, following the example of Hoffmann, Dostoevsky, Goya, Chagall and Mayakovsky.

His contemporary Yuri Daniel, a Jew, who was arrested on 12th September on his return from Novosibirsk, was a member neither of the party nor of the Writers' Union, but was well-known in Moscow as a poet and translator from various languages of the USSR; only his friends and the police knew that he too, under the pen-name of Nikolai Arzhak, had written stories that had been published abroad from 1961 onwards and had since found their way back to Russia (*Moscow Speaks, Hands, The Men of MINAP, The Expiation*, and others).

Both Sinyavsky and Daniel were men of distinction, notably superior in literary ability and perhaps also in force of character to the young people whose dissent took the form of romantic rebellion. While Soviet and western cultural circles were in turmoil, because they well knew that it was not an offence under the penal code to send manuscripts abroad, Sinyavsky and Daniel were accused of anti-Soviet activity because of the contents of their books (an aggravating circumstance being the fact that the American edition was edited by Boris Filippov, a representative of Russian culture in exile, who did not hesitate to describe Arzhak as the spiritual heir of Dostoevsky).

At this point there was another bombshell. In the middle of October Sholokhov was awarded the Nobel Prize. Though this seems to have been a coincidence, no-one could fail to see that, after the Pasternak episode, this major world tribute to Soviet literature, in the person of an author who, in spite of some anti-conformist gestures, had in substance always stayed on the rails of ideological orthodoxy, was bound to have repercussions on the trial of the two men. The prosecution had been presented with the obvious argument that, in view of the fact that Soviet fiction, published with the party's blessing, earned the country such flattering laurels, clandestine literature was obviously valueless and seeking success behind a pseudonym in the west was pointless.

It may have been self-satisfaction deriving from this that led to an unexpected gesture of comparative benevolence towards Solzhenitsyn, possibly a last attempt to win him over into becoming the advance-guard of a dialectical process within official literary society. The fact remains that *Literaturnaya Gazeta* totally unexpectedly published with great prominence on 4th November, 1965 an article by him on questions of language and style. The headline it was given was a Russian proverb: 'You don't season soup with tar; sour cream is better', which roughly amounts to saying that the right word should be used at the right time. The subject seemed to be non-political enough. In fact Solzhenitsyn, with the aggressiveness that was now usual with him whenever he had the opportunity of addressing the public, took the opportunity to attack one of the pundits of Russian culture, no less than the Academician Victor Vinogradov, who a few days previously, on 19th October, had published in the same journal 'Some notes on style' in contemporary Soviet writing.

'Vinogradov's article', Solzhenitsyn began, 'creates an unpleasant sensation, by its tone, the unsatisfactory choice of examples, the bad use he makes of the Russian language. . . . It is unnecessarily haughty, misunderstands the intentions of K. J. Chukovsky, is offensive in regard to F. Gladkov, S. Ozhegov, F. Kuznetsov. . . . The choice of examples is hasty, superficial, inconsistent; some are too obvious, too academic, others are wrong. . . . Above all, they are put forward in disorganised fashion, and do not help us either to understand the author's real thought, assuming that the article expresses any thought, or to overcome the defects of Russian as it is written.' Academician Vinogradov, Solzhenitsyn continued, severely criticised contemporary style, but in his turn offered very insufficient models. Instead of choosing expressive terms and concerning himself with reflecting the elastic harmony of the Russian language, he resorted from the outset to stereotype phrases, such as 'the national and aesthetic-artistic prospects', 'statistico-structural points of view', 'mass communications in modern culture', 'by virtue of powerful integration'. . . . His 'Notes on style' offended their sense of language and confused the issue instead of clarifying it; and it was at least curious that in an article on the Russian language in which the diary of Jules Renard was quoted twice there was no mention of Academician Vinogradov's predecessors who had been diagnosing defects and suggesting remedies since the nineteenth century. It would have been sufficient to recall Vladimir Dal and Herzen, who had courageously undertaken the task of promoting the progress of the language, as well as Andrei Platonov.

After this sarcastic beginning, Solzhenitsyn went on to argue the case for combining intelligent and sensitive preservation of traditional values with cautious and discriminating innovation. The Russian written language, he said, had been sick since the times of Peter the Great. Both its vocabulary and grammar and syntax had been negatively affected by authoritarian intervention, the influence of an educated class that thought in French, the unscrupulousness of translators, the haste of those who knew the value of time and thought, but not of words. The Russian vocabulary had been constantly impoverished by lack of effort to find the right word and by shame at the 'crudity' of certain Russian terms, which were considered inadequate to express lofty, modern ideas, and unnecessary recourse was often had to foreign words. Verbal substantives of neutral gender on the German model were favoured, for instance, while the so much stronger and more vigorous verbal substantives of masculine and feminine gender were neglected. Lavish use was made of abstract nouns, and the opportunities that Russian provided for the formation of adverbs had been neglected. Above all, the ability to handle words, to combine and arrange them with the delightful vigour still illustrated by proverbs, had been lost. The very structure of the Russian language had been disturbed. But there was reason for hope, since in the spoken language much less damage had been done. If writers, exercising due caution, succeeded in enriching their vocabulary, many hidden treasures would be restored to life and the whole of their literature would be strengthened.

The debate on language that had been opened in *Litera-*

turnaya Gazeta, Solzhenitsyn concluded, had produced numerous examples in favour of the case that he was making, but it was not a debate of the kind that went on for a month and could then be declared editorially to have been concluded. The issue was not that of finding a dozen guilty men and exposing them to public condemnation. Names must certainly be mentioned, for the purpose, not of making personal accusations, but of bringing errors to light. 'In my opinion, we are living through decisive decades, and there is still time to correct mistakes, discussing them all together, comparing one another, subjecting ourselves to severe criticism. It is we ourselves, with our hasty pens, who are responsible for the damage inflicted on the written language. We must go more slowly and check our course. There is still time to eliminate journalistic jargon, to correct the structure of the Russian language in order to restore to it facility and liberty of discourse. Following the advice of Dal, all of us together will gradually be able to substitute beauty for ugliness, brevity for length, clarity for obscurity, the expressive for the banal.'

Solzhenitsyn's article was as significant at the politico-cultural as it was at the strictly literary level. He did nothing to minimise the accusatory nature of an offensive that, through the authoritative Vinogradov, was directed at the whole of an establishment that was insensitive to classical values and problems of taste. At the same time he indirectly replied to those who accused him of stylistic traditionalism, using his usual technique of appealing to his colleagues to join in the defence of common values. The final quotation from Dal, the celebrated author of the *Dictionary* who extolled the virtues of the living language in the second half of the nineteenth century, was a reiterated tribute to the past and the necessity of a gradual, collective effort, by way of literary style, among other things, to revive the idea of a sincere, fresh, vigorous society that rejected bureaucrats and technocrats and restored individual taste as the standard of value. Solzhenitsyn's appeal to the responsibility of writers to regain a love of language was not mere self-defence; it was a rallying cry that was the more striking in that it appeared in *Literaturnaya Gazeta* while the debate on the principle of freedom of stylistic choice was at its height.

Meanwhile the campaign of protest against the arrest of Sinyavsky and Daniel continued vigorously, at home and abroad. Appeals to Sholokhov to intervene on behalf of the accused in his new prestigious rôle were sent from France, Japan, Italy, the Americas and India; and appeals were also made to Surkov, the First Secretary of the Writers' Union; to Furtseva, the Minister of Culture; and to Kosygin, the Prime Minister; telegrams were sent, among others, by the Pen Club and by Danish writers, Indian intellectuals, Swedish students and seventeen American writers, including Mary McCarthy and Arthur Miller, calling on them to continue along the path of toleration and legality opened up by the Twentieth Congress. All these testified to the literary value of Terz's work and pointed out the damage to the reputation of the Soviet Union that would be done by gagging a writer who, as Domenakh said, had been brought up in the spirit of the October Revolution and, so far from harming his country, protested against the absurd tyranny introduced into literature by Zhdanov.

The first reaction of the most prominent writers to this chorus of sorrow and indignation was one of embarrassment. Bella Akhmadulina, the poet Voznesensky, Surkov himself, and Tvardovsky, who expressed the opinion during a trip to Paris in November that the matter would be settled in accordance with the letter of the Soviet law and not on an ideological basis, were soon forced to change their minds when the Tass agency at last broke its silence and announced that Sinyavsky and Daniel had been arrested on the suspicion of having written, preserved and disseminated anti-Soviet literature. By this move the Kremlin not only indicated that it rejected foreign interference in what it considered an exclusively domestic matter but also, by again appealing to national sentiment, tried to undermine the significance of a protest demonstration organised in Moscow, again by SMOG, in Pushkin Square on 5th December (Constitution Day) at which two hundred students, mostly from the Gorky Institute, called for a public trial, 'the basis of a free democratic nation', for the two accused. The result of the demonstration was about twenty arrests, about ten expulsions from the university and from the Komsomol, the confinement to a psychiatric clinic of the sixteen-year-old girl poet Julia Vishnevskaya, the nineteen-year-old poet Leonid Gubanov, who was a contributor both to *Yunost* and to clandestine publications, and V. Bukovsky, who had been released a few months previously from the sentence imposed on him for 'parasitism' and being an editor of *Phoenix*.

Meanwhile the news from Stockholm was not encouraging; Sholokhov had refused to receive Mark Bonham Carter, representing Collins, the London publishers of Abraham Terz, and said he sided with writers 'who honestly look the Soviet authorities in the eyes and print their works at home and not abroad'. He pretended, in other words, not to understand that the Sinyavsky-Daniel affair again raised two questions crucial to Soviet society: whether it was obligatory for a Soviet writer to follow the rules of socialist realism in the restrictive interpretation imposed on it by the conservatives (and, if the answer were yes, whether it was a crime against the state to publish abroad, under a pseudonym, works that disobeyed aesthetic precepts); and what basis there was for the creeping fear among a large section of the intelligentsia, in view of the official silence about the case, that the authorities were going to conduct it behind closed doors, so that the public would not have the opportunity of seeing whether the alleged return to socialist legality was or was not being observed.

'The illegalities of power,' said a manifesto distributed at Moscow University on the occasion of the 5th December demonstration, 'have in the past cost the life and liberty of millions of citizens. The bloody past compels us to vigilance about the present.' It continued: 'Cries and slogans of any kind that go beyond calling for strict observance of the law are unquestionably harmful, perhaps actually provocative, and must be suppressed by those who take part in the meeting.' Thus the aim of the students' protest was unmistakable. Without for the time being going into the merits of the case against Sinyavsky and Daniel, the young dissenters presented themselves as the active wing of a movement that, with a view to exorcising Stalin's ghost, aimed at a democratic interpretation of constitutional liberties.

Immediately after the 5th December demonstration, as soon as the repressive measures taken by the authorities against the demonstrators became known, a group that called itself 'Opposition' pointed out, quoting Togliatti's memorandum, that 'the problem of greatest importance, both for the Soviet Union and for the other socialist countries, is that of overcoming the system of restriction and oppression of democracy and individual liberty introduced by Stalin'. (Those same weeks saw the publication of Nekrich's *22 June 1941*, on Stalin's grave military responsibilities, as well as a book by Oleg Antonov disputing the criteria applied to Soviet planning.) Sinyavsky's and Daniel's wives wrote letters to Brezhnev, the Public Prosecutor of the Soviet Union and the president of the KGB, and many friends and admirers of the arrested men sent protests to the most varied quarters, chiefly about the way in which the preliminary proceedings were being conducted, in which the accused men's guilt was already assumed.

Foreseeing which way the wind would be blowing at the trial, many denied that the works of Terz and Arzhak contained anti-Soviet propaganda, and appealed to Article 125 of the constitution, which guarantees freedom of speech and of the press (though 'in conformity with the interests of the workers and the aim of consolidating the socialist system'), Article 18 of the Penal Code (which states that 'judicial proceedings are always public'), Article 19 of the Declaration on the Rights of Man, to which the Soviet Union subscribed in 1948, which establishes the right freely to spread ideas by any means and independently of state boundaries. From the legal point of view, however, the crux of the matter lay in Article 70, in which, since the amendment of the penal code approved by the Supreme Soviet in December 1958, Article 58 of the 1926 code was now incorporated; this was the article under which Solzhenitsyn had been convicted and Sinyavsky and Daniel were now charged.

Article 70 provides for imprisonment for from six months to seven years, with or without banishment from two to five years, for 'agitation or propaganda tending to subvert or weaken the Soviet régime' or spreading 'slanderous fabrications denigratory to the Soviet political and social system'. If the prosecution succeeded in showing that the two writers had anti-Soviet intentions, the court would be within the law in convicting them. Hence the vigour of a campaign intended to emasculate the concept of slander in relation to the régime and the alarm felt by the progressive intelligentsia at seeing the decision whether or not a style of writing was a political crime put into the hands of judges unqualified in literary matters.

The trial took place in the presence of a public selected by the authorities (western journalists were excluded) and lasted from 10th to 14th February, 1966. It went through various phases and had juridico-political implications of various kinds that are too well-known in the west for it to be necessary to reiterate them. For our purpose the important point is that the central issue was whether or not Soviet writers had the right to depict reality in grotesque colours, to extract and distort elements of the truth in making imaginative literature out of history. It was, in short, the freedom of art that in non-repressive régimes has been recognised for centuries; and in particular the freedom of satire, long since accepted by democracies without being regarded as a threat to the security of the state.

However, in Italy and elsewhere the crime of public defamation still exists, legally exempting certain persons and institutions from ridicule, and the Sinyavsky-Daniel case showed that in the Soviet Union also it is necessary to contain smiles within limits beyond which the humorist, instead of reaching the heights of an absurd, surrealist fantasy, and hence providing his country with new artistic values, plunges into the abyss of satire, denigration and calumny and thus exposes himself to the rigours of the law.

The Moscow court seemed to have no doubts that Sinyavsky and Daniel had exceeded those limits. The use of pseudonyms in books published abroad was regarded as clear evidence of a bad conscience. The judges, prompted by the conservative wing of the party, the bureaucrats and soldiers, were most shocked at the content of 'libels', nearly always situated in Stalin's and Beria's time, based on the horrors of flat-sharing (as in Terz's *Fellow-Tenants*), the imaginary collapse of a city in which a hypnotist dictator claims to have achieved universal happiness (Terz's *Lyubimov*), the declaration of a 'day of public homicide' (Arzhak's *Moscow Speaks*), etc., etc., in which the authors satirised the personality cult, the servility of certain intellectuals and the duplicity of demagogues; in short, parodied with an imaginativeness that was hilarious or insolent, but was nevertheless dictated by love of country, a social condition that had wrought havoc with human relations, substituting hatred, cowardice and suspicion for the ideals of the revolution.

'Satire is an indispensable instrument of public health, a weapon against defects, a weapon against immobilism; without it society decays.' This obvious statement by the art critic Gerchuk in a letter to *Izvestya* made no more impact at the trial than did that sent to the court by another art critic, Golomshtek, in which he pointed out, correctly enough, that the problems raised by Sinyavsky – the breach between the individual and society, the contradiction between the growth of technical process and man's spiritual impoverishment, the relationship between ends and means – lay at the heart of contemporary civilisation. The whole trial was so conducted that the ideas and words of their characters were attributed to the accused, and an imaginary reality, populated with grotesque and petty figures, a kind of writing that used satire for the purpose of liquidating the sad heritage of Stalinism and made an appeal to personal responsibility, was regarded as a slanderous, or actually sacrilegious, picture of Soviet society (the public prosecutor called it 'public lavatory talk').

Sinyavsky was sentenced to seven years' hard labour in a camp and Daniel to five years, on the grounds that they had inspired feelings hostile to the régime and incited to revolt. This was the outcome, inevitable in view of the siege mentality that had been restored by the Kremlin, which regarded every disobedient writer as a smuggler of spiritual poison, of a long and tragic mistake about the relations between the arts and politics. Literature having been equated with propaganda, and words with reality, once more it seemed monstrous and blasphemous that artistic creation should obey laws different from those laid down in the penal code. Those like Sinyavsky, who in his self-defence rejected the obligation to make his own literary taste coincide with that imposed by the authorities, are described by forensic wisdom as authors of works characterised by 'Freudism, anti-Semitism, eroticism and mysticism' – all terms that are regarded as pejorative. Those, like Daniel, who claim that they love their country and their people, are considered to be perjurors. A writer who fails to offer his readers positive heroes, departs from socialist realism, and puts weapons into the enemy's hands by denouncing in ironic allegories the danger of relapsing into old errors, cannot be a patriot.

So complete was the *volte-face* that time seemed to have travelled backwards. The attacks on Sinyavsky and Daniel re-echoed with terrifying monotony those made in the twenties and thirties on Ilf and Petrov and Bulgakov, and those that later earned Zoshchenko the epithet of 'empty-head' and the withdrawal of his ration cards. The system encourages irony about the west, but refuses to accept it about itself, and declines to contemplate the possibility that pillorying evil might help to destroy it and that social and political life might benefit as a result. To the system irony is always 'corrosive', a sign of scepticism and bourgeois decadence, a vehicle of ideological disengagement and nihilism.

The conviction of Sinyavsky and Daniel created a tremendous stir, far greater than the expulsion of Tarsis from the Soviet Union that took place soon afterwards (in reality Tarsis was allowed to go; 'we gave him to the west, I hope you are pleased to have him,' Chakovsky said four years later), and produced what seemed a definitive breach both in the international *bloc* of the communist intelligentsia and in the Soviet Writers' Union. In France Louis Aragon announced his disagreement with the verdict in *l'Humanité*, the organ of the French Communist Party, and in Moscow Sinyavsky was expelled from the Writers' Union. This was made the more serious by the fact that the secretariat was careful to point out that the expulsion was based, not on the particular style of composition used by him, but on his having knowingly slandered the state, the régime, the party and the government. 'Soviet writers, at one with their people, always have supported, now support and will always support their state,' the secretary wrote in a letter to *Literaturnaya Gazeta*. *Pravda* said that 'Soviet writers and artists are completely free in their creative activity, in the choice of subject and form of their works, tell the truth about our life, our great ideas and their realisation, the feelings and aspirations of the builders of communism ... Sinyavsky and Daniel were tried, not as writers, but as persons conscious of criminal acts against the Soviet system.' A group of doctors of law declared that 'the trial was not directed at works of literature but at works of anti-Soviet propaganda concealed in a pseudo-literary guise'. This 'distinction', dictated by the need to reassure and simultaneously warn the intelligentsia, naturally produced precisely the opposite effect on progressive opinion. The conservatives of *Oktyabr* were almost alone in rejoicing at the verdict.

In the second half of March five citizens wrote to Brezhnev pointing out that the Sinyavsky-Daniel case, because of the way in which it had been prepared, conducted and presented by the Soviet press, 'has done greater harm than any anti-Soviet writing could to the world communist movement, our régime, the state, and our ideology'. Sixty-two Moscow writers, including Chukovsky, Ehrenburg, Shklovsky, Kaverin, Dorosh, Nagibin and Okudzhava, appealed to the presidium of the twenty-third party congress, held from 29th March to 12th April, for the two men's release (they themselves offered to stand guarantee for them). 'Conviction of the writers for their satirical works constitutes an extremely dangerous precedent, capable of putting a brake on the process of development of Soviet culture,' they wrote. 'Neither science nor art can exist without the possibility of expressing paradoxical ideas and creating exaggerated images. The complex reality in which we live requires expansion (and not restriction) of the freedom of intellectual and artistic experimentation. From this point of view the trial of Sinyavsky and Daniel has done greater damage than all the mistakes of those two writers.'

This lucid statement of the problem, this modern and alert awareness of the obstacles in the way of the development of Soviet culture, was answered at the congress by a furious onslaught by Sholokhov himself. 'I am ashamed', he said, to the accompaniment of thunderous applause, 'of those who have slandered my country and besmirched what we hold most dear . . . I am ashamed of those who tried and still try to go to their defence.' In the memorable twenties, he continued, when justice was administered by revolutionary tribunals, these 'mad wolves' would not have been treated like this. At a press conference in Tokyo he added that for his part he would have given them 'three times as much'.

The vigorous open letters with which Galanskov and Lydia Chukovskaya answered the Nobel Prize winner in their turn clearly demonstrated the degree of cultural maturity attained by that part of the Soviet intelligentsia that regarded the condemnation of Sinyavsky and Daniel as an offence against writers' dignity and freedom. While Galanskov denounced the 'old demagogue' and spoke of the vital function of clandestine literature, Chukovskaya dealt adroitly with the two principal aspects of the affair. She charged Sholokhov with showing a contempt for legality in regretting that martial law was not applied in peace time, and accused him of once more betraying the writers' duty, which was always and everywhere 'to clarify and bring to the consciousness of the individual the whole complexity, the contradictory nature, of the processes that take place in literature and history'. 'A book, a story, a novel, in short, all literary works, whether good or not, whether brilliant or insignificant, false or truthful,' she insisted, 'are not subject to any court, whether civil or military; they can be judged only by literature and public opinion. A court has no power over literature. All ideas must face other ideas, not labour camps and prisons.' And she ended in biblical tones: 'You have spoken as an apostate from literature. History will not forget your infamous speech, and literature will avenge itself, as it avenges itself on all who shirk the heavy duties that it imposes. It will condemn you to the maximum penalty for an artist: to sterility. And no honours, money, national or international literary awards will be able to remove that condemnation from your head.'

More than ever this was now a dialogue between the deaf; an unbridgeable gap yawned between two ways of regarding the relations between politics and the arts, and it was made still wider by the repressive measures taken immediately after the trial against some of those who gave evidence for the accused. The gap now ran through the heart of society itself. The Sinyavsky-Daniel case, which was discussed in public and in the press (in contrast to Stalin's time, when writers vanished without trace), represents an important milestone in the campaign of the Soviet progressive intelligentsia to obtain at least formal respect before the law and to establish their own right to express opinions about affairs of state. Sinyavsky and Daniel did not admit their guilt. That was sufficient to make a larger and larger number of Soviet writers feel promoted from the rank of servants of the party to witnesses to the truth. They armed themselves to campaign with unaccustomed vigour for a régime that would feel strong enough to be able to tolerate freedom of the arts and freedom of speech.

One of the secret weapons in this campaign was Solzhenitsyn's new novel, *Cancer Ward*, written between 1962 and the summer of 1966. In November of that year the author submitted the first part to the 'prose section' of the Writers' Union, which approved it. Nevertheless it was accepted neither by *Novy Mir* nor by other journals (surprisingly, some extracts were published on 7th January, 1967 in the Bratislava *Pravda*). The reasons for the Moscow rejections may once more seem obvious enough in retrospect, but at the beginning of 1966 something extraordinary had happened that may have suggested an unexpected change of attitude to Solzhenitsyn on the part of the authorities, though in fact it was merely another example of the dramatic surprises than can arise in the battle between authority and a section of the intelligentsia.

Just when the campaign against Daniel and Sinyavsky was at its height, the January number of *Novy Mir* published *Zakhar-Kalita*, a new piece by Solzhenitsyn. It was only a few pages long, and the fact that it appeared at all might have suggested an act of defiance, were it not for the suspicion that the authorities, having committed an act of spite against Vinogradov by permitting the publication of Solzhenitsyn's article on style in the *Literaturnaya Gazeta*, now proposed to make use of him for the purpose of exalting the value of the Russian tradition in the fact of the 'yellow peril'.

In *Zakhar-Kalita* Solzhenitsyn describes a bicycle trip (made in August 1962) to the plain of Kulikovo, where the Nepryadva and the Don converge, celebrated for the battle in which Prince Demetrius IV Ivanovich, afterwards known as Donskoy, the builder of the Kremlin, in 1380 defeated Mamay, the Great Khan of the Tartars. Solzhenitsyn found the place desolate and abandoned. An old monument to the prince's memory was disfigured by tourists' signatures, and some parts had been stolen by peasants of the neighbourhood. Against this melancholy background there stood out the strange figure of Zakhar-Kalita, a kind of inspector or watchman, in appearance half peasant and half bandit, wearing patched clothing and with a satchel slung from his shoulder and a sack which, apart from bottles and tins abandoned by tourists, contained two loaves of black bread and a 'guest-book', which he guarded as if it were a sacred relic. The man was illiterate and crude and frightened people, but actually he was the only person who cared about this place of patriotic memories. He was fanatical about his duties, and announced with pride that no-one had scrawled anything on the monument since he had been in charge of it. He left it only at night, to return to the village and have a meal and sleep in a hayloft. His pay was barely twenty-seven roubles a month, but that did not seem to worry him very much; his chief concern was the authorities' neglect of the monument. At night, when the place seemed to emerge intact from the shadow of centuries, Solzhenitsyn abandoned himself to reflection. Viewed in the light of centuries, history looked like a line drawn by a topographer, without curves or obstacles. However great a victory Kulikovo had been, it had not been a decisive one (because three years later the Great Khan had his revenge and burnt down Moscow, and Prince Demetrius had to submit to him). But Solzhenitsyn invited the reader to recall its symbolic significance; that day Russia had begun the struggle for her liberty.

Even though the *nihil obstat* for *Zakhar-Kalita* was obtained without excessive difficulty, only in moments of the most unbridled optimism could it be hoped that *Cancer Ward* would slip past the censor in a fit of absence of mind. This novel in fact presents an even gloomier picture of the Soviet world than *The First Circle*.

That the novel is woven of poetry and probably represents the highest peak reached by Russian literature this century matters little to those who believe that it should be imbued with the spirit of socialist optimism. The title alone, and the fact that the scene is a surgical ward set among the complaints of the sick, is sufficient for the state to feel justified in concealing its mistrust of the author behind solicitude for the serenity of mind of the people, who must not be distracted from work by being reminded of death. The stupidity of the bureaucrats is great, almost as great as the disturbing quality of the book. It reverts to the issues of *The First Circle*, which in some ways it deals with in even greater depth, and restates Solzhenitsyn's basic theme, that resistance to physical pain and consciousness of the moral abjection to which fear can lead are yardsticks by which the dignity of man can be measured in a world in which putrefaction of the flesh does not necessarily mean putrefaction of the conscience.

Cancer Ward is more tightly constructed than *The First Circle*. The action is almost exclusively confined to the limits of the ward but, thanks to the exploration of minds and memories, there is even more elbow-room for the orchestration of the themes, covering a wide range of experiences, moods and characters, that Solzhenitsyn presents in his favourite fashion, that of a great realist mosaic in the Tolstoyan tradition, rich in historical and psychological overtones and touches of lyricism. The 'thriller' element that added suspense to *The First Circle* is here submerged in a grey world of medicines, X-rays, the smell of infected bandages, and a babble of national languages; yet *Cancer Ward* is less gloomy, because from the premise that no-one has the right to make choices for others it deduces a principle the observation of which makes peoples and individuals the arbiters of their own fate.

Cancer Ward was written almost contemporaneously with *The First Circle* (some paragraphs are interchangeable), but is less closely involved in political issues and has a greater imaginative sweep; the obvious symbolism by which the cancer ward stands for the Soviet Union, populated by arrogant burueacrats, men released from labour camps now faced with the prospect of death, as well as other suffering mortals, is absorbed into the vision of a world in which everyone is put on the same level by the death that awaits the ideologies, fragile constructions of the mind destined to be worn away by time, conquered by the force of the spirit that ultimately triumphs in the history of humanity. The belief that Solzhenitsyn, quoting Pushkin, has made his own, that he is living in an abject century, in which man is either tyrant, traitor or prisoner, does not lead to resignation or any pietistic plenary indulgence for man. Compassion is counterbalanced by an ever more vigorous appeal to the individual's sense of responsibility, for the individual is the active cell in society, even if the latter deprives him of all rights. Perhaps a damaged soul that has been deprived of its place and meaning in society thereby reveals its own nature as a fragment of the universal spirit, which puts into it its own metahistorical values.

The witness to this truth in *Cancer Ward* is Oleg Kostoglotov (for whom Solzhenitsyn draws on his own experience as a cancer patient in the Tashkent hospital, on which he also drew for his 1960 story *The Right Hand*, published in *Grani* at Frankfurt in 1968). Kostoglotov, who was convicted under Article 58 of the Penal Code when he was a first-year student, is sent to hospital in an unspecified town in the south of Russia on 23rd January, 1955, suffering from a stomach tumour. He has had an operation two years before, but the surgeons attached to the labour camp in which he was then confined were negligent, and the condition returned in the autumn of 1954 when, after serving his seven-year term, he was banished to Kazakhstan as an 'administrative deportee'. He does not have much reason for hope in the future even if he survives as a result of the treatment he is now receiving, for he has been sentenced to perpetual banishment. This circumstance is vital to his rôle in the book. Knowing he will never be free again (though in the final chapters, when he hears talk of a possible amnesty – the time is shortly before the Twentieth

Congress – some hope revives) he might well feel, that, having been transferred from police to medical supervision, he has lost the faculty of free will, has become an object manipulated by others, a grain of sand carried by the wind of life towards objectives programmed by higher powers. That is undoubtedly the condition of the weak, of the average Soviet man who entrusts himself body and soul to the party, is brought up in a marmoreal idea of socialism, does not know the feeling of revolt. It is precisely against this voiding of the personality that Solzhenitsyn fights, giving a significance to the struggle that is the more dramatic in that Kostoglotov, stricken with cancer and condemned to perpetual banishment, seems to have no more reason to rebel. Instead the man is inflexible in his spirit of resistance.

When he is discharged after two months in hospital, cured of cancer but deprived of his virility by the hormone treatment he has had, and walks through the streets of the town, his spirit of independence, enriched by suffering and proud in the knowledge of having attained full interior liberty, has been so fortified that he is able to decline the aid of Vera Gangart, the young woman doctor in whose charge he has been; Vera, whether motivated by love or by compassion, has offered to put him up in her house on the day of his discharge. And he preserves the honesty and integrity that has hitherto enabled him to confess his sufferings and to which he would no longer be able to have recourse if, aware of the impossibility of his aspiring to conjugal happiness, he agreed to tie his fate to that of a woman. He does not modify his view of the world for this reason. 'Whatever he looked at in life, a grey spectre and a subterranean rumbling weighed down on everything.' On the exhilarating day of his discharge the two things that most strike him are an apricot tree in blossom and a news item about a zoo monkey blinded by a malicious visitor who threw tobacco in its eyes; a reminder of the senseless cruelty that spoils the pleasure in life.

It is this combination of revulsion at the absurdity of life with the consolation of overcoming it with love and controlling it with knowledge that gives *Cancer Ward* its supreme poetical value, and at the same time clarifies the nature of Solzhenitsyn's humanism, in which awareness of living in a tragic period of history brings about a fusion between Christian pessimism and certain existentialist moods and the still living doctrine of Kropotkin and Solovyev that repudiates every form of socialism that inculcates hatred. 'Social life cannot be built on hate . . . we wish to love; that is what ethical socialism must be . . . a society in which all relations, principles and laws spring from morality and from morality only.'

The ideological content of such statements may seem slight. In reality, in the socio-political context of a country that for nearly half a century has sacrificed the elementary rights of the individual to the myth of a collective morality, it has a revolutionary potential proportionate only to the artistic quality of the work in which it is contained. Oleg is surrounded by a whole gallery of 'shocking' characters who draw attention to individual destinies precisely to the extent that, when faced with the fear of death, they reacquire their true personal identity and reveal their humanity by the strength of character they have been able to preserve.

Typical from this point of view is the tragic figure of Rusanov, a bald hierarch with gold-rimmed spectacles and a wife with a fur coat, who is in hospital with a suspected cancer of the neck. For the first few days he rages and storms with his usual arrogance, because doctors and nurses do not treat him with the solicitude to which he is accustomed, and then, when he recovers his health, he is panic-stricken at the news of the rehabilitation of a friend whom he denounced as a saboteur in 1937–38, and fears he may be confronted with his victims and charged before the Supreme Court with having given false evidence. It is not only Kostoglotov whom Solzhenitsyn contrasts with Rusanov, who sums up in his person the misdeeds of a Stalinist bureaucracy that is essentially stupid and self-seeking even if it acts in good faith, and is disgusted with the new times and always ready to accuse decent people of ideological sabotage in order to defend itself against remorse for its crimes. All the other patients are better than he, if only because their worry about the prospects of survival is tempered by humility and hope, and sometimes also by self-irony, the virtue of the strong.

Once again Solzhenitsyn makes much of his gallery of women characters. These include Asya, a young girl with a great desire for life and happiness, who amid tears offers her tender breast to be kissed by Dyomka, a boy whose leg has been amputated; Lyudmila Dontsova, the head of the radiological department, who herself has a stomach tumour; the noisy cleaning woman Nellya; Zoya, the blonde nurse and medical student, who takes off her white coat and responds with a festive dance and some kisses to Oleg's suggestion that she should come and live with him at Ush-Terek, in the virgin lands of Kazakhstan; the melancholy Vera, torn between the memory of her fiancé who fell in the war and the disturbing feelings roused in her by Oleg; Aveta, Rusanov's poetry-writing daughter, the quintessence of ambitious youth, ready for any compromise for the sake of adapting herself to the consumer society now on the point of coming into being in the Soviet Union. Solzhenitsyn's women are embodiments of different aspects of femine psychology as moulded by the conflict between a warm and compassionate nature and the precepts of the party; and they provide the counter-chant to a chorus that expresses in robust and powerful tones (critics speak of a Beethoven-like power) a whole range of political and moral issues firmly rooted in the recent history of the Soviet Union and for the most part arising out of the contradictions of the system.

After the pattern of *The First Circle*, we are reminded of the controversy about sincerity in literature roused by Pomeranchev's essay, and irony at the expense of the Writers' Union re-echoes in the sermon inflicted by Aveta, who duly takes her stand on the neo-Stalinist line, on the timid Dyomka, whose life is dominated by literature. We think of the quarrel between Kostoglotov and Rusanov, from which there emerges a bitter denunciation of the social and economic inequality that the régime has not succeeded in eliminating; of the conversation between Dontsova and an aged doctor friend, which goes into the problem of the sexual education of the young, work rates, and hospital organisation, and Oleg's talk with the stretcher-bearer Anatolevna, who in 1935 was deported to Leningrad with her whole family and witnessed the revolting spectacle of children being invited to repudiate their parents. Above all, we see it in the discussion between Kostoglotov and Sulybin which sums up the tragedy of the Old Bolsheviks who did not have the courage to speak out against Stalin, accepting extermination or suicide instead, and now, if they survived, despised themselves for their cowardice.

It is here, in Chapter 31, that Solzhenitsyn most clearly states the rational and realist nature of his position, associating himself with Bacon in pointing out that men's fear of being left in isolation, outside the group, is responsible for their disastrous refusal to live by pure experience and their succumbing to prejudices: they subject themselves to the idols of the theatre (the authoritative opinions of others by whom they allow themselves to be guided) and the idols of the market-place (the errors deriving from social ties), all dominated by the atmosphere of terror. The Solzhenitsyn of *Cancer Ward* mistrusts every theory that claims to lead men to happiness, and rejects the Soviet official line. His response to the official obligatory optimism is to recall the frailty of the flesh, the fertility of doubt, the biological laws that regulate man's life and can be changed only in the course of millennia. As against Stalinist communism, he sets up an ethical socialism based on men's meeting each other on terms of equality. As against what he regards as the disaster of allowing oneself to be indoctrinated from above, he sets up the joy of thought, of working out a point of view about one's own life. Kostoglotov, the author's mouthpiece, seems to be stating a truism when he says that no-one in the world can say anything final, because in that case life would stop; in reality what seems to be a minor heresy is the result of deep meditation about the mystery of being, a painful awareness of the crime done to the whole of humanity when a defenceless individual is tormented or his freedom of judgment violated. Neither the attacks on Stalin ('the cannibal'), nor the criticism of Soviet institutions, nor the contempt for the hierarchy that is apparent would have led to such persecution of Solzhenitsyn if he had not, through the mouth of a pariah, denounced the betrayal of the revolution represented by the proclamation of dogmatic truths and the use of historicist excuses for violence.

The discussion on *Cancer Ward* that took place in the 'prose section' of the Writers' Union on 17th November, 1966 was dominated by awareness of the dangers threatening such an aggressive writer, as well as the necessity of proclaiming the artist's right to freedom of expression. The relations between Solzhenitsyn and the union were going through an extremely delicate phase. Solzhenitsyn had finished the first part of the novel and had circulated it in manuscript (this was the version that reached the west at the end of 1967 and was attributed by the Italian publisher to 'an anonymous Soviet author'), and it had been rejected by *Novy Mir*. But he still had hopes of finding a publisher for it in his own country, while his enemies were busily working to prevent this.

The discussion in the 'prose section', which ended with a warm invitation to the periodicals *Zvezda*, *Prostor* and *Moskva* to accept the novel (the invitation was duly declined), was considered by the dogmatists to be a totally unacceptable act of defiance, almost amounting to a revolt by the base against the leading cadres. Criticisms of *Cancer Ward* were certainly made in the course of the discussion, but the atmosphere was extremely cordial; at the end of the meeting Solzhenitsyn himself confessed that, in contrast to anything that might have happened at Ryazan, this was the first time he had ever had the opportunity of listening to the opinions and criticisms of qualified colleagues, and he had been encouraged by the experience to improve his work ('having nothing but the page in front of me, and having few readers, I was becoming less and less exigent towards myself'). The writers with whom the discussion took place in fact formed a group sufficiently homogeneous to be able to work out with the author a line of interpretation of the novel and its artistic values to oppose to the predominantly political judgment of its detractors.

In seeking the meeting Solzhenitsyn was obviously trying to force the censors' hand, putting on them the onus of suppressing a work recommended for publication by qualified judges, but he also wanted an outside view of the work. He believed in his talent, but during those years the pride of the solitary artificer was less than the ambition to see himself in print in his own country, openly to fulfil his mission as witness to the truth; if the experts, who undoubtedly knew more about the Moscow ropes than he did, recommended a few cuts here and a few changes there, he was willing to listen to them, so that *Cancer Ward* might be published in Russia and the castle of provocations and speculations built up by the police and the west might collapse.

His discussion with his colleagues of the 'prose section' confirmed that his was not a solitary voice in the wilderness; the moral reasons that impelled him to fight the neo-Stalinists were widely echoed among the writers, who seemed nearly unanimous in solidarity with him and found a kind of absolution for their own timidities and anxieties in his courage and talent. The objections of those who, like N. Asanov and

Zoya Zedrina (the zealous denouncer of Sinyavsky), were opposed to the book, pointed to its socially negative aspects and complained of the nebulousness of certain pages, were insufficient to drown the chorus of praise.

Borsagovsky compared Solzhenitsyn to Tolstoy and Salty-kov-Shchedrin, and spoke of the power with which, rejecting all prefabricated pictures of man, he solved the problem of the positive hero. Kaverin, almost anticipating the citation by the Nobel Prize committee, said that *Cancer Ward* was imbued with the profound sense of conscience that had always animated Russian literature. 'All attempts to silence Solzhenitsyn are doomed to failure,' he continued. 'He cannot write differently from the way he writes.' Leo Slavin said that his social diagnosis was exceedingly accurate, he was strong and crude, like Dostoevsky, and the book was one of the most important of recent years. L. Kabo said that by confronting them with death it made them think of essentials, in contrast to what they had been brought up to do by Soviet literature; and Arkady Belinkov went even further; Solzhenitsyn's work, he said, heralded the rebirth of Russian spiritual life.

Criticisms were confined to pointing out excessive realism here and there and to details in relation to certain characters. Some regarded the character of Rusanov as excessively caricatured, others complained of excessive imagery, and others again complained of Solzhenitsyn's reluctance to forgive, but no-one doubted his quality as an artist. Even those who felt doubts about the civic virtues of *Cancer Ward* admitted his uncommon talent. The aged Kaverin said that his spiritual freedom and need of truth made him better than any of them; they had hidden these things from themselves and lost them in contradictions; Solzhenitsyn represented the birth of a new literature. That was the sense of the whole discussion, with the corollary that the writers reaffirmed their claim to be judged by those who understood literature instead of by administrative bureaucrats. 'The Rusanovs are not only a danger of yesterday,' Yuri Karyakin said. 'They are still alive and waiting for their hour to come.'

It was for this reason that Solzhenitsyn, when he replied to the discussion, after expressing his thanks and promising to do his best in the second part of the novel to deserve the praise he had received, denied the charge of having been too hard on Rusanov. The principle that laid it down that when

David, pushed forward by untrustworthy allies, had no arms other than his own faith, while Goliath mobilised all the forces of the party and the state to prevent a revolt of consciences. There is a moving and also a melancholy quality about the former's defiance of the giant, and the combat that ensued behind a pink-painted façade. Before the fourth congress of the Writers' Union, held in May 1967, the dissenters did not succeed in expressing themselves on a scale proportionate to the shock caused by the Sinyavsky-Daniel trial. Tvardovsky's exclusion from the party central committee, which was the penalty imposed upon him by the Twenty-Third Congress for having published and praised Sinyavsky in *Novy Mir*, seemed to act as a brake on the liberal-minded intellectuals, a number of whom, to avoid the danger of being classified as 'socially dangerous', returned to the shores of prudence on which well-informed and scholarly individuals such as Georgy Breytburd, the translator of *The Leopard*, had established themselves for some time. To destroy the weed of Italian neo-avant-gardism and to prevent that 'provincial extravagance' from putting down fresh roots in territory where experimentalism has always had the flavour of opposition to the régime, Breytburd wrote in *Novy Mir* that 'the aspiration to blow up the "decrepit foundations of European humanism" recalls some of the appeals of the Chinese Red Guards'; and he also said that 'the positions of the extreme aesthetic formalists by no means excluded "ultra-left" political extremism of the Chinese type.' 'One of the important problems of present-day literary life,' he said, in an attack on Giuliani, Guglielmi and Sanguineti, 'the problem of the artist's social rôle, has been resolved by the neo-avant-garde in over-simplified and negative form. . . . When literature confines itself within the limits of linguistic experimentation and ceases to look at the world, becomes basically ideological, the reader is naturally the last thing that it considers.' In other words, this condemnation of the Sixty-Three Group was based, not on any critical assessment of the innovatory function of experimentalism, of a minority movement within a traditional literary culture, but on its refusal to wage an ideological battle on the lines of ortho-dox Marxism and the realist code. 'The renunciation of ideology,' Breytburd declared, without seeming to understand the ideological nature of the neo-avant-gardist revolt, 'is a renunciation of moral values, of the artist's responsibility for his work.' From this to political denunciation was only a short step. 'In reality the creators of experimental pseudo-novelties serve the masters of the cultural industry. . . . Thus a para-doxical situation arises in which a work of art, the aim of which is criticism of the system, is swallowed up by the system itself, is tranformed by it into an article of commerce, and functions within the limits laid down by the latter . . .' That was because 'the deepest roots of neo-avant-gardism lie in the very reality of neo-capitalism. . . . The rejection of the aim of painting a picture of the world and the possibility of knowing it by means of a scientific vision of reality contains the essen-tial link between the ideas of the representatives of the neo-avant-garde and the ideologies of neo-capitalism. The neo-avant-garde is not merely a product of neo-capitalist society, but accords with it on all essential questions, and this remains the situation in spite of all the anti-bourgeois state-ments made by the neo-avant-gardists.' This may be true, but the interesting point in the present context is the use made of it by part of the moderate intelligentsia, which is always ready to accuse those who leave the official tram-lines of collusion with Maoism and capitalism.

So once more the initiative was left to the younger and more audacious. After a silent demonstration organised on 14th March, 1966 by the novelist Aksyonov, Bella Akhma-dulina and General Grigorenko, and an open letter to Brezh-nev written by a number of scientists, a Ministry for the Defence of Public Order was set up on 26th July which, on the pretext of the struggle against hooliganism, gave an addi-tional turn of the screw to the repressive system. (In September suitable amendments to the penal code laid down penalties for disseminating false information and unauthorised publications and organising demonstrations in the streets.) Nekrasov was the only well known writer who had the courage to sign a letter of protest; the majority were content to look on, sur-reptitiously reading the *White Book on the Daniel-Sinyavsky Case*, in which Alexander Ginzburg (the editor of *Syntax* in 1959–60) collected a large number of documents and evidence about the trial, 'so that the voice of public opinion shall not cease or weaken until those who have the country's destiny more at heart than their own return to us'.

Meanwhile *Tetrad*, a new clandestine literary review, appeared, and the poets Vladimir Voskerensky and Evgeny Kushev revived after nearly a century the radical review *Russkoye Slovo*, now the organ of the so-called Ryleyev Circle that took its inspiration from the Decembrists, adopted the motto 'Culture, truth, honour', and announced that it wished to educate the young in patriotic virtues and a kind of anti-dogmatic cultural revolution. *Phoenix* also arose from the ashes five years after the first number came out (and among other things exhumed Mandelstam's 'Fourth Prose' written in 1930). In the interval the group gathered round its editor Yuri Galanskov had refined its critical sensitivities, and by publishing articles on literature, politics, history and religion (there was one by Sinyavsky on Yevtushenko) it tried to make its presence felt in fields wider than that of those whose aspiration was the freedom of artistic creativity. The police had sufficient appreciation of this state of affairs to begin 1967 with a wave of arrests. The poet Vladimir Batshev had been exiled to Siberia in 1966 for 'having devoted himself to so-called literary activities without being a member of the Writers' Union'. Those now sent to prison were Ginzburg (because of the *White Book*), Galanskov, Vera Lashkova, Dobrovolsky, and a few days later, for yet another demonstration in Pushkin Square (on 22nd January), which called for their release and the amendment of Article 70 of the Penal Code, Vladimir Bukovsky, the teacher Ilya Gabay, Igor Golomshtek, who had given evidence for Sinyavsky, and General Grigorenko, who was about to publish his *Stalin and the Second World War*.

There was another instance of a phenomenon that was to become a permanent feature of the scene. Apart from the extreme wing of dissenters who went on their way unperturbed and paid the price in their own person, a group of writers and artists came into being who protested through legal channels. Most of the dissenters, however, though convinced of the rightness of their cause, remained on the sidelines, yielding to the old temptation of Oblomovism. Not even the news in March that twenty-five intellectuals of the Berdyaev Circle had been arrested in Leningrad (Ogurtsov and Vagin were to be condemned in December to fifteen and thirteen years respectively for establishing a 'Christian Social Union for the liberation of the people' and maintaining contacts with foreign countries) induced the writers who called themselves progressive to set aside their personal differences and go out into the streets with the 'hotheads'. In their view, publication of Bulgakov's *The Master and Margherita*, certain hints in *Novy Mir* (which actually published something by Edoardo Sanguineti), and some unexpected liberal gestures were reassuring signs of a relaxation of tension that must not be prejudiced by foolhardy action. It would not be the moderate progressives who would rock the boat; nevertheless the fact remains that sometimes the resistance they put up in the face of pressure was firm enough to persuade the censorship to act with a great deal of circumspection.

This was what happened in the film world, where a battle had been in progress for some time between a small group of script writers and directors and the bureaucratic machine. Dissent in the film world has to take a form very different from that in the literary world, for the very good reason that it cannot declare itself and make an impact on public opinion in the form of completed work; the censorship intervenes at the scenario stage and the necessary approval and finance are refused, and if film-makers continue to suggest subjects considered inappropriate they end by losing their salaries. But if they are willing to renounce popular success and are content with a distribution of only about fifty copies of a film instead of the two or three thousand usual in the case of innocuous productions, they may succeed in persuading their supervisors, who are always in search of an alibi, to agree to subjects that are more modern in nature or are to some extent critical of society or include formal innovations or outbursts of lyricism. Innumerable examples show how hard the struggle is.

An attempt was made in 1965 to set up an 'experimental studio' that would constitute a kind of 'free zone' for the young – the task was entrusted to Chukray and Pozner – but it came to nothing. The most striking example of the obstacles that can be put in the way of a film even after the scenario has been approved is *Andrei Rublev*, which the director Andrei Tarkovsky started writing with Andrei Mikhalkov-Konshalovsky in 1962. Shooting was completed in 1966, but it was not seen in public until 1969 at the Cannes Festival, where it was shown *hors concours* and without Soviet official backing. It took three years to persuade Tarkovsky to make the cuts demanded by those who maintained that it contained too much realistic violence, mysticism, and polemics in the representation of the relations between art and authority. Tarkovsky first flatly refused to make the cuts, and then threatened to make an international protest if anyone dared use the scissors on his film without his consent, and he thus managed to keep his superiors on tenterhooks for a long time. Then the film was definitely shelved, and today the only hope of seeing it is abroad. But Tarkovsky succeeded in saving the reputation of the Soviet cinema and showed that its creative vein is anything but exhausted.

The fourth congress of the Writers' Union, held in Moscow from 22nd to 25th May, 1967, provided Solzhenitsyn with an opportunity of raising the level of protest to that of denunciation of the structure of the neo-Stalinist system itself, as distinct from merely its violent repression of the rights of literature. The mood he was in at the time is revealed by the interview he gave in March to the Slovak writer Pavel Ličko, published in the *Kulturnyj Zivot* of Bratislava. After recounting the salient features of his life, he went on to express his ideas with a clarity and precision that caused his interviewer to remark that the way his mind worked reminded him of a computer. 'Looking at the world through the eyes and with the intuitions of the artist,' Solzhenitsyn said, 'the writer discovers many social phenomena before others and in unexpected forms. Therein lies his talent, and from this there follows his duty to tell society what he sees, or at least to tell it what is unhealthy and represents a danger. . . . Russian literature has always addressed itself to the suffering. With us it is sometimes claimed that one should embellish reality and write about tomorrow; but that is a fallacy, that justifies lying. The literature that results from it is a dangerous form of cosmetics. . . . The writer's primary obligation is to man rather than to society. The life of the individual is not always identical with that of society, the community does not always help the individual. . . . Man is a physiological and spiritual entity before he is a member of society.

'In our time,' he went on, 'in which technology is becoming the master of life, prosperity is considered the supreme objective and the religious spirit is declining everywhere, the writer has special duties, and must occupy more than a place that

141

has been left vacant. In regard to the problem of the relations between his own time and eternity the writer cannot maintain a position of equidistance from both. If his works are to be merely topical, if they do not look at the world *sub specie aeternitatis*, they will have a short life. If, however, he devotes too much attention to eternity at the expense of the present, his work will lose colour, strength, breath. The writer is always between Scylla and Charybdis; he must forget neither the one nor the other. . . . On the other hand, it is not an irreparable error if society is unjust to a writer; to him that must serve as a test. It is not a good thing to spoil artists too much. In many cases society has been really unjust to a writer, but the latter has nevertheless succeeded in fulfilling his mission. The writer must be ready to put up with injustice; that is one of the hazards of his mission. The writer's destiny will never be an easy one.'

These ideas were soon to be restated in Solzhenitsyn's letter to the fourth congress of the Writers' Union, though in more combative form, as if to imply that willingness to put up with injustice did not mean surrender to tyranny. As he was not a delegate and could therefore not hope to address the congress, he adddressed his letter of 16th May, a few days before the opening date, to the presidium, the delegates, and the editors of literary newspapers and reviews. In resolute tones he called on the congress to face two problems, the censorship and the union's duties towards its own members.

'The Writers' Union,' he began, 'can no longer tolerate the enslavement that our literature has suffered for decades at the hands of the censorship, an illegal institution not provided for by the constitution that, camouflaging itself behind the emblem of Glavlit, allows illiterates arbitrarily to interfere with writers' work, preventing them from expressing opinions on the moral life of man and society. Excellent works by unknown young writers are nowadays rejected solely because they "would not get by". Many members of the Writers' Union, including delegates to this congress, are aware of not having resisted the pressure of the censorship; they have agreed to change pages and titles for the sake of seeing their works published. . . . The greater part of our literature sees the light in distorted form.' This was the more serious as the criteria applied by the censorship changed before their very eyes. Some labels ('ideologically harmful', 'corrupt', 'counter-revolutionary', 'anti-Soviet') that had been applied to writers such as Dostoevsky, Yesenin, Mayakovsky, Akhmatova, Bunin, Bulgakov, Platonov, etc., had been dropped or changed in a short space of time. Sometimes only his death succeeded in reviving an author's name; so it had been with Pasternak, whose poetry was now actually quoted at official ceremonies. 'But the posthumous publication of books and authorisation for the return of these names does not compensate either for the social or for the artistic damage done to our people by these monstrous delays and the enslavement of the artistic conscience.' Writers of the twenties such as Pilnyak, Platonov and Mandelstam had at a very early stage denounced the beginnings of the personality cult and the character of Stalin, but they had been eliminated or silenced instead of being listened to. 'Literature cannot develop within the limits of "this can be done, that cannot".' A literature that did not breathe the atmosphere of the society of its time, that did not dare to communicate to society its own pain and anxiety, that was not in a position to give warning about threatening moral and social dangers at the right time, did not deserve the name of literature; at most it could aspire to be called cosmetics. Such a literature did not even enjoy the confidence of the people, and the books that constituted it were not for reading but for pulping.

'Our literature,' Solzhenitsyn went on, 'has lost the position of pre-eminence that it enjoyed in the world at the end of the past century and at the beginning of the twentieth century, as well the splendid experimentalism of the twenties.' Because of the restrictions to which it was subjected, the literary life of their country now presented itself to the whole world in a form incomparably poorer, more uniform and more mediocre than it really was. This damaged the country in the eyes of the world and was an impoverishment of world literature; if the latter had at its disposal the fruits of their literature, freed from its fetters, it would be deepened by their spiritual experience, and the whole artistic development of the world would take a different course, would be strengthened, would attain a new level of development. Solzhenitsyn concluded his diagnosis by proposing a radical course of treatment: the abolition of all censorship, whether open or secret, and of the obligation imposed on publishers to submit every page of print for approval. This was the least that an association of writers jealous of their liberty of expression could subscribe to in a democratic country.

After calling on his colleagues to reflect on his basic point, Solzhenitsyn went on to attack the Writers' Union, which not only had never defended its members but, through its governing body, had contributed to persecuting those of its members who were the targets of insult and slander. He mentioned about a dozen names of writers whom the union had thus abandoned to their fate, and recalled that it had docilely handed over to imprisonment or deportation more than six hundred absolutely innocent writers. He therefore proposed that the constitution of the union should be amended to assure the defence of writers who were exposed to slander and unjust persecution. To demonstrate the urgency of this step he recapitulated the trials and tribulations to which he had himself been subjected.

(1) Just under two years previously his novel *The First Circle* (consisting of thirty-five printed sheets) had been confiscated by the political police and published without his knowledge or consent in a limited edition accessible only to a restricted group. He had had no way of ensuring that this should be publicly discussed at the Writers' Union or of preventing abuse or plagiarism.

(2) In addition to the novel, his literary files, dating back fifteen or twenty years and including matter not intended for publication, had been confiscated. Extracts from these files, selected for tendentious purposes, had been published for the use of a few readers. His verse drama *The Feast of the Victors*, which he had written from memory in a labour camp, when he had a four-digit number on his back and 'condemned to die of starvation, we were forgotten by society and no-one outside the camps spoke out publicly against (such) repressions'. This play, which he had repudiated a long time ago, was now attributed to him as his latest work.

(3) 'For three years an irresponsible campaign of slander has been conducted against me, who fought in the war as a battery commander and was decorated in the field. It has been said that I was condemned to the labour camp for common crimes, that I handed myself over to the enemy as a prisoner of war (which I never was), that I "betrayed my country" and "served the Germans". That is the interpretation put on the eleven years I spent in labour camps and banishment for

criticising Stalin. Persons in positions of public responsibility spread these slanders in secret instructions and at various meetings. I have tried in vain to put an end to them by applying to the executive committee of the Writers' Union and to the press; the committee did not even answer me, and no journal published my letters. On the contrary, in the course of this year the slanders from public platforms have increased. Use is now made of material from my files, it is distorted, and I have no way of replying.'

(4) In spite of its approval by the 'prose section' of the Moscow branch of the Writers' Union, the first part of *Cancer Ward* could not be published either in serial form (five periodicals had rejected it) or complete (it had been rejected by *Novy Mir*, *Zvezda* and *Prostor*).

(5) His play *The Stag and the Camp Prostitute* had been accepted by the Sovremennik Theatre in 1962, but its performance had not yet been authorised.

(6) The screen play *The Tanks know the Truth*, the play *The Light that is Within Thee*, the novella *The Right Hand*, and the *Miniature Tales* could not be produced or published.

(7) The stories of his that had appeared in *Novy Mir* had never been published in volume form and had been rejected everywhere (by the Soviet Writers Publishing House, the State Literary Publishing House, and the Ogonyok Library), thus remaining inaccessible to the general public.

(8) He had also been denied any kind of contact with readers, such as reading extracts from his work in public (of eleven reading evenings that had been authorised nine had been forbidden at the last moment in November 1966), and he had also been banned from reading his works on the radio. 'The mere fact of giving someone a manuscript to read or copy, which the scribes of ancient Russia were permitted to do five centuries ago, is now a crime in our country.'

'My work has been stifled and defamed,' Solzhenitsyn concluded, and he asked whether, in the face of such gross violation of his rights, the congress would decide to come to his defence. 'My mind is at rest,' he said. 'I know that I shall do my duty as a writer in any circumstances, and perhaps with greater success and authority from the grave than while I am alive. No-one will ever succeed in blocking the path of truth, and I am ready to die for its sake. Will the many lessons that we have had finally teach us that so long as a writer is alive his pen must not be stopped? Such behaviour has never ennobled our history.'

What was the impact on the congress of a letter that raised far wider than personal issues and put all writers on their guard against a state of affairs in which any one of them might find himself at any time? About eighty of Solzhenitsyn's colleagues supported him, demanding in vain that the letter should be read and freely discussed at the congress. On 26th May Georgy Vladimov wrote that it would be a disgrace to allow Solzhenitsyn's appeal to be passed over in silence, for he was 'the writer that Russia needed above all at that moment'; and the aged poet Pavel Antokolsky sent an indignant letter to Demichev, who was responsible for ideological matters on the central committee. In short, a great deal of noise was made, but no-one was willing to give battle, except in words, even to force the secretariat of the union to reply to the letter immediately. The fact of the matter was that since the Sinyavsky-Daniel trial the atmosphere had seemed unhealthy to many, and the circumstance that most of the members of the union were ageing also had its effect (the average age of the delgates to the fourth congress was sixty; only twelve per cent were under forty).

The greater part of the liberal intelligentsia had chosen the path of non-collaboration with the bureaucratic apparatus, under the illusion that in the eyes of public opinion this would signify open dissent. What happened in practice was that the dissenting minority that came out in open opposition to the leadership outflanked the moderates on the left and put them back among the forces that out of timidity acted as a brake on democratic development in the Soviet Union. In this situation the figure of Solzhenitsyn became a symbolic link between the young dissenters, most of whom were not members of the Writers' Union, and those of his colleagues who sympathised with him, were lavish in their expressions of sympathy, but were willing to make a fuss only when they themselves were victims of injustice.

This was the position of the poet Andrei Voznesensky, who, like Ehrenburg and Yevtushenko, did not attend the congress, but on 22nd June wrote a long letter to *Pravda* protesting against the 'lies' and 'stupidities' disseminated by the Writers' Union to justify the government's decision to refuse him a visa for a visit to the United States. 'This is not a matter that concerns me alone, it concerns the destiny of Soviet literature, its honour, its prestige in the world. How long will the Writers' Union continue resorting to these methods? Obviously the executive committee of the union does not consider writers to be human beings. ... Many other colleagues are treated like me. Our mail is not forwarded, sometimes others answer it in our name. We are surrounded by boors and chameleons, lies, lies, lies, crudities and lies. I am ashamed of belonging to the same association as certain other people.' (But there were some who were ashamed and ended up in prison. Vladimir Bukovsky, Evgeny Kushev and Vadim Delone, who had taken part in a demonstration protesting against the arrest of Ginzburg and Galanskov on 22nd January, were tried *in camera* on 30th August, 1967 and sentenced to deportation.)

On 12th June Solzhenitsyn had an interview with the secretariat of the union to ask for a reply to his letter and in particular to clarify the situation in regard to the publication of *Cancer Ward*. The situation was complicated and full of perils. In Italy the journal *Panorama* remarked that Solzhenitsyn's manuscripts had a strange fleetness of foot, and in fact *Cancer Ward* was already in the west, with Mondadori, the Milan publisher. But Solzhenitsyn tried to cover himself, to put it beyond a shadow of doubt that if the book were published abroad before it was published in the Soviet Union it was not his fault. At the meeting on 12th June he therefore asked for the backing of the Writers' Union to secure its speedy publication in some Soviet journal. The results of the interview seemed encouraging. The secretaries Markov, Voronkov, Sartakov and Sobolyev (Fedin chose not to be present) said that the executive committee considered it its duty publicly to refute the slanders in circulation about him and undertook to use their best endeavours to secure the earliest possible publication of the book.

But three months later no-one had moved a finger (in the meantime Solzhenitsyn's letter to the congress had caused a great stir in other communist countries besides the Soviet Union). *Novy Mir* was now willing to print *Cancer Ward*, but the Writers' Union had neither expressed an opinion on it nor done anything to check the slanders, which in the meantime had grown to enormous proportions (there was even a rumour that he had fled to Egypt or England). In another letter of 12th September he wrote: 'Perhaps the secretariat hopes that by letting the affair drag on to infinity my work will gradually evaporate, so that the problem of whether or not to include it in the national literature will no longer arise. ... If things are left like this, we shall not succeed in preventing the book from being published in the west. After the absurd procrastination of all these months, the time has come to say that, if this happens, it will clearly be through the fault (or perhaps the secret desire?) of the secretariat of the Writers' Union of the USSR. I therefore insist on my novel being published without delay.'

All that he obtained was an extraordinary meeting of the union secretariat on 22nd September, attended by about thirty members of the hierarchy, Melentev, of the cultural section of the party central committee, and Solzhenitsyn himself. There was a prelude during the morning beforehand. According to Belinkov, one of the secretaries, Voronkov called a meeting in his office for the purpose of agreeing on the line to be taken in the afternoon. He read a letter from Sholokhov pointing out that they had the choice between the following courses: 'Who is Solzhenitsyn? (i) A madman; (ii) not a writer; (iii) an anti-Soviet slanderer. What shall we do? (i) Put him in a mental hospital; (ii) expel him from the Writers' Union; (iii) send him to prison.' The official meeting, with Fedin in the chair, lasted from one to six, and resembled a trial. Fedin said that he took offence at the peremptory tone of Solzhenitsyn's letters. ('In the last resort it is he himself who is holding up the course of things by his pretensions. I have discerned no trace of professional solidarity in his letters.') Solzhenitsyn replied by denouncing another diversionary manoeuvre by his enemies. 'I have learned that someone has suggested that in order to form an opinion of the novel *Cancer Ward* the secretaries of the executive committee should read the play *The Feast of the Victors*, which I have repudiated, have not read for ten years, and all the copies of which I have destroyed, with the exception of that which was confiscated and is now being distributed.' He vainly pointed out that this play had nothing whatever to do with his present work, and that he had protested against its illegal confiscation. His accusers changed the subject and tried to convict him of connivance with bourgeois propaganda abroad by consenting without protest to his letter of 16th May being broadcast in the west before the congress opened. Solzhenitsyn denied that this had happened, and

148

added: 'I feel that a very significant use is made here of the word "foreign", attributing extraordinary authority to it, and almost implying that foriegn opinion is to be held in the very highest esteem. Perhaps that is intelligible in the case of those who devote their time to travelling abroad instead of to creative work and flood our literature with sketches of foreign countries. But to me it sounds strange. I have never been abroad, and there is no time in my life for getting to know foreign countries. Nor do I understand how it is possible to be so much more sensitive to foreign views than to those of our own, genuine public opinion. Throughout the whole of my life I have only had the soil of my own country beneath my feet. I listen only to its pain, and it is only about it that I write.'

Eventually the discussion turned to *Cancer Ward*. Someone asked whether the novel had been rejected or accepted by *Novy Mir*. Whose authorisation did *Novy Mir* need to publish a novel, and who had the power to grant it? Tvardovsky was asked to clarify the position. He said that in general the question of publication or non-publication came within the competence of the editorship, but that, in view of the situation that had arisen in connection with this author, it was the secretariat of the Writers' Union that must decide.

Voronkov arose and said that, since Solzhenitsyn's letter had appeared in the 'filthy bourgeois press', 'the working comrades and comrades of the pen' of the Writers' Union no longer had any intention of helping him, as they had once undertaken to do. If Tvardovsky thought it necessary to publish the novel and the author agreed to revisions, let him publish it. What had the secretariat to do with it? Tvardovsky agreed that the deliberations of the secretariat were sometimes not sufficient, and referred to the case of Alexander Bek's *New Destination*; this novel had been approved by the Union, but *Novy Mir* had not yet received permission to publish it. (Kaverin had said at the meeting in November 1966 that Furtseva, the Minister of Culture, had been personally opposed to it.) So there they were, back at the beginning again.

After this picturesque exercise in buck-passing, it was clear that the union had neither the strength nor the will to defend its members against open or secret intervention by the censorship. Most of the secretaries seemed to see nothing disturbing in this situation, and Solzhenitsyn went on hammering away at his point. If it were desired to prevent *Cancer Ward* from appearing in the west before it was published in the Soviet Union, the *nihil obstat* must be given immediately. But who was to give it? Certainly not his 'working comrades of the pen'. 'For two and a half years these comrades have quietly looked on at the way in which I have been oppressed, persecuted and slandered.' Once more he reiterated details of the treatment to which he had been subjected: the failure of the newspapers to publish his denials; the withdrawal of *One Day in the Life of Ivan Denisovich* from the public libraries; the malicious rumours of all sorts that had been spread about him ('if they said that I was a believer in the geocentric system and lit the fire when Giordano Bruno was burnt at the stake, I should not be in the least surprised').

The discussion became grotesque. Simonov made distinctions and differences; he was opposed to the publication of *The First Circle*, but was in favour of publishing *Cancer Ward*. Tvardovsky confirmed that *Novy Mir* was willing to publish *Cancer Ward*, 'with certain modifications, of course', and invited the union to deny the slanders to which Solzhenitsyn had been subjected, but he joined the prosecution in criticising him 'for the inadmissable and inopportune form he chose in approaching the congress, sending the letter to so many persons'.

The majority, led by Voronkov, persisted in evading discussion of the literary merits of Solzhenitsyn's work apart from its political implications. First of all, they said, he must protest 'against the filthy use' made of his name by their 'western enemies', and must realise that while a 'colossal global battle' was being fought Soviet writers were soldiers whose duty it was to defend their government, their party and their people. All the old political arguments were trotted out again; Solzhenitsyn had suffered in the camps, but he had not been the only one, and he saw only the black side of the past; even among the communists who had been deported in 1937 there had been some who had preserved intact their faith in the party and the country, and this year, the fiftieth anniversary of the October Revolution, it was stronger than ever. Solzhenitsyn had set out, not to represent Soviet reality in his novels, but merely to take a personal revenge. The incomparable Kozhevnikov said that *Cancer Ward* caused revulsion by its excessive realism and tendency to excite all possible and imaginable fears. And what was this 'insistence' on the publication of a novel that the author had not even 'revised'. 'With us,' he continued, 'all writers willingly follow editors' advice and do not force their hand.' Another secretary, Ozerov, said that a whole series of cuts should be made in the book, above all to prevent the author from smuggling in his own philosophy of ethical socialism through the personality of the principal character. Surkov said that if the book were published 'it could be turned against us, and do us more harm than Svetlana's memoirs'. 'Our readers are of course too advanced and shrewd to be diverted from communism by any wretched book, but to us the works of Solzhenitsyn are more dangerous than those of Pasternak.' This was because 'Pasternak was a man detached from life, while Solzhenitsyn has a lively, combative temperament and a very definite ideology. He is a man who has ideas.'

So the meeting went on for five hours, in an atmosphere of increasing tension very different from that of ten months earlier, when the 'prose section' had agreed on Solzhenitsyn's artistic merits. This time there was little sympathy for his books. Those most willing to grant him a certain talent (though there were some who thought his writing 'sickening and without a ray of light') were also the most opposed to its publication and the most hostile to Tvardovsky's proposal that *Cancer Ward* should be revised; they said he should be expelled from the Writers' Union unless he repudiated the novel as well as *The Feast of the Victors*. The last speakers displayed such rancour, such a tendency to blame their own pettiness on Solzhenitsyn, that the latter, defending the novel's realism (someone had suggested that the title was symbolic), pointed out that some of those present might themselves one day have the misfortune to suffer from cancer.

Thus the discussion ended up in a pitiful wrangle, with Solzhenitsyn undertaking to make a public protest against the west, but only if the Writers' Union undertook his defence and published his letter to the congress, while his furious 'colleagues' insisted that it was he who must take the first step, after which they would decide what to do. But he could give up any idea that there was any prospect of his letter being published. 'Now that the west has got in first, there is no more reason to do so,' was Fedin's excuse. The final exchanges showed the impossibility of reaching any understanding. 'You must tell us,' Surkov said, 'whether you repudiate the role of leader of the political opposition in our country that the west attributes to you.' 'I cannot believe my ears,' Solzhenitsyn sarcastically replied. 'A man of letters and leader of the political opposition? How do you reconcile the two things?'

No verbatim report of the meeting is available. The information we have comes from Solzhenitsyn's own account, distributed by him to the members of the Writers' Union; it was published in *Viesnik* at Zagreb in June 1968. In view of the source, it is possible that it may contain inaccuracies, that Solzhenitsyn may have tended to show himself in as favourable a light as possible and may have been led away into colouring certain passages. However that may be, the meeting unquestionably served once and for all to clarify the attitude to him of the secretariat of the Writers' Union. Except for Tvardovsky and a few others who tried to adopt a conciliatory position, both the secretaries on the one hand (or at any rate most of them) and Solzhenitsyn himself on the other behaved in a way that radicalised the conflict. Mutual asperity may have been sharpened by a general belief that they had been overtaken by events, because the strings in the case were now being pulled by the party and the police.

In all probability Solzhenitsyn and his enemies also knew that a plot was already in hand to get *Cancer Ward* published in the west as quickly as possible and to attribute responsibility for this to him, thus establishing definite proof of his infamy. If the novel had been published immediately in *Novy Mir* this manoeuvre would have failed, so the tug-of-war was now between Fedin, the leader of the conservatives, and Tvardovsky, who was strong in the support of his twenty-four editors belonging to the literary section. Tvardovsky succeeded in persuading Solzhenitsyn to make a few changes in the novel here and there (among other things, an unkind reference to Ehrenburg was deleted, as well as a reference to the deportation of the Chechens and Kalmuks), and planned to publish it in the January 1968 issue of *Novy Mir*. But Fedin had the upper hand; his intervention (perhaps inspired by Brezhnev himself) caused the production of *Novy Mir* to be stopped while the first eight chapters of the novel were being set up in type, and it appeared late, in February 1968, without the first part of *Cancer Ward*, which was published in the spring in Milan, Paris and Frankfurt (in the latter in *Possev* and *Grani*, both Russian *émigré* publications). The latter claimed in a telegram to Tvardovsky on 8th April, 1968 that it had decided to publish the novel knowing that the Soviet government had itself exported copies. It is difficult to establish with certainty what truth there may be in this; Victor Louis, the Soviet journalist, who was stated by *Grani* to have lent himself to this manoeuvre by acting as courier, denied it; his name was again mentioned in connection with Svetlana's and Khrushchev's memoirs.

Henceforward Solzhenitsyn's work was an ideological commodity in which both east and west speculated unscrupulously. In the Soviet Union the campaign of slander against him increased rather than diminished. At a meeting of journalists in Leningrad on 5th October Zimyanin, the editor of *Pravda*, called him a vindictive schizophrenic with an obsession about the labour camps, and in a reference to *The Feast of the Victors* regretted the times when writers were sent to prison for stuff of that sort. 'He won't go hungry,' he said. 'He is a physics teacher, let him do his job instead of thinking himself a genius.' The Writers' Union showed signs of life on 25th November, but only to reiterate that Solzhenitsyn should be the first to make a public statement, and the latter replied in a letter of 1st December with a series of questions to the secretariat. What was the union doing to defend him? he asked. What was it doing to persuade the government to sign the International Copyright Convention, to secure the restoration of his confiscated papers, as well as *The First Circle*, as the secretary Ozerov had promised, to print an anthology of his works, as Simonov had proposed, or to stop the illegal publication of extracts from his files?

Thus in the second half of 1967 the situation was bleak indeed. The atmosphere grew more and more threatening. Tension was increased by news of political trials at which heavy sentences were passed, and there was a haunting fear of the grave personal consequences to which the slightest indiscretion might lead. Solzhenitsyn had taken the measure of his enemies' hatred of him (as they had of his contempt for them), and he had been able to note the western readiness to exploit his personal drama. He had also been able to count his real friends. These were few.

Meanwhile, to complicate matters, the publication in the west of Evgenia Ginzburg's account of sufferings in Stalin's camps, and her warning that such tragic errors must never be allowed to happen again, had repercussions in the USSR, and Soviet literary circles looked at the past and wondered about the present and the future in a high degree of disarray. There was near-unanimity in condemning the crimes of Stalin, but only a few saw a threat to their own work in the resurgence of repressive measures and the denigration and slander of anti-Stalinist writers. Not even the example set them by the Writers' Congress held in Prague, which loudly applauded Solzhenitsyn's letter attacking the censorship and called for the independence of the arts as a matter of urgency, moved them to take a courageous stand. Most of them were insensitive to the principle of liberty of expression, which propaganda had for generations denounced as a bourgeois myth, and were ready to believe that Solzhenitsyn was a vindictive and alarmist victim of megalomania and paranoia. They even thought it legitimate that the police, if they suspected him, should ransack his private papers and that publishers should refuse to spend state money on equivocal works in which denunciation of Stalin implied between the lines denunciation of a system that, all things considered, conferred notable privileges on writers – widespread popularity, considerable creature comforts, holidays and rest homes.

Whether because of the habit of accepting orders from above or the decline of the hold of ideology on the country as a whole, most of Solzhenitsyn's fellow-writers deplored the taking of dramatic steps that exposed them to the danger of reprisals or forced troublesome examinations of conscious on them. That does not mean that they adopted the conservative and reactionary line of individuals such as Kochetov, who was spoken of with irony in the most varied circles. It meant waiting for the Kremlin to unfreeze the situation, for certain democratic values that were established in the minds of a minority to obtain official sanction. Respect for authority had worked such havoc that those who did not agree with the bureaucratic apparatus felt a sense of guilt, believed themselves to be black sheep, and found temporary relief from their inhibitions only in vodka. They both envied the courage of a Solzhenitsyn and detested him. They would have liked to join the young people who demonstrated in the streets, because at heart they still had generous impulses, but at the same time they hated them as spoil-sports who indirectly justified the strengthening of police controls. They were souls suspended in a limbo shot through with pallid gleams of light and icy fears. If the Soviet régime were one day to collapse, thousands of writers would join in the popular rejoicing and display as evidence of their anti-communism the works now locked up in their desks. But now the only course was to hold their peace; it mattered little that silence reigned in the House of Sleep, barely broken during the nights blanketed with snow by the Voice of America, the BBC, and Radio Free Europe.

One who did not throw in the sponge, however, was Tvardovsky, whose journal increasingly stood out as one of the few life-rafts left to writers who, however cautiously, wanted more elbow-room for literature. On 15th January, 1968, that is, after Fedin had stopped the publication of *Cancer Ward*, Tvardovsky wrote him a long letter that plainly showed that the *Novy Mir* group wanted to use the Solzhenitsyn case as a moral lesson for Soviet writers as a whole. Tvardovsky said in effect that he did not claim that Solzhenitsyn was an author to be accepted without any reservations whatever, but for a complex series of reasons he was now at the focal point of two opposite trends in the social conscience of their literature, one of which was pushing forward while the other was pushing back. This was confirmed by the fact that they had been discussing the case for months, growing indignant about the form of his letter to the congress (which was to be condemned) and pretending to ignore its content, and actually declaring this to be wrong and harmful to Soviet literature while in fact it was irrefutable. The insistence that if he were to survive as a writer and as a citizen he must first of all reply to the anti-Soviet campaign in the west was a gesture that belonged to the past, when orders were given to confess, to renounce, to sign. 'These "renunciations", these "confessions", damage us enormously, establishing an image of the writer as a man who is morally volatile, devoid of any sense of dignity, and capable only of carrying out orders from above; which in point of fact amounts to the same thing.'

Among the many methods suggested for cutting the Gordian knot, someone had proposed that Solzhenitsyn should merely express his attitude to the west in a letter to the secretariat of the union that would be put in his file and remain unknown to anyone outside the secretariat. Tvardovsky protested against this. 'Is it possible that the solution of the whole tangle should depend on a secret piece of paper? That is the situation that we have reached; a document of two or three pages becomes more important to us writers than a completed novel of 600 pages that in the opinion of most of those who have read the manuscript would constitute a precious ornament of and a subject of pride to our literature.'

They had taken more interest in the publication of *Cancer Ward* than the author himself, Tvardovsky went on, fearing that this was going to be a repetition of the Pasternak story, and he took the opportunity of pointing out that the novel was at the head of a queue of a whole series of worthy and valuable works, such as Simonov's *Hundred Days*, Bek's *New Destination* and E. Drabkina's *Winter Journey*, that were being held up by the censorship even though they had not been formally banned. 'Let us speak frankly,' Tvardovsky went on. 'You know as well as I do that in the whole history of world literature there has never been a single instance in which the persecution of an individual of talent or the attacks directed at him, no matter where they came from, have been successful. ... In our case it is much better to run the risk of making a mistake in permitting the publication of a book than to try to prevent a mistake (assuming that that is possible) by preventing its publication. And in the existing circumstances I really think that you are faced with the double danger of confirming with your signature either a shameful decision or an equally shameful hesitation. ... I have now known you for thirty years and I have heard a great deal about you from Marshak and others who knew you at Leningrad; it is the general opinion that Fedin is a man of honour and a person capable at any time of helping a colleague or acting in defence of his rights. And I myself had confirmation of that in 1954, when things were going badly for me. ... But today I feel it my duty to tell you things that will displease and perhaps offend you. They are, however, things that I have already said in a recent meeting on this same subject. You know the proverb; dogs that bark don't bite. I am outspoken, and probably I have often shown myself in a bad light by failure to control myself. It is not in my nature to measure my words, and any kind of intrigue or duplicity, all the things that are nowadays held up as examples of "tactics" and diplomacy, are totally alien to me. The fact remains that the harshness with which I replied to you during our last meeting, in the presence of Markov and Voronkov, was due to what was to me the incomprehensible irritation with which I heard you speak of Solzhenitsyn. How is it possible to speak in that way of a man and a writer who for every page and every line that he has written has paid more in his person than any of us who are called on to judge him? He has undergone the greatest ordeals that a human being can suffer, war, imprisonment, and a killing disease. And now, after his marvellous début in the world of letters, he is faced with yet another ordeal, perhaps a trial, provoked by circumstances of a non-literary nature — open slander, a ban on his name being mentioned in the press, etc. . . .

'Two days ago, while I was sitting at my desk rereading this letter, I received a telephone call from the State Publishing House. They said to me: "In the fifth volume of your complete works there is an article on Marshak in which you mention the name of Solzhenitsyn. . . . Our instructions are . . ." Needless to say, I refused to delete it, even at the cost of the volume's not being published, but it is astonishing that certain things can happen.'

Tvardovsky's letter to Fedin should be read in the context of the tangled and often ambiguous story of the relations between the *Novy Mir* group and the secretariat of the Writers' Union, a drama that took place behind the scenes rather than in the full light of day. But a quite different series of events in that same January 1968 provides confirmation of the fact that the radicalism of the conflict led to the establishment of a united group of dissenters inside the union that sided firmly with those who demanded a return to legality and freedom of expression.

The trial of Galanskov, Ginzburg, Dobrovolsky and Vera Lashkova took place in Moscow on 8th to 12th January, in a much less intimidating atmosphere than that of the Sinyavsky-Daniel trial, and several members of the union (Bella Akhmadulina, Aksyonov, Babayev, Bogatyryov, Y. Golisyova, Iskander, Rudnichky, Edlis) signed a petition calling for publicity for the proceedings and free access to the court. The physicist Pavel Litvinov, grandson of the former Foreign Minister, and Larisa Bogoras (Daniel's wife) denounced to the western liberal press the witch-hunt atmosphere that pervaded the trial, in which one of the accused, Dobrovolsky, played the part of *agent-provocateur*, and they appealed to world public opinion for a retrial of the case, which was 'in no way better than the disgraceful trials of the thirties', in accordance with all the rules of law.

As soon as the sentences were made known (Galanskov was given seven years, Ginzburg five, Dobrovolsky two and Vera Lashkova one) twenty-four Moscow students wrote to Litvinov expressing solidarity with him; this was the first instalment of what was to be a voluminous correspondence. A few days later, on 16th January, at a meeting of writers who were members of the party, Grigory Svirsky, a writer who worked for the best-known journals, attacked the censorship on the lines that had been made notorious by Solzhenitsyn's letter; his speech cost him expulsion from the party. He said that the censorship, far from restricting itself to the potection of military and state secrets, had submerged the whole of Soviet literature with the blind cruelty of a flood. The writer was humiliated, deprived of the right of communicating his thoughts and feelings to the people; he felt himself to be a second or third-class citizen. He quoted a long series of examples illustrating the contradictory behaviour of Glavlit; works that criticised Stalin were invariably cut, while those that praised him escaped the scissors, and their authors were actually rewarded by the government. 'Lenin said that one must not lie even to one's enemies,' he said. 'With us one lies to one's friends. How many lies there have been in recent years. Lies about Pasternak, Solzhenitsyn, Vosnesensky, Yevtushenko, Evgenia Ginzburg, Okudzhava. . . . We have grown so used to lies that sometimes we do not trouble even about the plausibility of the accusations, and we force writers to lie in the name of a so-called higher discipline. . . . Yes,' Svirsky went on, though the chairman tried to silence him, 'we demand liberty. But not liberty outside the party, of which we are flesh and blood. The interests of the party are our own interests.' They demanded liberation from the reactionary clique that betrayed the party line with impunity and lent plausibility to the claim of their enemies abroad that the errors resulting from the personality cult were the natural consequence of the communist system. 'Let us speak frankly,' he said. 'What divides the Writers' Union into two groups is neither genres nor age nor literary passions, but the Twentieth Congress.'

In conclusion he quoted his own novel *State Examination*,

which exalted the courage of those who defended the freedom of science in 1949-53 but had been held up by the censorship for thirteen years. 'The elimination of controversial books is an exceedingly dangerous symptom; it means that people who think are not wanted, because in the arbitrary conditions in which we live a man who thinks is potentially a heretic. We are still stuck with the Jesuit style, which consists in building up the outside wall of a church to the upper storey, behind which there is hidden something very different from what appears at first sight. Behind the façade of fine speeches and promises there is Glavlit, equipped with incredible powers, that succeeds even in thwarting the official policy of the central committee. To those comrades I put an anxious question: When will they remove the barriers erected in the path of a literature that studies life? The time has come to fight all those who think neither of the people nor of the international communist movement and offend the dignity and prestige of our country.'

Svirsky put his finger on the sore spot, pointing to the Stalinist bureaucrats ensconced in the censors' offices as the source of the poison that prevented Soviet literature from advancing along the path opened up by the Twentieth Congress, and his speech did not fall on infertile ground. A few days later, on 25th January, the authoritative Venjamin Kaverin wrote an open letter to Fedin criticising him for opposing the publication of *Cancer Ward* in *Novy Mir*. 'There is not an editor's or publisher's office at the present time in which it is not known that Markov and Voronkov favoured the publication of the novel, and that approval was refused only because you opposed it. That means that the novel will continue to circulate in thousands of manuscript copies, that it will be published abroad, that we ourselves are putting it into the hands of Italian, French, British and German readers; what will happen is precisely what Solzhenitsyn has more than once energetically tried to prevent. How is it possible for a leading figure in the Writers' Union to believe that he is punishing a writer by handing him over to foreign literature? He is punished by being given a world-wide fame that our enemies will exploit to their advantage. Or is it perhaps hoped that Solzhenitsyn will change his mind and his way of writing? That is ridiculous in the case of an artist who has provided us with a rare example of a burning vocation and continually reminds us that we write in the language of Chekhov and Tolstoy. ... You are assuming a very grave responsibility, obviously without realising it. A writer who puts a noose round the neck of another writer gains his place in the history of literature, not for what he has written himself, but because of the other writer's works. You are becoming, perhaps without suspecting it, a target for the loathing, indignation and discontent of the whole of our literary world. And this can be changed only if you find in yourself the strength and courage to reverse your decision.'

Fedin stood firm, however, with the result that between March and July dissent spread at the most varied levels, in spite of Brezhnev's order to increase vigilance against 'persons greedy for publicity who for the sake of acquiring a reputation accept the praises of our enemies and fall easily into their net' (the reference to Solzhenitsyn was unmistakable). Also the first numbers of a new clandestine journal, *Chronicles of Current Events* began to circulate. It was published quarterly, and from April 1968 was to be the richest source of information on the progress of dissent and repression. Letters of protest to the judges, to Podgorny and Brezhnev calling for the restoration of legality (signed among others by writers such as Paustovsky, Kaverin, Aksyonov and the woman poet Novella Matveyeva) alternated with appeals to the United Nations Commission on Human Rights for intervention in defence of the freedom of expression of opinion.

In March a dozen intellectuals (again including Larisa Bogoras and Pavel Litvinov, as well as the philosopher Boris Shragin, the teachers Ilya Gabay and Yuly Kim, the philologist Yury Glazov, the historian Pyotr Yakir, and the Old Bolshevik writer Alexei Kosterin) protested to the conference of communist parties in Budapest against the increasing number of trials for crimes of opinion and the inhuman conditions in which thousands of political prisoners were kept. Also in March the poet Vadim Delone, writing in *Literaturnaya Gazeta* and *Komsomolskaya Pravda*, recalled the suppression of all the attempts made to enable the youngest generations of writers to express themselves by way of the legal communist youth channels instead of in the clandestine press. ('What the Stalinist theory of the intensification of the class struggle during the construction of communism has led us to is well-known ... it is a crime against the country to inculcate into the young the myth of "enemies of the people" '.)

The Pan-Russian Christian Social Union, inspired by the ideas of Berdyaev, was dissolved in April. In May Ilya Gabay and the physicist Kadyev were tried at Tashkent for having shown solidarity with the Tartars who wanted to return to the Crimea, from where Stalin had deported them in 1944 on the pretext that they were collaborating with the Germans. General Grigorenko, who was in the front rank of the protesters, was arrested and sent to a mental hospital. 'It is a return to the times of Stalin, when the whole country was held in the grip of terror,' said a statement made among others by Pyotr Yakir, who had spent fourteen years in a labour camp, and Yesenin-Volpin, who was speedily sent off to the company of the insane, to the protests of about one hundred mathematicians.

In June there was a purge in the university town of Novosibirsk, and on the 20th of that month a letter to the Writers' Union from Arkady Belinkov was distributed. This was a very violent document, breathing a profound hatred of the régime, which was described as dominated 'by a handful of conspirators who have seized power and decide the fate of an oppressed people' for whom 'another Nuremburg trial is being inexorably prepared'. 'I return you my membership card of the Writers' Union,' he wrote, 'because I consider it unworthy of an honest man to remain in an organisation that serves with dog-like devotion the most cruel, inhuman and pitiless political régime of the whole of human history. Artists and scholars of this exhausted and abject country, all you who have preserved a trace of dignity and decency, return to yourselves, remember that you are writers belonging to a great literature, and do not serve a régime that is now rotten; fling your membership cards in their faces, withdraw your manuscripts from their publishing houses. . . . Despise them . . . and despise their petty, verbose, sterile and pitiless state, which will always praise its own victories and successes with the sound of the drum.'

As for Solzhenitsyn, he went on living through agitated months. Some extracts from *Cancer Ward* appeared in *The Times Literary Supplement*, and the first version of the novel was published in the original Russian by Mondadori of Milan early in 1968. On 16th April he sent to all the members of the Writers' Union a copy of his letters to the secretariat of 12th September and 1st December, 1967, together with his account of the meeting of 22nd September, and declared the secretariat, which had allowed nearly a year to pass without a reply, to be responsible for the situation. 'Nothing has changed to the present day,' he said. 'My papers have not been returned, my books have not been published, my name is banned. I have several times warned the secretariat of the danger that, in view of the wide circulation that my books have now had for some considerable time in our country, they would finish up abroad, but it has not only not approved the publication of *Cancer Ward*, which is now in proof in the editorial office; it has done everything to stop its publication, even preventing the Moscow "prose section" from examining the second part of the novel. Now that the inevitable has happened, let my writer colleagues decide whose fault it is.'

Two days later, on 18th April, Solzhenitsyn returned to the attack with another letter to the secretariat and members of the Writers' Union and to *Novy Mir* and *Literaturnaya Gazeta*, based on the telegram sent to Tvardovsky by *Grani* ('The Committee for State Security has sent to the west another copy of *Cancer Ward* through Victor Louis to prevent its publication in *Novy Mir*; we have therefore decided to publish the work at once'). He protested against all unauthorised publication of his work, asked what were the relations between Victor and the KGB, complained that literature had been reduced to such a state that works were becoming 'profitable merchandise for the first trader provided with a passport', and concluded with a statement ('the works of our authors should be published at home and not handed over as prey for foreign publishers') which would have disarmed those who charged him with connivance with the enemy if there had been any desire to do so. He went still further.

On 21st April, in a letter to *Literaturnaya Gazeta*, he said that it had been stated in *Le Monde* (the news had been published in Paris on 13th April) that parts of *Cancer Ward* were to be published without his authorisation in various western countries by publishers such as Mondadori and The Bodley Head, who were quarrelling with each other, taking advantage of the fact that the Soviet Union was not a signatory of the International Copyright Convention. 'I declare,' he went on, 'that no foreign publisher has received the manuscript of this novel or authority to publish it from me. Not having given the rights to anyone, I do not recognise either present or future editions of the novel as legal. Similarly I regard as illegal all changes in the text (inevitable in view of the uncontrolled multiplication and dissemination of the manuscript) and all unauthorised film or theatrical versions. I already know by experience that *One Day in the Life of Ivan Denisovich* has been ruined by haste in all the translations; the same fate obviously awaits *Cancer Ward*; but, apart from money, literature also exists.'

Solzhenitsyn's letter was published in the west (in the Italian Communist organ *Unità*, after its confiscation by the customs at Moscow airport from its bearer, Vittorio Strada), but not in the Soviet Union. *Literaturnaya Gazeta* took its time. It waited while another edition of *Rakovy Korpus* was published in the original by Einaudi in Italy in May (the Italian version published by Il Saggiatore was attributed to an anonymous Soviet author) and a Russian edition of *The First Circle* was published by the Fischer Verlag at Frankfurt, and it took note of Solzhenitsyn's letter of 21st April only on 26th June in an article entitled 'The ideological struggle. The writer's responsibility'. This declared that Solzhenitsyn had remained deaf to the warnings of the Writers' Union about the use made of his name by reactionary western propaganda, and it rejected the personal slanders (it admitted he had fought at the front, had been decorated, accused of anti-Soviet propaganda, condemned to labour camps and rehabilitated in 1957). But it accused him of not having taken part in the social life of the Writers' Union. 'He preferred taking another path, that of attacks on the basic principles of Soviet literature.' Not only that; in contravention of ordinary standards, on the occasion of the fourth writers' congress he had caused to be circulated 250 copies of a letter of his intended to cause a scandal by stating that Soviet literature was in a state of oppression and by denigrating its achievements. There was no justification for his demand that the constitution of the Writers' Union should include a clause guaranteeing the defence of all its members who were the object of unjust and slanderous persecution, because it would put the constitution in open conflict with the normal standards of the state, which already offered these guarantees to all its citizens. It was false that the organs for the security of the state had searched his files and confiscated manuscripts of his at Ryazan, though it was true that, after the frontier police had found derogatory writings in the luggage of a foreign tourist, the house of 'a certain citizen' Teush had been searched and that anonymous manuscript copies of works of Solzhenitsyn had been confiscated there, including *The Feast of the Victors*, in which the Soviet army was represented as 'a gang of idiots, roughs, marauders and vandals', and Captain Nerzin, who helped traitors to the country to desert and join up with General Vlasov, was held up as a hero. Solzhenitsyn's behaviour at the meeting held at the Writers' Union on 22nd September had been plainly demagogic; instead of rejecting the provocation of the western press, he had peremptorily demanded the publication of *Cancer Ward*, 'which from the ideological point of view, in the opinion of the secretariat, was in need of radical changes', and later he had shown himself ready to haggle with the secretariat, declaring himself willing to make some concessions. His reply to a letter from the secretariat of 25th November had made it clear that he wished to continue using western public opinion as a tool with which to exercise pressure on the Writers' Union. In April 1968 he had in arrogant tones attributed to the Writers' Union responsibility for the publication of *Cancer Ward* by western reactionary publishers, and he had written a tendentious account of the meeting held on 22nd September. Finally, he had refused to denounce the enemy *provocateurs* of his country, even when he knew that foreign publishers were about to publish *The First Circle*, which was 'explicitly slanderous of our social system'. 'At this point it is clear that Solzhenitsyn has adopted the role attributed to him by our ideological enemies. . . . The writer Solzhenitsyn could have devoted his abilities to his country instead of to those who harm it. The bitter fact is that he has not wished to do so. Now it is up to him to find a way out of the blind alley into which he has driven.'

So much for the article in *Literaturnaya Gazeta* (which also took the opportunity to scold Kaverin, who had 'joined the enemy chorus' with his open letter on *Cancer Ward*, which had been made use of by the foreign radio). Lidya Chukovskaya, whose vigorous attack on Sholokhov we mentioned above, answered what she called this 'painful' article in a long typewritten reply distributed in July 1968. She explained, for the benefit of those who did not yet appreciate the fact, that Solzhenitsyn was persecuted and slandered only because he had been among the first to unmask Stalinism; this was a serious crime because, with a few exceptions, 'the editors of journals deliberately delete from all articles everything that recalls the disappearance of our compatriots in Stalin's prisons and camps'. Why was *The First Circle*, for which Solzhenitsyn had signed a contract with *Novy Mir* in 1964, now described as 'a base slander on our social system'? Had the novel changed, or had the social system? 'No, the climate has changed; the order has surreptitiously been given that the past must be wrapped in mist.' Because of the necessity of inventing an excuse for penalising an author who disobeyed orders by continuing to unmask Stalinism in *Cancer Ward* and *The First Circle*, *Literaturnaya Gazeta* applied a worn-out denigratory terminology to him without taking the slightest trouble to inform its readers what his works consisted of or what he said in his letter to the congress, and actually quoted excerpts from works he had repudiated. 'I do not deny', Lidya Chukovskaya concluded, 'that receiving our riches from foreign hands is a great misfortune, a great humiliation to our people, to all of us. There is, however, only one way of avoiding it, by ourselves publishing the important works of Soviet literature.'

Two other letters were also written. One was from J. F. Turkin, a contributor to *Literaturnaya Gazeta*, who refused to go on working for it so long as it was edited by Chakovsky. The other, dated 4th July, 1968, was sent to *Literaturnaya Gazeta* and *Novy Mir* by Alberto Mondadori, the Italian publisher, who defended himself against the charge of literary piracy in publishing the manuscript of *Rakovy Korpus* in the anonymous form in which it had reached him. 'A book', he wrote, 'is a message that is addressed to someone, is in search of an addressee. Not he who publishes it, but he who prevents its publication violates its nature, betrays its mission. Every book, if it is born of genuine and honest experience and displays indisputable literary qualities, must reach the readers for whom it is written, as much in your society as in ours. If you wish to accuse us, accuse us for good reasons, and not for carrying out our duty which, as publishers and thus cultural organisers, is that of acting as link between authors and readers, i.e., printing and distributing books. Courage, Soviet friends,' Mondadori concluded. 'Why do you slander your country by creating the impression that after fifty years the foundations of communist society are so weak as not to be able to stand up to the distribution of a book in which a writer honestly relates his experiences? I do not believe that that is the case, though there are reactionaries in the west who have an interest in believing it and causing it to be believed. Do not supply them with ammunition. Act so that all can love your country and your people without reservations.'

Solzhenitsyn's friends and enemies might have gone on endlessly exchanging blows in a manner that seemed to be becoming a permanent feature of the cultural landscape (at the end of July, there was another wave of protests at the arrest of Anatoly Marchenko, a worker who in his *My Testimony* described his experiences as a political deportee from 1960–1966) but for the dramatic shock to a large part of the intelligentsia, as well as to a large part of the rest of the world, caused by the Soviet intervention in Czechoslovakia. To the anti-Stalinist writers the Russian tanks in Prague represented an application on the international scale of the technique of obscurantist repression of which they had daily experience in their relations with the censorship. To weaker spirits discouragement was piled on humiliation. Few believed the version of the facts put out by Moscow; the arguments with which the Kremlin sought to justify itself, and even the terminology, too closely resembled those used in the internal struggle against liberalising elements for the latter not to note with dismay the dimensions of a neo-Stalinism that they had hoped to exorcise by passive resistance. While the majority of those who had preached the writer's duty to stand up for the truth and not bend to tyranny chewed over their indignation and shame in silence (only Yevtushenko, so far as is known, sent an insolent telegram to Kosygin and Brezhnev), the small fringe of those who took up the torch of peaceful open protest at the risk of burning themselves again went out into the streets.

The demonstration in Red Square at midday on 25th August, 1968 by seven sympathisers with the Czechoslovak communists (Larisa Bogoras, Konstantin Babichky, Vadim Delone, Pavel Litvinov, Vladimir Dremlyuga, Victor Feinberg and Natalya Gorbanevskaya) symbolised the marriage between political and cultural dissent. It was now clear that the principles of the freedom of expression of opinion and of a nation's freedom to choose its own path, respect for legality in daily practice and respect for national sovereignty, were inseparable in the context of a modern socialism that repudiated ideological absolutism and imperialist terror. It was just as clear that the penalties imposed on the demonstrators (Litvinov, Larisa

Bogoras and Babichky were sentenced to five, four and three years' banishment respectively), the subsequent sending of the woman poet Gorbanevskaya to a mental hospital, and the repressive action taken at Gorky University, where protest against the events in Czechoslovakia was liveliest, showed the determination of the Kremlin to strangle at birth a new relationship with public opinion.

An opportunity of striking a pact that would reinforce democratic convictions was provided by the death of Alex Kosterin, an Old Bolshevik anti-Stalinist writer who, on regaining his liberty after seventeen years' imprisonment, devoted himself to the defence of national minorities (the Volga Germans, the Crimean Tartars, the Chechens, Turks and the Ingush, all victims of Soviet centralism), returned his party card in a protest against the intervention in Czechoslovakia, and was duly expelled from the Writers' Union on 30th October, 1968. Some hundreds of persons gathered at his funeral on 14th November, 1968 and listened to nearly a dozen speeches in his praise, including one by General Grigorenko (who chiefly praised his civil courage in advocating Leninist democracy as against totalitarianism and accused the Writers' Union of having morally murdered him), and another by the historian Yakir, who said that Kosterin regarded Czechoslovak socialism as the alternative to capitalism and Stalinism.

The pomposity of the speeches, the pathetic pride in defying the authorities who tried to prevent tribute being paid to Kosterin, did not diminish the significance of a demonstration in which the chief themes of dissent merged in the principle of loyalty to the ideals of Lenin. There seems to be justification for suggesting that at the present time the most fertile soil for protest is that in which the seeds of a return to the origins of the revolution are germinating, while episodes of revolt against the system itself remain marginal. This return to the origins being impossible in a profoundly different historical context, the myth acts as a stimulus towards a wider consciousness of the human dignity which the Stalinists trampled on and of which Solzhenitsyn continues to be the most prestigious and inflexible standard-bearer.

The police, the bureaucracy, the conservatives are well aware of this, and hence the special venom with which they harass him (in November *Oktyabr* denounced him for allegedly travelling round the country to collect evidence about popular discontent). Actually at this time Solzhenitsyn was unable even to go on teaching at the Ryazan school. He applied to be transferred to the Moscow branch of the Writers' Union, but this was rejected because his official place of residence was Ryazan. He left his house as little as possible, but every now and then the windows were broken.

On his fiftieth birthday on 11th December, 1968 he received telegrams of congratulation from all over the world, as well as an anonymous letter praising Stalin to the skies and comparing him, Solzhenitsyn, to a goose flapping its wings. 'History will put everyone in his place,' the letter said. 'Having earned the praise of the west, you have earned the contempt of your people. Greetings to your friend Nikita and don't take offence.' Next day Solzhenitsyn wrote a letter to *Literaturnaya Gazeta* which it did not publish. 'I sincerely thank all those who have sent me good wishes, and I promise them never to betray the truth,' he said. 'My only aspiration is to meet the expectations of Russian readers.' That he succeeded in doing so was confirmed a few months later by the results of a public opinion poll carried out by the Novosibirsk Institute of Sociology among subscribers to *Literaturnaya Gazeta* with a view to finding out, among other things, who their favourite Soviet authors were. The two most popular were Paustovsky and Solzhenitsyn. The choice of the silent majority could not have been more comforting.

CHAPTER EIGHT

A visit which I made to Moscow in the summer of 1969 provided the opportunity for a number of meetings with Soviet writers and for gaining a first-hand impression of the oppressive atmosphere, relieved by an occasional feeble breath of fresh air, in which the intelligentsia were living at that time of perplexity. Conversations with these people were cordial, sometimes a trifle emotional. They were never cheerful, never marked by the sparkle of wit or humour that indicates the detachment of those who feel themselves above the interview game. All of them betrayed in their manner pain or anger at having been surprised at the pearly hour that belongs either to a dawn or a sunset, depending on which way you look at it. They were men rich in human sympathy and often of acute and wide-ranging intelligence but, even when they hid their feelings behind a proud mask, they were dispirited by a more than fifteen-year struggle into which they had poured enthusiasm and anxiety with nothing to show for it but the suspicion that they were playing the part of outsiders, living on the fringe of the cultural debate of the seventies.

Their embarrassment appeared most plainly in their almost physical inability to take part with European and American colleagues in developing, let us not say a theory of literature, but merely a point of view on the development of modern taste. Talking to a foreigner, they did not renounce self-questioning about the need to regard literature as something other than an ideological tool, but they did so with such timidity, and often so inhibitedly (as if mistrusting themselves) as to rule out any possibility of an answer usable in their socio-political context. We know the reason why; the great themes of contemporary literary life – the relations between art and ideology, between fiction and the human sciences, between tradition and linguistic revolution, the real or presumed crisis of the novel – have such slender roots in Soviet soil that a breath of wind, or even the fear that discussing the subject might produce a breath of wind, are sufficient to inhibit the adoption of any point of view that departs from the Stalinist tram-lines.

There is a specific reason for Soviet writers' reluctance to face an ideal confrontation at inter-continental level on the future of literature in the contemporary world. So far from having accustomed themselves to the idea that, through no merit of their own, they have evaded the grim alternative between being the régime's servants or its victims, pride and fear make them cling to the myth of self-sufficiency; hence their reluctance to intervene openly in a debate that would link them with the west. But if the system acts as a powerful gag, that does not necessarily mean that they are also blind-folded. We have seen that threats are no longer sufficient to silence determined dissent. Protest no longer has to 'choose liberty' in order to be able to express itself; political action is an exceedingly thorny path, requiring a high degree of physical and moral courage, but it is more fruitful than escape abroad, because it affects men's consciences and disturbs them. The fact remains, however, that to Soviet writers who grew up under a system of terror, the idea of cultural self-sufficiency, combined with the habit of talking in whispers while looking over their shoulder, provides a kind of excuse for the gap that exists between their vocabulary and that of the west; and younger generations took this in with their mother's milk.

Drawing up a catalogue of the ideas round which the socio-cultural debate of the seventies revolves in Europe and America and comparing it with the contents of a Soviet journal of the same period painfully illustrates the extent to which the many fields of enquiry that have long been familiar in the west, but have now to be looked at in a new light because of the phenomena of mass culture, e.g., the function of art and the dislocation of the intellectual at the present day, are sterilised by the primitive formulae of a Marxism-Leninism to which the mechanical reiteration of recent years, the process by which they are automatically dug up again after half a century, gives an archaeological flavour.

In spite of the breach that is slowly coming into being between official literature and the nucleus of public opinion round which a new national consciousness shows signs of beginning to form, the cultural apparatus, and even the repertoire of themes in prose and verse, trail a long way behind the state of maturity reached by average taste, which the fifth column, the cinema, feeds with small mouthfuls of western trends. In the absence of freedom to experiment and to engage in the adventure of discoveries in self-expression without supervision by a censorship that keeps the consumers of ideas in the state of a minority, the basic media of mass communication (the press, book publishing, radio and television) fail to respond dynamically to the social demand for cultural goods.

The working out of artistic and moral values for the seventies is taking place in a kind of limbo. 'Costume' novels situated in the Stalin era and fiction inspired by the war years meet the needs of different generations of readers united by the problem of whether they should be proud of the past or ashamed of it. But, apart from that, a whole series of consumer demands are developing that are disappointed, both at the lowest 'thriller' level of literature (invariably populated with American spies and ex-Nazis who commit the most fiendish crimes) and at the higher level of serious fiction. These demands arise in the academic world, the professions, the world of science and technology, where there is no toleration of the writer who acts as loudspeaker for the party, has become fossilised in the rôle of 'worker with words', and by enclosing himself in the iron ring of socialist realism has excluded himself from the literary civilisation of the second half of the twentieth century and simultaneously isolated himself both from socialism and from realism.

That part of the public that foreshadows, however vaguely, the cultivated society of tomorrow, shows no mercy to the poet, novelist, critic, who continues to sacrifice his liberty of imagination to the myth of literature as an auxiliary service. At best he is accused of acting as a brake on a phase of development in which a less rigid relationship between the people and culture might have been established, and at worst he is a target for the sarcasm that is the reward of the false prophet.

However, the fact that the process by which the writer is being stripped of his halo is taking place in such a critical atmosphere is also due to the circumstance that the man in the street was brought up at school and by the party press to idealise him for political reasons, to approach a work of art with veneration as a sublimation of the community. Having been placed for decades on the pedestal reserved by the régime for the Hero of Propaganda, the Soviet writer of strict observance, and also his *alter ego*, the waverer, is threatened with a fall in the social hierarchy as disastrous as his ascent was dazzling.

Thus the resulting picture is one of insecurity in a bitter provincial isolation, marked both by infantile and senile but basically reactionary traits. The Soviet man of letters, comparing developments in his field with the progress made by the scientists and in the economic field, has the choice between banging the table with his fists and taking refuge in the siege mentality. It is a tense situation, liable to lead to neurotic outbursts or heart attacks, and the outcome is either rage or surrender to the standardised literary product.

The way of escape from drowning in the swamp of commonplaces is a narrow passage, parallel to that used by the mass of non-party members, carpeted with appeals to the benevolent function of criticism, along which there moves, resisting as far as possible the pressures of thrusts and counter-thrusts, the fringe of the intelligentsia that is generally called 'liberal', by analogy with the nineteenth-century opponents of absolutism. It is a treacherous and hazardous path, because the old guard has sown it with traps, but it is the only hope of establishing a fertile relationship between the writer and the society of his readers, between the Soviet writer and Europe.

The summer of 1969 found the traffic of ideas in a state of crisis. So long as work was in progress to clear the road of the huge landslides produced by the latest trials of writers and the invasion of Czechoslovakia, all advance was blocked. According to the pessimists, the rule of the Khrushchev era had been reversed; instead of two steps forward and one step back, it was now two steps back and one step forward.

The Writers' Union bore a heavy responsibility for this state of affairs, and the list of grievances at that time was made the more significant by the fact that many authors asked that to avoid reprisals their names should not be mentioned. 'The union has never defended us; on the contrary, it has always harmed us,' said a literary critic who was a contributor to *Novy Mir*. 'On the pretext of helping us and avoiding difficulties with the censorship, it imposes small-minded editors on journals, and always looks with suspicion at trouble-makers who try to bring about a kind of professional solidarity among its members based on the liberty and universality of literary work. Though legally independent of the party, it has never taken up a position in opposition to authority, has never expressed an effective independent line to stimulate the feeble process of democratisation that is making headway among the intelligentsia. It has always followed in the foot-steps of the central committee of the party and, if it has some-times created the impression in its discussions of wanting to touch on unseemly matters, it was because it was reflecting at that moment the short-lived successes of the "liberals" in the battles at the top. It has never attempted to work out a coherent, organic alternative to the grim ideological totali-tarianism of the authorities. It confines itself to acting as a barometer. In stormy weather its servile frenzy makes it more royalist than the king, and when it calms down again it con-tents itself with ordinary administration. The Writers' Union is one of the many Soviet superstructures in which the bureau-cracy shows itself in its true light; it rouses itself from torpor only when occasion arises to lay about itself. What action did it take, for instance, to further the rehabilitation of the many authors who were disgraced in the Stalin era, or in more recent times died in an odour of less than perfect sanctity? The committees for the preservation of the literary heritage that it establishes after every writer's death are supposed, in co-operation with his family, to help in securing publication of his unpublished work or works that have been out of print for some time. In practice, if he is still out of favour with the authorities, they serve only to bury his memory as well. When Solzhenitsyn accuses the union of having handed over more than 600 writers to their fate as political prisoners, he is merely stating the sober truth.'

A young fiction writer said: 'If only the union performed a trade union function in relation to the publishers. It does not even discuss the criteria by which publishers decide on the number of copies to be printed. As is well known, in the Soviet Union authors' royalties are paid on the number of copies printed, not on the number sold. Theoretically this offers some advantages as compared with the injustices that arise in the west from the operation of the laws of the market; in practice the distribution of a book depends on its degree of political conformism and thus, in the absence of any link between supply and demand, neither creates nor respects any hierarchy of values.' Bulat Okudzhava said: 'Look at my case. A million copies of my book of poems *A March of Great Spirit* could easily have been printed in view of my growing popularity as a *chansonnier*. In fact only 40,000 were printed. The principal bookshop in Moscow received exactly thirty copies, not one of which was put on sale, because the assistants drew lots for them among themselves.'

A somewhat similar state of affairs exists in regard to periodicals. Restrictions on paper supplies mean that the number of copies printed is related to the number of subscribers, but in the case of journals that are considered dangerous the number put openly on sale is very limited indeed. For many years it was difficult to find the latest number of *Novy Mir* on the Moscow bookstalls, but there was never any shortage of *Oktyabr*, the mouthpiece of the conservatives.

'If at least the Writers' Union worked to get Russia to join the Berne Copyright Convention,' a middle-aged poet said. 'Solzhenitsyn has pointed out that it would be a sure way of protecting us from unauthorised translations made abroad and from buccaneering commercial competition in getting them out first. Instead, the union spends its time cautiously regulating the foreign travel of its members, weighing the advantage to be gained from instructive accounts of the life of peoples struggling against imperialism and colonialism against the risk of the traveller's showing himself to be a weak communist in order to please the bourgeois public.'

The general impression gathered from my meetings with Soviet writers in the summer of 1969 was that the barriers erected by those who denied writers the right of flexible participation in the creation of a modern literary society were growing higher and higher. While the idea that the justification of a work of art lay only in itself continued to be heretical, the theory that a writer, working with such infinitely variable material as human nature, should express himself as he wished about what he wished was utterly abominable. Pessimists said that the students who in their letters of solidarity with Pavel Litvinov called for the publication of Brodsky's verse, Remizov's and Zamyatin's stories, Mandelstam's poems and Pasternak's prose, would grow old before their wishes were met.

The sharpest barbs were of course reserved for Glavlit, the central authority on questions of art and literature responsible to the Council of Ministers. 'It is enough to make one's hair stand on end,' one of those interviewed said. 'Not one of us knows where he is. The situation has certainly deteriorated since Solzhenitsyn described it in his letter to the fourth congress of the Writers' Union two years ago. His scathing denunciation of police outrages and the arbitrary actions of the censorship, carried out by boorish officials at artists' expense, probably sealed his fate for good. He pointed out that the greater part of our literature appears in distorted form. If it has lost the pre-eminent position it had in the world at the end of the nineteenth century and the experimental brilliance of the twenties, it is because it has been prevented from developing and from appearing less poor and insipid than perhaps it really is. Solzhenitsyn had a thousand reasons to protest; he is the greatest writer that the Soviet Union has today and, strong in his experience of Stalin's camps, he carried out the duty of defending in his person the dignity of all his colleagues, even those who consent to changes being made in their texts and titles for the sake of seeing their work in print.

'But in one way his intervention, and the campaign conducted throughout 1967 and 1968, did more harm than good. Glavlit, concerned at the amount of support that Solzhenitsyn had among intellectuals, redoubled its vigilance. Not only did it dig in its heels in forbidding *Novy Mir* to publish Bek's novel, but it also postponed *sine die* the rehabilitation of poets such as Mandelstam, Voloshin, and Khodasevich and tightened the screw a little on everyone. Those who pay the highest price of course are the writers of medium level, who neither can nor (perhaps out of loyalty to the régime) want to send their manuscripts to the west.

'The first station of the cross is at their work desks when, to adapt themselves to the requirements of the censorship, they distort their imagination, eliminating psychological situations and details and engaging in Byzantine contortions of syntax. The second sees them standing cap in hand in front of the editor of the journal in which they hope to see their work published in instalments, in accordance with the Russian custom. At this point the tragi-comedy, the haggling over characters and adjectives, begins. The editor – the man of confidence that the Writers' Union has on every journal – tries to divine what there may be in the manuscript on his desk that would be displeasing to Glavlit. The author begins by declaring his complete confidence in the editor's taste and discrimination, and then, if he encounters resistance, tries to persuade him that, according to his personal information, the wind is blowing in such-and-such a direction at this particular moment, with the result that greater tolerance can be expected. It is at this stage of the negotiations, when officially the censorship has not yet intervened, that changes are often made in authors' works, especially in passages touching on the conflict between the generations, or in which young vagabonds or women of easy virtue appear, or the Stalinist terror is criticised, or the necessity of war is indiscriminately denied, or a character's moral crisis is not attributed to his detachment from proletarian society.

'When this phase is over (though the novelty of the last few months has been the increase in the number of writers who do not accept impertinent interference in their work and prefer to tighten their belts), the work passes into the hands of Glavlit. At this point tragi-comedy tends to turn into tearful melodrama. Beween 1956 and 1964 the powers of the bureaucratic oligarchy assembled in Glavlit were reduced. Its duty was only to make sure that nothing coming from the printing presses contained infringements of military secrecy or morality. After Krushchev's fall, its former functions of ideological control were restored. In that Counter-reformation atmosphere you can imagine the zeal with which Stalinist-trained censors, conscious of the restoration of their rights as guardians of the system, applied the (often contradictory) instructions of their superiors. Remember that at the time of Daniel's trial *Izvestya* saw evidence of his guilt in a passage in which he describes certain women as "resembling castrated men . . . with short legs, like pregnant basset-hounds, or with long legs, like ostriches, who hid swellings and bruises under their clothes, drew in their corsets, and padded out their breasts with cotton-wool".'

And if Glavlit refused its *imprimatur*?

'Glavlit does not refuse its *imprimatur*, which is the number printed with other information (number of copies printed, type of paper used, the names of the censors) on the last page of every book and periodical. If it detects the scent of heresy, it withholds its *imprimatur*, but denies that it is unwilling to grant it. It merely indicates that the author must wait. The editor, pressed by the author for information, is told that the time is not right, let him try again later – say in a month, or a year, or twenty years. Only if the author has a private saint in paradise, i.e., a friend in the cultural department of the central committee of the party, can he hope that the "right time" will ever come.'

Ginzburg pointed out the relativity of the idea of anti-Soviet propaganda in a letter to Kosygin in December 1965. 'When criticism comes from below,' he wrote, 'it is anti-Soviet propaganda; but if it comes from above and has been incorporated in congress resolutions, it is the party line.' A young woman writer, asked if the situation had improved, if there were any firm principles at that time on which Glavlit based its decisions on which works strengthened and which weakened the Soviet system, replied with a smile: 'Where dogmas would be useful, if only to make life less complicated for us, they are lacking. Theoretically, the list of "isms" regarded as heretical is the same as thirty years ago. All the ramifications or irrationalism, from formalism to anarchism, from mannerism to abstract art, and everything suspected to be of bourgeois origin, from nationalism to cosmopolitanism, from psychologism to naturalism, are in the Glavlit black book. But bans are not always enforced with the same rigidity, and not even we know why. The work of Katayev, for instance, which is akin to a great deal of experimentation in the west, was given the *imprimatur*.

'In recent months things have been easier for some very cautious experimental work, intended for a very restricted public, than for some works addressed to a wider public that are regarded as having a depressing effect, being too critical of the older generation, insufficiently imbued with enthusiasm for the communist panacea, and tending excessively in the direction of humour.'

The censorship also has consequences of a different kind. It has unquestionably led to tremendous over-estimation of the merits of clandestine literature. The story is told in Moscow of a father who was able to get his son to read Tolstoy only by having *War and Peace* typed out in full and presenting it to him as a banned book. Typists who type poems or novels they think are unlikely to be published generally make an extra carbon copy, which they sell on the black market. In the case of one book that was stopped by the censorship while it was being set up in type, the operators pulled extra proofs at night of the few pages that had been set and sold them at a high price.

It cannot of course be claimed that all the manuscripts that circulate surreptitiously in this way are of a high literary merit. But it is thanks to the censorship that art and literature still have such an extraordinary power of attraction, are able to stand up to the competition of scientific achievements, and occupy the first place in the hierarchy of values to be recovered in the future.

It is beyond the power of Glavlit to persuade the educated public opinion of the Soviet Union that printing Ezra Pound, Borges or Malaparte, republishing Joyce, Gide, or T. S. Eliot after all these years, rehabilitating Mandelstam, Voloshin, Khodasevich, Gumilyov, Zamyatin, Remizov, would have such a disturbing effect on the people as to destroy their will to tend blast furnaces or thresh the grain. The argument that workers' money must not be spent on printing books regarded as anti-revolutionary is folly. A revolution that after fifty years is still afraid of some writers has devoured itself.

Above all, it is beyond the power of Glavlit to persuade the public conscience that a writer should be disgraced (and starve if he loses the confidence of publishers and periodicals) merely because he refuses to tell what the party considers to be the truth. While things are in their present state in Moscow, the only persons who have reason to rub their hands with glee are scholars who specialise in the establishment of genuine, original texts. There are Soviet poems of which as many versions exist as the places in which they appeared. Anyone who set about reconstructing the original, eliminating all the changes made by author and publishers to satisfy the censorship on every occasion, would have endless material to work on and a hobby to last him until well into old age.

'We are living through years of difficulty and uncertainty, torn this way and that by contradictory instructions from men engaged in a stealthy struggle among themselves. To-day hypocrisy is triumphant, and I feel old and tired.' That was Bulat Okudzhava's summing up of the situation.

It was in this grim atmosphere that the Kuznetsov case exploded at the end of July 1969, when that author, having left Russia on the pretext of travelling for the purposes of study, sought political asylum in England.

Anatoly Kuznetsov, deputy secretary of the Tula branch of the Writers' Union, a member of the party since 1955 and a member of the editorial committee of *Yunost*, is not a writer of high rank, but his gesture made a big impact, because it represented the only course open to a Soviet intellectual who had neither the strength of mind to go on swallowing humiliations and insults, waiting for better times to come in which he might hope to have a free outlet for his talent, nor the civil courage to join the small platoon of 'internal' *émigrés* willing to face imprisonment or confinement to a mental hospital for the sake of continuing the struggle in their own country for socialism with a human face.

As soon as Kuznetsov was granted political asylum he wrote three letters, to the Soviet government, the central committee of the Communist Party, and the Writers' Union. Of these the most important is the second. 'After seriously reflecting on the matter for many years,' he said, 'I have arrived at the most complete rejection of Marxism-Leninism. I believe that to-day that doctrine is completely out of date. . . . It is absolutely incapable of resolving the contradictions of modern society and, what is worse, it has led and threatens to continue to lead to terrible social tragedies. I can no longer remain a member of a communist party that bases its policy on that doctrine, and I therefore ask to be removed from the list of members of the Communist Party of the Soviet Union.'

This letter is significant for two reasons. In the first place, it rejects a doctrine that the majority of Soviet intellectuals continue to accept while denouncing its twists and turns and deviations; and it implicitly uses this rejection as justifying his flight to the west, implying the impossibility for a Soviet intellectual who has left the Marxist-Leninist church of continuing his work without the blessings conferred by faith. 'After long reflection and much practical experience,' he said in his letter to the Writers' Union, 'I have realised the complete falsity, the stupidity and the reactionary nature of "socialist realism". The most terrifying failure and periods of total frustration that debase official Soviet literature are due, I am firmly convinced, to the dictatorial imposition of "socialist realism" and in particular to the doctrine that imposes on literature a content desired by the party.' Again the implication is that the apostate, attributing the failure of his country's literature to the official doctrine, feels professionally as well as morally absolved of guilt in taking a step with the rightness of which most of his colleagues would not agree.

Nevertheless the Kuznetsov case forms part of the picture of the collective neurosis of the Soviet intelligentsia induced by the identification of the party with cultural life. This is confirmed by the long statement he made to the *Sunday Telegraph*, in which he announced his change of name to A. Anatol. In this statement, which was naturally prominently reproduced by the whole of the anti-communist western press, he said: 'I simply cannot live there any longer. This feeling is something stronger than me. I just cannot go on living there. If I were now to find myself again in the Soviet Union, I should go out of my mind. If I were not a writer, I might have been able to bear it. But, since I am a writer, I cannot. Writing is the only occupation in the world that seriously appeals to me. When I write I have the illusion that there is some sort of sense in my life. Not to write is for me roughly the same as for a fish not to swim. I have been writing as long as I can remember. My first work was published twenty-five years ago. In those twenty-five years not a single one of my works has been printed in the Soviet Union as I wrote it. For political reasons the Soviet censorship and the editors shorten, distort and violate my works to the point of making them completely unrecognisable. Or they do not permit them to be published at all. So long as I was young I went on hoping for something. But the appearance of each new work of mine was not a cause for rejoicing but for sorrow. Because my writing appears in such an ugly, false and misshapen form, and I am ashamed to look people in the face. To write a good book in the Soviet Union, that is still the simplest thing to do. The real trouble begins only later, when you try to get it published. For the last ten years I have been living in a state of constant, unavoidable and irresolvable contradiction. Finally I have simply given up. I wrote my last novel *The Fire* with no feeling left in my heart, without faith and without hope. I knew already in advance for certain that, even if they published it, they would ruthlessly cut everything human out of it, and that at best it would appear as just one more "ideological" pot-boiler. (And that is, incidentally, exactly what happened.) I came to the point where I could no longer write, no longer sleep, no longer breathe. . . .

'A writer is above all an artist who is trying to penetrate into the unknown. He must be honest and objective, and be able to do his creative work in freedom. These are all obvious truths. These are the very things which writers are forbidden in the Soviet Union. Artistic freedom in the Soviet Union has been reduced to the "freedom" to praise the Soviet system and the Communist Party and to urge people to fight for communism. The theoretical basis for this is an article which Lenin wrote sixty years ago on "The party organisation and party literature", which laid it down that every writer is a propagandist for the party. His job is to receive slogans and orders from the party and make propaganda out of them.

'This means that writers in Russia are faced with the following choice:

'(a) Simply to go along with this idiocy – to let their brains and their consciences have no effect on their actions. If Stalin is on top, then praise Stalin. If they order people to plant maize, then write about maize. If they decide to expose Stalin's crimes, then expose Stalin. And when they stop criticising him, you stop too. There are so very many Soviet "writers" who are just like that. But real life will not forgive a man who violates his conscience. Those writers have all become such cynics and spiritual cripples and their hidden regret for their wasted talent eats away at them to such an extent that their wretched existence cannot be called life but rather a caricature of life.

'It would probably be difficult to think up a worse punishment for oneself than to have to spend one's whole life trembling, cringeing, trying fearfully to get the sense of the latest order and fearing to make the slightest mistake. Oh God!

'(b) To write properly, as their ability and consciences dictate. It is then one hundred to one that what they write will not be published. It will simply be buried. It may even be the cause of the author's physical destruction. It is a sad thought that Russia has long and deep "traditions" in this connection. The best Russian writers were always persecuted, dragged before the courts, murdered or reduced to suicide.

'(c) To try and write honestly "as far as possible". To choose subjects which are not dangerous. To write in allegories. To seek out cracks in the censorship. To circulate your works from hand to hand in manuscript form. (But not anti-Soviet works, because then they would arrest you!) To do at least something: a sort of compromise solution. I was one of those who chose this third way. But it did not work for me. The censors always managed to bring me to my knees.

'My anxiety to save at least something from what I had written, so that something would reach the reader, meant only in the end that all my publicised writings were neither genuine literature nor utterly contemptible, but something in between. They were some kind of unlikely product of a deal between the censorship and an author's conscience.

'However much I protested or tried to prove some point, it was like beating my head against a wall. Literature in the Soviet Union is controlled by people who are ignorant, cynical and themselves very remote from literature. But they are people with excellent knowledge of the latest instructions from the men at the top and of the prevailing party dogmas. I could not force my way through their ranks. Yevtushenko managed to achieve a little in this way, Solzhenitsyn managed a little more, but even that is all over now. The cracks were noticed and cemented up. Russian writers go on writing and keep hoping for something. It is a nightmare.

'So for a quarter of a century I went on dreaming about a happy state of affairs which is unthinkable for a Soviet writer – to be able to write and publish his writings without restriction and without fear. Not to choke off his own song. To have no thought for party instructions, government-appointed editors and political censors. Not to start trembling at every knock on the door. Not to be hiding his manuscripts away in a hole in the ground almost before the ink on them is dry. Oh, the number of holes I have dug in the ground to conceal my jam jars full of "dangerous" and "doubtful" manuscripts. I could not keep them in my desk, because whenever I was not there my flat could be broken into and searched and my manuscripts confiscated, as happened with Solzhenitsyn and many others. My writing desk in fact had no drawers at all. The Russian earth itself served as my desk and my safe. It became a real mania for me to be able to see my writing published in the form in which I had written it. I wanted to see it just once, and then they could do what they liked with me. Yes, in that sense I was a sick man, I was a maniac.

'As a boy I saw books being burned in Russia in 1937, under Stalin. I saw books being burned in 1942 in occupied Kiev, under Hitler. And now it has pleased God to let me know in my own lifetime that my own books are being burned. Because, now that I have left the Soviet Union, my books will of course be destroyed there too. Some books or other are always being destroyed there, so why should my books be an exception? In fact I pray that my published works should be destroyed down

182

to the very last one. Since they are not what I actually wrote and wanted to say to my readers, that means, after all, that they are not my books! I dissociate myself from them.

'And so: I hereby, publicly and definitely dissociate myself from everything which has been published under the name of "Kuznetsov" in the USSR or has appeared in translation from Soviet editions in other countries of the world.

'I solemnly declare that Kuznetsov is a dishonest, conformist, cowardly author. I renounce this name.

'I want to be, at last, an honest man and honest writer. All my writings published from this day onwards will bear the signature "A. Anatol". I request you to regard only such works as being mine.'

There is no reason to suppose that in this confession Kuznetsov-Anatol dramatised reality more than was to be expected under the emotional impact of his flight from Russia. There is growing evidence that such charges have serious foundations, though they should not be generalised.

Though it did not create so much of a sensation, there was the precedent set shortly beforehand by Arkady Belinkov, who in 1968 emigrated to the United States after thirteen years in labour camps. Belinkov is the author of novels and of works on Tynyanov, Platonov and Olesha in particular that are openly hostile to the Soviet régime. ('It is not you,' he wrote to the Pen Club, 'but we who defend freedom, dying in the camps, going into exile, facing hunger, suffering and death.')

A rebel such as Amalrik disapproved of the course chosen by Kuznetsov. 'I understand your reasons,' he said, 'but to me a writer's true freedom is his interior freedom, and Russian society today needs men capable of attaining that freedom by way of conquering fear.' Nevertheless it is significant that the conflict that arose from Kuznetsov's action was between those who thought him a hero and those who thought him a deserter or traitor, and that he felt it necessary to state that in spite of everything he deeply loved his country.

This confirms yet again the anomalous nature of a society that conducts the ideological debate in terms of faith, and thus forces a writer who breaks with the system to repudiate his name and his work to re-establish a virginity he feels he has lost. Kuznetsov is neither hero nor deserter, but merely an extreme case in a tragic situation. In order to be able to express himself in accordance with his conscience he felt he had to be reborn, thus embodying an elementary need of individual freedom that outweighs the claims of alleged collective interests. The reasons given for his flight may have been a cover for reasons of a different kind (Moscow tried to extract itself from an embarrassing situation by describing him as a depraved good-for-nothing). But, in the absence of evidence of this, Kuznetsov can claim to symbolise the drama of an intelligentsia that can establish its moral dignity only by civil suicide.

Kuznetsov's flight took place barely three months before Solzhenitsyn's expulsion from the Writers' Union. It presented his enemies with the opportunity of excommunicating him for which they were waiting; the meeting at Ryazan in fact began with a statement proclaiming the necessity of reinforcing the communist conscience of the writing community after Kuznetsov's disgraceful flight. As the centenary of Lenin's birth drew nearer, the elimination of the voice of dissent became more and urgent, so that the world might be presented with a picture of a solid and unshakable Soviet Union, and in the second half of 1969 the pressure that had been applied since the beginning of the year was greatly increased. In fact the harmony of the picture had been disturbed on 22nd January when, in the ceremonial atmosphere of a reception in honour of the cosmonauts, an assassination attempt was made in the Kremlin itself.

'In order to awaken Russia', Second-Lieutenant Ilyin, of the Leningrad garrison, fired at a car, hoping that Brezhnev was in it. There was no magnification of this incident by the authorities, but neither was there any minimisation of the increasing number of acts of repression against recalcitrant intellectuals (these included another sentence on Marchenko, the arrest at Tashkent of General Grigorenko, the bearer of a letter signed by 2,000 Crimean Tartars, and of the physicist Kadyev); and, above all, a large-scale reorganisation was put in hand in the editorial offices of cultural journals. After pin-pointing the most dangerous elements and sentencing them to labour camps or mental hospitals – in many cases those concerned, so far from concealing their opinions, proclaimed them by signing protests with their name and address – the Stalinists in the Kremlin wanted to clean out all the remaining corners in which the germs of criticism might still persist. It was a slow but methodical and relentless large-scale operation conducted with the aid of the political police, and suspicion of ideological tepidity, indiscipline or merely slackness was regarded as firm evidence.

The dismissal of Yevtushenko, Aksyonov and Rozov from the editorial committee of *Yunost*, the Communist Youth organ that had sometimes gone too far in ridiculing the hypocrisy of their elders and had often adopted anti-conformist positions thanks to the writing of Vosnesensky, Vinokurov, Novella Matveyeva, Sluchky, Plisechky, etc., heralded the new purge, which was intended to reserve positions of responsibility to the totally dependable. More and more intellectuals were sent for by the police and discreetly warned not to 'play the enemy's game'. Articles 70-72 and 190-91 of the Penal Code (concerning anti-Soviet propaganda and organising activity and slandering the Soviet social system) were a sword of Damocles suspended over the heads of hundreds of artists, writers and scientists who had contacts with foreign countries by reason of their work.

Novy Mir was quivering on the brink; Tvardovsky's presumption in publishing articles, stories, poems that looked reflectively or pessimistically at the past or present ('I can no longer write/I am in a state of crisis/My mind is dumb', Vosnesensky confessed in a poem) was considered a potential crime. A particularly ferocious stance was adopted by the Slavophiles, who could not forgive Tvardovsky for printing the works of so many foreigners, thus showing insufficient appreciation of patriotic values. Those who had expressed pleasure at the Paris award to Solzhenitsyn of the prize for the best foreign book of the year and now found indirect ways of supporting the award to him of the Nobel Prize for Literature were considered criminals; anyone who went to see him at Obninsk, in his little *dacha* with its pink asbestos roof (two rooms on the ground floor, and a workroom with balcony upstairs) in which he lived an extremely retired life, content with his work, the smell of the woods and the friendship of simple people, was considered unreliable.

The whole of the intelligentsia were under observation. Behind the screen of a tolerance that above all concealed a fear of scandals breaking out, the ancient mistrust of the demagogue and the bureaucrat for the artist and man of letters had surfaced again; the standard-bearers of liberty of conscience were pointed to as the foolish servants of the bourgeoisie that was perpetually lying in wait.

It was among these darkening shadows that the decision was made to expel Solzhenitsyn from the Writers' Union, in the hope of condemning him to civic death; and it was in this frosty atmosphere that the figure of Solzhenitsyn and his work stood out with the brightness of a flame; he stood for the generation that had suffered most, and he was the hope of the young. In October 1967 he wrote to three students who had sought him out on the relationship between conscience and justice (the letter reached the west only two years later).

'Justice has been the common patrimony of mankind throughout the ages,' he said. 'And it does not cease to exist for the majority even when in some places it has been obscured. Evidently it is an idea innate in man, since it has not been possible to find any other source for it. It exists if at least a few individuals exist who feel it. Love of justice seems to me to be a feeling different from the love of people (or at any rate only partially to coincide with it). In times of mass decadence, when the question is asked: "What for? Whom are the sacrifices for?" one can certainly answer that they are for the sake of justice. There is nothing relative about it, just as there is nothing relative about the conscience. In fact, justice is the conscience, not the personal conscience, but that of the whole of humanity. Those who clearly recognise the voice of their own conscience generally also hear the voice of justice. I believe that in any social question (or historical question, if our knowledge of it is not only hearsay or derived from books but our minds are touched by it) justice will always suggest a way of action (or thinking) that is not in conflict with one's conscience.

'And as our intelligence is generally not sufficient to grasp, understand and foresee the course of history (and "planning" it, as you say, has shown itself to be absurd), you will never err if in every social situation you act in accordance with justice. That gives us the opportunity of being constantly active, without a moment's rest.

'Please do not tell me that everyone interprets justice in his own way. No. They can shout, get the better of it with their vocal chords, beat their breasts, but the internal rhythm of the heart is as infallible as the beliefs of the conscience. (Also, in private life we sometimes try to smother the voice of conscience.)

'I am sure, for instance, that the best among the Arabs realise now that in accordance with justice Israel has a right to live and to exist.'

CHAPTER NINE

At the beginning of the book we mentioned the repercussions of Solzhenitsyn's expulsion on the Writers' Union (the membership of which had now risen to 6,800) and the questions it raised for the Soviet intelligentsia and the communists of the whole world. The most important feature was the radicalisation of the line-up and the extension of dissent, or rather of awareness of its politico-cultural implications, from a non-homogeneous group of intellectuals to wider areas of public opinion, the bond between them being indignation at the major violations of legality concealed behind formal respect for the constitution. To a considerable extent the protest coming from below was often more determined than that of the writers, who were going through another period of bewilderment and disarray. The excommunication of Solzhenitsyn disturbed the weak, the purge of the journals isolated the most restless, the efficiency of the police methods persuaded many that the times were not ripe for fresh challenges. Only a handful of intrepid spirits remained in the breach.

In May 1969 a letter was sent from Moscow to the United Nations, signed by a so-called 'Action group for the defence of civil rights in the USSR', consisting of about fifteen intellectuals and workers who collected about forty signatures for their appeal, in which they enumerated violations by the régime of the right to freedom of opinion and freedom of expression and appealed for United Nations intervention. The gesture had a more than symbolic value; it showed that dissent, at any rate at the level of the boldest spirits, was trying to organise itself and reach an international audience in declaring its mistrust of the state apparatus and of justice as exercised in the country.

Unless there is a palace revolution, no-one will ever know whether there is a silent majority with secret leaders among those competing for power at the top (the inability of the police to eliminate the *samizdat* might be evidence of this) which delegates its own secret feelings to the extreme dissident wing. The great mass of public opinion, indoctrinated by half a century of propaganda to regard every campaign for human rights as a bourgeois plot seems to have no difficulty in believing that those who appeal to an international tribunal are *ipso facto* enemies of their country. Those obsessed with the idea that the world is divided into faithful servants of the cause and odious traitors find confirmation for their suspicions in the passage in Kuznetsov's letter to the Moscow government in which he says that he will not again shake hands with a Soviet official until the Soviet Union guarantees unconditional liberty for Czechoslovakia and permanently withdraws its troops from that country. A statement such as that, made by a writer who in the opinion of many deserves to be shot as a deserter, is sufficient in the eyes of the perplexed to justify the invasion of Czechoslovakia by Warsaw Pact tanks. Thus it was not by chance that in August 1969, a year after the Prague passion, there were only fifteen signatures (including those of Yakir, Gabir and Natalya Gorbanevskaya again) to an appeal stating that 'a nation that oppresses another nation cannot be free or happy'. The lever of patriotism continues to be used by the propaganda machine with an ease that is increased by the growing threat represented by the Peking schism, the intolerance of many communist parties of Soviet leadership, and growing economic difficulties at home.

Pari passu with the tightening of the screw by the Kremlin, the protest of the intelligentsia is transformed into a general discontent, regresses into a collective ill-humour that is more irritated than comforted by the voice of some isolated dissident cursing the party. It was this kind of resentment that was earned by the nineteen-year-old girl student Valeria Novodvorskaya, who on 5th December, 1969 distributed an ironic 'Hymn to the Revolution' in the Hall of Congresses at the Kremlin:

> Thank you, party,
> For all you have done and are doing,
> Thank you, party,
> For our hatred of to-day.
> Thank you, party,
> For our servile phoneyness.
> For our indolence,
> Treachery and duplicity,
> Thank you, party,
> Thank you, party,
> For all the fictions and lies,

All the spying and denunciation,
The shooting in the squares of Prague,
For all that you are wiping out,
For the paradise of factories and houses
Built for crimes,
For the black and oppressed world
Of old and new torture chambers.
Thank you, party,
For our bitter lack of belief
In the empty shells of lost formulae,
In the misty darkness of early dawn.
Thank you, party,
For our distress and despair.
For our cowardly silence,
Thank you, party,
Thank you, party,
For the burden of our condemned truth
And for the shooting in future struggles
Thank you, party.

The same resentment was earned by Bukovsky, who immediately after his release wrote an open letter to Mikis Theodorakis, the Greek musician imprisoned by the colonels for his pro-communist ideas. 'Dear Mr Theodorakis,' he said, 'I do not know you personally, and I can judge you only from what is published in the Soviet press, but it seems to me that you are in a better position than anyone to know the meaning of a police state, the persecution of dissidents and the struggle against illegality in such conditions. As an artist you cannot be indifferent to the fate of those deprived of the freedom to work; as a former political prisoner you cannot be indifferent to the fate of those who openly defend citizens' rights. Nowadays these problems are no longer those of a single nation only, but of the whole of mankind. The fact that dissidents are persecuted in our country, that some of them are confined to psychiatric hospitals, that some authors are prosecuted for their writings and their beliefs, must be authoritatively and objectively confirmed in the eyes of the world, to prevent deceit or slander from being believed. You are a man whose objectivity and honesty are not doubted by the Soviet government or by world political opinion. Also you have gained exceptional popularity and respect in our country. There is no reason why you should be refused permission to visit Soviet labour camps, prisons and mental hospitals, unless there is a desire to conceal the facts and the arbitrary and illegal behaviour of some authorities. Some years ago the government of our country announced that there were no more political prisoners. Today it is no longer in a position to repeat that claim, because the world knows the names of many persons arrested and sentenced in recent years for political reasons, as well as the situation of the camps and hospital-prisons in which they are confined. You would be able to visit the writers Sinyavsky, Ginzburg and others in their camps; you would be able to see General Grigorenko and the woman poet Natalya Gorbanevskaya surrounded by degenerates and luna-tics. You would be able to se the writers Amalrik and Mar-chenko, the religious writer Levitin-Krasnov, the poets Delone and Gabay, shut up together with common criminals. You would be able to ask the poet Galanskov about the medical treatment he is receiving. You would be able to observe the conditions in which they live and taste the food they are given. In short, you would be able to compare the way in which political prisoners are treated in Greece and in the USSR. It is essential that information of such importance should be made public, so as to contribute to the cause of the struggle for civil rights and democracy, but above all to help the innocent who are suffering. The Soviet government may refuse you permission to visit the places of detention, but will not refuse you an entry visa. In that event I am ready to introduce to you a number of former political prisoners who have spent long years in the places mentioned above, and I am in a position to offer you genuine evidence. As one former political prisoner to another, I appeal to you to help our comrades, the political prisoners in the USSR.'

Theodorakis does not seem to have accepted Bukovsky's in-vitation, but instead, in the first half of 1970, after two or three sensational demonstrations, there were dozens of calls to order by the KGB and sentences by the courts. The year 1969 ended with the removal of Yuri Rybakov from the editorship of *Teatr* and his replacement by the conservative Lavrentyev, and with the news of hunger strikes by political prisoners on the occasion of International Human Rights Day; and 1970 began with the announcement that Svetlana Allilueva had been deprived of Soviet citizenship, the expulsion of Ennio Caretto, the Moscow correspondent of *La Stampa* of Turin (followed in

October by that of John Dornberg, the correspondent of *Newsweek*), an attack in *Sovietskaya Rossiya* on the poet Stanislav Fedotov (who had the temerity to claim that Stalin's purges were the forerunner of Hiroshima), and the convictions of Valeria Novodvorskaya, who was accused of schizophrenia, the poet Gabay, and Mustafa Dzhemilyov, the leader of the Crimean Tartars.

Thus in Lenin's centenary year the whole of the police and judicial apparatus could be said to be concentrating on the objective of rationalising the suppression of new centres of revolt, above all bearing in mind the impact that incidents of dissidence were having on western communist parties (it was to these that Yuri Galanskov was to send an appeal from prison, calling on them to use their influence for the democratic development of the Soviet system, while Yuri Daniel's son appealed to Graham Greene to do something for his father, who was transferred from a camp to prison and then released in September 1970).

This concern was very evident in the warning issued by Demichev, the man responsible for the cultural policy of the party, against the dissidents in the Soviet Union and the other east European countries, as well as against those other communists, especially in Italy, who showed that they had 'detached themselves from class positions' and were being influenced by capitalism. 'Pluralism, with the legalisation of bourgeois ideology and propaganda,' he said, 'leads to counter-revolution,' and he claimed that 'real innovation in art is incompatible with experiments in the modernist style. ... Sometimes even in the USSR attempts are made to interpret the freedom of artistic creativity from abstract and anti-scientific positions, claiming a subjective right of self-expression.' The result was the appearance of works 'intended to cause a sensation, of a repugnant political odour'. If, therefore, the artist did not want to diverge from the correct path, he must ensure that 'the needle of his compass coincides with the guiding line of communism'. The basic problem, analysis of the factors that contribute to determining that guiding line, is obviously evaded here.

The progress made by obscurantism is shown by a comparison of Demichev's statement with an article by Alexei Rumyanchev that appeared in an outburst of liberalism in *Pravda* in 1965. 'True creation', it said, 'is possible only in an atmosphere of enquiry and experiment, of free expression and the clash of opinions. . . . A fruitful development of science, literature and art requires the presence of different schools and trends, different styles and genres in emulation with each other.' The disorientation and bewilderment of the intelligentsia is hardly surprising in view of the contradictory statements made with party approval in the course of a few years.

Meanwhile the struggle continued. In January and February four young foreigners, the Belgian Victor Van Brantengam, the Italians Teresa Marinuzzi and Valtenio Tacchi, and the Norwegian Gunnar Gjengseth, were arrested and sentenced and then expelled for protest demonstrations in Moscow and Leningrad which, the court decided, were acts of hooliganism. Also in February, the police had a great deal of trouble trying to remove from circulation an open letter to Brezhnev attributed to the nuclear physicist Andrei Sakharov appealing to the party secretary to 'remove people's gags' so that they might freely discuss the country's most important problems ('public examination of the country's real problems' was Sakharov's suggested remedy for the 'mutual lying' that had caused the Soviet Union to lose the race to the moon and the economic competition with the United States). During the same month, while the news was circulating that there had recently been sixty-three arrests for crimes of opinion, the tussle between Tvardovsky and the conservatives reached its inevitable outcome.

His repudiation in a letter to *Pravda* of 4th February of all responsibility for the publication abroad (in Italy in *l'Espresso*) of the poem 'By right of memory', 'provocatively and without authority' printed under the title of 'On the ashes of Stalin', was of no avail. On 11th February *Literaturnaya Gazeta* printed Tvardovsky's letter and simultaneously announced that the secretariat of the Writers' Union had decided to appoint two deputy editors, D. G. Bolshov and O. P. Smirnov, to the staff of *Novy Mir* to assist him and to replace the editors Vinogradov, Kondratovich, Lakshin and Sats, who were notoriously loyal to him, by the more reliable Kosolapov, Ovcharenko, Remenchuk and Taurin (who presided at the meeting at Ryazan at which Solzhenitsyn was expelled). True, the same issue of *Literaturnaya Gazeta* severely took to task the conservative ringleader Kochetov, whose tedious novel *But What do You Really Want?* among other things contained an attack on

Italian communists as '*embourgeoisé* philistines' (it was easy to identify the character of Benito Spada with Vittorio Strada, the Italian Communist Party's greatest expert on Russian literature). But that did not diminish the significance of the ham-stringing of *Novy Mir*, hitherto the greatest bulwark of moderate opposition to the grim and reactionary fanaticism of the dogmatists and Slavophile nationalists. Obviously Tvardovsky's position, already weakened by the pressure of those who attacked him for his support of writers who had since been disgraced, was finally undermined by Kuznetsov's flight, Solzhenitsyn's excommunication and the more and more brazen use made of *Novy Mir* in the west, where it was held up as a stronghold of dissent, though all it had done was to follow the trend set by the Twentieth Congress and stand for a more elastic ideological commitment, besides encouraging rejection of the phoney and a taste for literary experiment among its readers.

Tvardovsky, deprived of the support he had hitherto had in the Kremlin that had enabled him to stand up to his enemies' attacks (the most severe of which was a letter, signed by eleven writers, denouncing *Novy Mir* as 'anti-patriotic' in *Ogonyok* in August 1969), immediately drew the consequences and resigned his editorship, as his enemies wanted him to do. He was replaced by Vasily Kosolapov, who had himself had to give up the editorship of the *Literaturnaya Gazeta* for having published Yevtushenko's *Babi Yar*.

Tvardovsky's resignation was greeted in the west as a refusal to surrender to the guardians of conformism and a sure sign that official reaction was being met by growing resistance on the part of the progressive intellectuals. In reality his resignation was merely the inevitable result of his defeat. In his time he had won three Stalin Prizes, but now had to pay the price of ideological tepidity, and obediently accepted the inevitable. Confirmation of this was his resignation from the vice-presidency of the European Community of Writers in protest against the 'ultimatory and demagogic' statement it made after Solzhenitsyn's expulsion. He had always fought for Solzhenitsyn, but the grotesque situation arose that he now broke off relations with the international organisation that defended the author closest to his heart and fell in with the Writers' Union's denunciation of Giancarlo Vigorelli for destroying with his own hands 'the fruits of more than a decade of efforts to promote collaboration between European authors'.

The reply of the Writers' Union to the Comes appeal was delayed for nearly three months, and took the form of a letter by Nikolai Gribachev published in *Literaturnaya Gazeta* on 18th February, 1970. It made it clear that the official attitude to Solzhenitsyn was now stabilised. On the one hand it tried to disparage him by representing him as a writer 'who used traditional means of expression' and had earned the admiration of the bourgeois press above all because of the sensational nature of his brazen political tendentiousness. 'Perhaps to you, Signor Vigorelli, he seems a giant against the background of contemporary literature,' the letter said, overlooking the fact that Lukács, commenting on *The First Circle* and *Cancer Ward* in 1969, had once more described him as the author who best succeeded in combining the heritage of the socialist realism of the twenties with the tradition of Tolstoy and Dostoevsky, and said that those who compared him with Svetlana were guilty of slander. On the other hand, it continued to put pressure on him to leave the Soviet Union. 'Solzhenitsyn has a good house, he is safe and sound, and no-one will put obstacles in his way if he decides to strengthen Italian literature, or any other, with his own activity. All the roads are open, *bon voyage* to him.' The reply already given by Solzhenitsyn was: 'I remain. Let them go to China, if they want to.'

The repetition of the invitation to emigrate was a sign of the uneasiness of the authorities in the face of a writer who had now acquired the most widespread popularity in the country and in whose case it was no longer possible to take the now usual course of confining him in a mental hospital, which was what they did at about this time to General Grigorenko (the methods employed at these establishments were described by Bukovsky, Amalrik and Yakir in an interview with William Cole before he was expelled from the Soviet Union). Grigorenko who, it was decided, was not in full possession of his faculties, was sent to a mental hospital, as had already happened to him in Khrushchev's time, but in the meantime he had taken the opportunity of distributing copies of a letter he wrote to the journal *Historical Questions of the Communist Party of the Soviet Union* (published in Italy under the title 'Stalin and the Second World War') that shows little sign of mental disturbance. The former holder of the chair of cybernetics at the Moscow Military Academy, defending A. M. Nekrich's *22 June 1941* from the attacks made on it in that journal, blamed Stalin for the huge losses suffered by the Soviet Union at the beginning of the Second World War; it was his fault, he claimed, that the Red Army, disorganised and decimated by the political purges, suffered reverses that cost the country millions of dead and brought the Germans to the gates of Moscow. Considering that this irreverent attitude on Grigorenko's part was accompanied by an outspoken campaign for a return to socialist legality and for the return of the Tartars to their home in the Crimea, his confinement in a mental hospital (a procedure that reduces the risk of political prisoners' dying on their hands, which is always liable to lead to a scandal) was, in its way, a logical reaction on the part of a régime that considers swimming against the stream to be evidence of insanity.

It was at the cost of enforced amnesia that some writers succeeded in remaining on the crest of the wave. At the end of February 1970 an anthology of poems by Yevtushenko sold like hot cakes. But the poet forgot to include in it *Babi Yar*, *Stalin's Heirs*, and *Let there not be another 1937*, which had made him famous in the years of the thaw.

Meanwhile, after an international ideological conference of communist parties had proclaimed the necessity of intensifying the struggle against right-wing opportunism, left-wing adventurism, and all attempts to revise the teachings of Lenin, a campaign against Solzhenitsyn proceeded along the lines of defamation and sarcasm. On 4th March *Sovietskaya Rossiya* published a poem by Mikhail Vladimov:

No, he has not gone abroad,
And does not seem even to want to go.
In his native country, where he was born,
He lives next to his garden and cabbage-patch.
As a man of letters he is a member
Of a certain organisation,
But he obeys different rules.
With every day that passes
His vocation is more definitely to denigrate
And his passion sacrilege.
His pages are distorting mirrors
Each worse than the last.

He digs, seeking in the strata of the years
Only shortcomings and disasters.
He does not see the road, but the drain,
He does not see the workshop, but the waste.
And more than anything else he is comforted
By the moment when he secures from Them
Applause coming from Over There.
His sting-like pen
Scratches, transpiring poison. . . .
He is here in body, but his spirit
Has long since fled Over There.

Solzhenitsyn in fact remained at home, spiritually as well as physically, bound up in the drama of a country and a culture that was most significantly summed up in his own person. In March 1970 he left Ryazan and now lives as the guest of the cellist Rostropovich in his *dacha* at Zhukovka, near Moscow. To emphasise his determination not to follow the path taken by Kuznetsov, and at the same time to circumvent traps that might be laid for him by the Soviet authorities, in March 1970 he entrusted the protection of his foreign rights to Dr Fritz Heeb, a Zürich lawyer to whom he gave three instructions:

(1) Henceforward to prohibit all unauthorised publication of his works, to take steps against the misuse of his name, and to take proceedings against anyone who made compromising statements about him;

(2) to check the quality of the translation of future editions of his works and to ask for improvements when necessary;

(3) to prevent film, radio or television adaptation of his works.

Dr Heeb was authorised to state that Solzhenitsyn's royalties were paid into blocked accounts and in the event of his death would be used in accordance with his wishes. Henceforward publication of Solzhenitsyn's works would require the approval of the author or his representative.

Will this be sufficient to stop those in the Soviet Union who, looking for a legal pretext to silence him, have claimed that the royalties accumulated by him in the west are used to finance anti-Soviet subversive organisations? This seems improbable, in view of the fact that having recourse to Dr Heeb was not dictated merely by the need to have his interests in relation to foreign publishers legaly protected after his

197

expulsion from the Writers' Union. No doubt the KGB continues to smuggle to the west manuscripts by him that can be used to aggravate his position (the most recent case was that of the play *A Candle in the Wind*, first published in *Grani* in Frankfurt, and then in England and Italy).

Faced with the double threat of the KGB on the one hand and western anti-Soviet journals on the other, both of which are interested in the political exploitation of his work, only two courses are open to him. Either he can lock up his works in his desk and keep them for posterity (after completing *The Gulag Archipelago*, another story about Stalinist camps, he was working on a historical novel called *August 1914*), or he can continue tirelessly denouncing provocative manoeuvres, e.g., the use made of *The Feast of the Victors*, the repudiated work of his, the only copy of which was confiscated by the police (in December 1969 the French Writers' Union publicly appealed for its non-publication in the west in order to avoid providing more ammunition for his enemies), or of 'Prussian Nights', the similarly repudiated poem written in prison that *Die Zeit* proposed to publish without authority in Hamburg.

So far, protected by the silent consent of the humble, he seems to have chosen the path that enables him to keep the flame of resistance and inspiration alight, but this is obviously the more dangerous course. It forces him to keep a careful check on all his movements, to suspect those around him, for even an imprudent friend could involuntarily play the part of an *agent-provocateur*. It does not protect him from the KGB; given a suitable opportunity, and if the matter were put into the hands of individuals who denied him the privilege of belonging to the 'non-torturable class', the secret police could easily accuse him of having connived in the expatriation of anti-Soviet writings and bring him before a court that would find arguments to justify sending him back to a labour camp. Nevertheless, the power of attorney granted to Dr Heeb, in anticipation of the possibility that someone might take compromising action in his name, absolves him from the suspicion that he would allow himself to be used by the enemies of the Soviet Union. He has thus indirectly gone some way to meeting the Writers' Union, which insisted on his declaring his attitude to the west.

This gesture, following his expulsion, was also of course inspired by the desire to reduce friction with the authorities and gain space and time in a struggle that grows more and more involved. The attitude of the liveried intellectuals was stated at a meeting of the Society for Danish-Soviet Friendship in Copenhagen by Alexander Chakovsky, editor of *Literaturnaya Gazeta* and the author of the historical novel *The Siege*, in which Stalin is described as 'the brilliant father of the people'. 'Solzhenitsyn is a talented writer,' he said, but 'it is sad to see him using his talents to damage his country.' Referring to passages in which Solzhenitsyn writes about Soviet soldiers in realistic terms, he added that it was 'an odious insult to the people to describe those who fought against the Nazis as rabble'. That is the usual refrain; the refusal to admit weakness and error among the factors that constitute human truth.

This short-sightedness, however, is not shared by the whole of the moderate intelligentsia. A striking appeal to the régime to take a longer view, to adopt a wider and more modern outlook in relation to the country's development, finally to overcome the siege mentality, and engage in a process of democratisation that would strengthen the prestige of socialism was made in a long letter to Brezhnev, Kosygin and Podgorny on 17th March, 1970 by three important Soviet personalities, the physicists Andrei Sakharov and Valentin Turchin and the historian Roy Medvedev. Sakharov is well-known for his *Progress, Coexistence and Intellectual Liberty*, which denounces the intoxication provoked by mass myths and ideological rigidity, and Roy Medvedev for his monograph on Stalin entitled *Facing the Tribunal of History*. The letter said that, in spite of the efforts made in the most varied sectors, wide areas of the national life were in difficulties (disorganisation and stagnation in the economy, diminution of the national product, slow and unequal progress in the field of the services, decline of productivity, accentuation of the gap, both quantitative and qualitative, between the Soviet Union and the United States). The cause of this unsatisfactory state of affairs did not lie in the socialist structures, the letter said, but in the anti-democratic manner in which these structures had been articulated since the times of Stalin, the gap existing between the party and state apparatus and the intellectuals, the lack of a wide exchange of information and ideas, the preference shown, as against those who possessed independence of judgment, for those who displayed verbal devotion to the party but in reality were concerned only with the advancement of their own interests. 'Just as no economic reform can yield fruit without due reforms in the field of administration and information, so must the intelligentsia, if it is to carry out its social function, see the abolition of restrictions that produce reciprocal mistrust and a total lack of reciprocal understanding.' The letter went on: 'How can prison, the labour camp and the mental hospital for individuals who have expressed their dissent within the limits of legality and in the field of ideas be justified? ... It is inadmissible that writers should be imprisoned because of their works. It is not possible either to understand or to justify certain absurd and irremediably disastrous steps, such as the expulsion from the Writers' Union of the most important and popular Soviet writer, who in the course of all his work has always expressed himself in profoundly patriotic and human terms, and the dispersal of the editorial staff of *Novy Mir*, which gathered round itself the most progressive forces in the Marxist-Leninist field.' Urgent steps must be taken to revive an enthusiasm similar to that of the twenties, and to prevent the Soviet Union, not merely from declining to the rank of a second-rate provincial power, but of heading for disaster.

The three signatories – who in many respects re-echoed the alarming political testament of the economist Evgeny Varga, which was denounced as a forgery by the Kremlin – proposed that the authorities should immediately undertake a programme of democratisation, involving the giving of wide publicity to information about the country's problems, increased contacts with foreign countries, the establishment of an institution for the study of social opinions, an amnesty for political prisoners and publication of the verbatim reports of their trials, the independence of the judiciary, complete liberty of travel for Soviet citizens, the organisation of industrial associations possessing a wide degree of autonomy, a press law and the abolition of the censorship, a more open system for selecting candidates for party and government posts, and full rights for nationalities deported in the times of Stalin. In the field of foreign policy, the Soviet Union should abandon its excessively Messianic ambitions.

So much for the letter of Sakharov, Turchin and Roy Medvedev, who so far at any rate have been left unpunished. But it is significant that the professional writers, who should have been the first to react to suggested reforms that would do away with their enforced servility, allowed this excellent opportunity to pass without publicly pronouncing on or supporting it. The third congress of the Writers' Union of the Russian Federal Republic, which took place in the palace of the Kremlin at the end of March, when the letter was already circulating, totally ignored it (meanwhile the trial had opened at Gorky of three students, Kapranov, Ponomarev, Ziltsov and the history teacher Pavlenkov; it ended with sentences of seven, five and four years). There was a struggle between propressives and conservatives, but it was confined to the preparatory stage of the congress, that of the election of delegates (observers noted that Kochetov ended up at the bottom of the list).

The fact remains that not one of the 522 delegates elected to represent 3,590 writers spoke at the congress in favour of freedom of information. The congress, indoctrinated by *Sovietskaya Rossiya*, which complained on the opening day of the existence of 'ideologically immature' books (referring to Solzhenitsyn, it said that 'it is obvious that lack of ideological principles is incompatible with wanting to remain in the ranks of the Writers' Union') was another triumph for conformism. As if nothing had happened in recent years, the president of the union, Leonid Sobolyev – who at the end of the conference was succeeded by Sergei Mikhalkov, a writer of children's books well known for having charged Solzhenitsyn with not having reached 'the *avant-garde* level of social consciousness' – pedantically reiterated that the yardstick of Soviet literature was 'loyalty to the principles of the party', denounced the 'furious attack of the sinister forces of our benevolent and cunning enemy, international imperialism', and declared that the writers' task was to create 'good literature about people and socialist work'.

Alekseyev, the editor of *Moskva*, denounced the 'ideological laxity' and 'lack of discipline' shown by some writers and held up Kochetov's novel *The Angle of Incidence* as an example to be followed; and Fyodorov, after accusing Yevtushenko of vanity and Voznesensky of bad taste, described allegations that there was any conflict between writers of the older and younger generations as a bourgeois propaganda manoeuvre.

The Moscow correspondent of the Italian communist *Unità* wrote in concern: 'The idea seems to be prevalent that there is a "bourgeois culture" on the offensive against progressive and Marxist positions, that there is a situation describable as "subversive imperialist activity" at work in the field of ideology instead of the presence, among the younger generations and intellectuals in the capitalist countries themselves, of an opposition culture that draws its growing strength from its own living and undogmatic links with Marxism and revolutionary movements and peoples.' The situation in fact is that ideological hardening of the arteries now prevents the régime from recognising as its own, as nourished from the same sources, any innovatory ferment that takes place outside the sacred confines of the Soviet fatherland. So great is the fear of revisionism, particularly after the sensation caused by the defection of personalities such as Garaudy and Fischer, as to make it over-estimate the force of penetration of bourgeois culture, if only in order to affirm Soviet primacy. The reassuring message that the congress sent to the central committee of the party provides conclusive evidence of the obtuseness and folly that aggravates the condition of a senile organisation. 'The wide discussion of the sectors' ideological and creative problems,' it said, 'has clearly demonstrated that the writers of the Russian Federation are closely united round the Communist Party and are devoting themsélves to still more active participation in the work of construction of a new society and the formation of the new man.' Not a voice was raised to ask whether the objective of the new man, which had been pursued for half a century, might not perhaps be more attainable if socialist structures were revived by the fresh air of liberty of culture.

It is impossible to say whether any of the seed-beds of the current widespread dissent will produce the purge that will rid Soviet culture of the dogmatic curse that has stifled literature for three generations, or whether the clearance will be practicable only by means of a development that will relegate part of that dissent to the margins of cultural life because of mistrust of the anti-communist elements contained in it. For the presence in the clandestine opposition of trends hostile not just to the practices of the régime, but to the system itself is shown by a document distributed in the middle of 1970 in which a secret organisation calling itself the 'Democratic Movement' claimed to include among its members 'materialists and idealists, atheists and believers, socialists, communists and nationalists,' and declared that 'the results attained in recent decades are too modest and insignificant to justify all the tears, misery, suffering and sacrifices of human life that the Russian people has had to face'. The document said that to make up for lost time ('after more than fifty years of socialism, in relation to the capitalists we are still a generation behind in everything regarding the material tenor of life, and a whole age behind them in everything regarding human rights') the Soviet Union should be transformed into a union of genuinely democratic republics governed by representatives of all parties and non-party groups, that free elections should be held, that judicial, legislative and executive power should be withdrawn from the Communist Party, that the secret police should be disbanded and political prisoners released, that industry should be partially restored to private enterprise, and that Soviet troops should be withdrawn from other countries.

The distribution of documents of this type, so obviously counter-revolutionary as to rouse the suspicion that they may have been deliberately planted by the police, is certainly helpful neither to a relaxation of tension between the progressive intelligentsia and the masters of the Kremlin, nor to the encouragement of an ideological debate between various cultural trends the merely provisional conclusions of which might lead to notable changes of route. Public controversies about recent literary works seem to be more interesting, since dynamic potentialitics are contained in them. An instance is the clash of views about Ivan Shevtsov's *In the Name of the Father and the Son* and *Love and Hate*, two neo-Stalinist and anti-Semitic novels in which Solzhenitsyn, Voznesensky and Bella Akhmadulina are held up to ridicule without their names being mentioned. *Komsomolskaya Pravda* said that the first of these novels was 'full of vulgarity and ignorance,' but *Sovietskaya Rossiya* praised it for denouncing 'the anti-artistic trends of the bourgeois west, parasitism, idealisation of the *dolce vita*, the lies, crimes, snobbism and reactionary essence of Zionism'. This journal was in its turn attacked by *Pravda*, expressing on this occasion the alarm felt in certain party circles at the revival of the Stalin cult. A mediocre novelist in fact became the occasion for a tragi-comic ballet.

But once again the astonishing feature is not so much the conflict of views, which might contain the seeds of a fertile critical pluralism, as the stubborn, reactionary concentration of both sides on the content of the book instead of on its quality. It is this archaic notion of literature, accompanied by non-recognition of elementary rights, that gives such an absurd and barbarous flavour to the persecution of the undisciplined intelligentsia, the purging of the journals, the censorship in the theatre – Voznesensky's *Look at Yourselves in the Mirror* was withdrawn from the repertoire of the Taganka Theatre in Moscow for 'ideological deficiencies' – the support given to the monumental in art, as a result of which the Soviet Union was still represented at the thirty-fifth Venice *biennale* by portraits of Lenin by the sculptor Andreyev and the muscular canvases of Deyneka (while no official blessing was given to the exhibition of Soviet abstract art that opened at Lugano in October 1970), the obstacles put in the way of films such as Alov's and Naumov's *A Bad Joke*, Kontsalovsky's *Assia the Lame*, Gershtein's *Turn, Comrade*, Abuladze's *The Prayer*, Yoseliani's *The Fall of the Leaves*, Parazhanov's *The Fire Horses*, Klimov's *The Adventures of a Dentist*, Daneliya's *Thirty-Three*, which were either held up on the pretext that they were in need of technical revision or a few copies only of which were distributed in peripheral areas or shown to restricted groups. It is in fact the archaic nature of the mental landscape in which official critics battle in Moscow and the provinces for the favour of the authorities that causes observers so often to regard the representatives of dissent as reflecting the dawn of a new cultural as well as ethical consciousness.

That Solzhenitsyn is the most distinguished harbinger of that dawn was again shown in June 1970 in the case of the biologist Zhores Medvedev (brother of the historian) who, after vigorously attacking the new followers of Lysenko's theory of the influence of the environment on genetic mutations, wrote a paper, which was circulated secretly, on the humiliating procedures to which they are subjected if they wish to go abroad. When Solzhenitsyn was expelled from the Writers' Union Medvedev wrote an open letter in his defence and now, as soon as he heard the news of his friend's arrest and confinement in a mental hospital, Solzhenitsyn made a public statement on 15th June condemning it in terms that summed-up all the indignation of international opinion at this horrifying police action. 'Incarcerating advocates of free thought, healthy people, amounts to spiritual murder,' he declared. 'It is a variation of the gas chambers, even more cruel because of the prolonged torture inflicted on those who are to be killed. Like the gas chambers, these crimes will never be forgotten, and all those involved in them will be condemned for all time, as long as they live and after their death.'

Referring to the crimes attributed to Medvedev, but painting a kind of self-portrait, Solzhenitsyn said that 'it is just because of the diversity of his talents that he has been accused of abnormality, of having a dissociated personality. It is because of his sensitivity to injustice that he is said to be mentally sick, unadapted to the social environment. If you think differently from the way in which you are ordered to think, you are abnormal, because all well-integrated people must think in the same way. . . . The régime uses servile psychiatrists, breakers of their [Hippocratic] oath, to certify dissidents as insane. One must have a really limited vision of the world to believe in the possibility of going on living counting on force only, constantly ignoring the claims of conscience.' Doctors and police had gone to Medvedev's home, bound him and taken him to a mental hospital without even a warrant. This was 'something that may happen to any one of us tomorrow'.

This statement was dated 15th June, 1970. At a meeting of the Academy of Science in Moscow next day, presided over by Petrovsky, the Minister of Health, a group of distinguished scientists, including Peter Kapitsa, Mikhail Leontovich, Nicolas Selenov (winner of a Nobel Prize for chemistry), and Andrei Sakharov, protested against the treatment of Medvedev. Barely twenty-four hours later he was released, and only four months later he was officially appointed to a research post at the Institute of Animal Psychology and Biochemistry at Borovak. Another who got off more lightly than expected was the Leningrad mathematician Revolt Pimenov, who in October was accused of spreading 'false statements insulting to the Soviet people and social system'; instead of being sentenced to three years in a labour camp, which was the general expectation, he was condemned, with the physicist Boris Weil, to five years' banishment.

Observers rightly regard these circumstances as eloquent. At a time when the party is forced to delegate a considerable degree of authority to science and technology to assure the country's economic development and prestige, the struggle between ideological orthodoxy and freedom of thought ends in victory for the scientists over the gendarmes. The theory that scientists, if only to defend their own privileges, may one day adopt a liberalising rôle similar to that which at the time devolved on writers in Hungary and Czechoslovakia was indirectly supported by the alarm shown by *Sovietskaya Rossiya* at the lack of ideological commitment of the young scientists at Akademgorodok, a scientific centre in Siberia, who were accused of having formed 'an exaggerated idea of their rôle in society' and were therefore invited to attend 'philosophy seminars'. (At the end of November 1970, *Pravda* similarly called to order the scientists of the Lebedev Institute of Physics.)

For the time being the stand taken by Solzhenitsyn on behalf of Medvedev, and the visit paid the latter in hospital by Tvardovsky and Kaverin, confirmed the trend for the literary and scientific opposition to unite on the common ground of their need for freedom of expression and enquiry, which is the prerequisite for any ideological practice, as was so plainly indicated at the end of the year in Andrei Amalrik's self-defence and in the setting up, again at Sakharov's instigation, of a 'committee for human rights' as a quasi-legal alternative to the rebelliousness of the 'action group for civil rights' which was inspired, among others, by Yakir and Bukovsky.

Amalrik, the author of *Will the USSR Survive until 1984?* and *Involuntary Journey to Siberia*, who was given a three-year sentence at Sverdlovsk in the Urals, had unreservedly condemned the 'mediaeval witch-hunt atmosphere' created by political trials. 'You can put me on the index of prohibited books,' he said, 'but no court has the right to condemn anyone for his ideas. . . . Everything that is happening can be explained only by the fear felt by the régime, which sees danger in the spreading of any opinion contrary to its own ethic and the directives of the bureaucratic summit. . . . But your fear does not change reality; the ferment of ideological liberation now in progress is irreversible.'

He appealed to Article 125 of the constitution and the Declaration of Human Rights in justification of his refusal to discuss his opinions in court, or to produce evidence, or reply to questions put by the judges or the lawyers in the course of a trial the outcome of which had been decided in advance; the same attitude was also implied in the action taken by Sakharov, together with two other young physicists, Andrei Verdoklebov and Valery Chalidze. The 'committee for human rights', while declaring its determination to act within the limits of Soviet legality and in 'consultative collaboration' with the authorities, aims essentially at working as an organisation of political dissent, to the extent that any move that raises questions related to the liberty of the subject expresses the restless state of public opinion and of non-party members in particular. In proposing to 'encourage steps towards the creation and application of guarantees for human rights, to lend assistance to those interested in constructive enquiry into the theoretical aspects of the problem of human rights and the study of those problems in socialist society, to promote legal education by methods including the dissemination of international and Soviet documents relating to the laws on human rights,' Sakharov is taking advantage of his privileged position as a scientist to condemn the lack of legal guarantees of which the literary dissidents complain in relation to the censorship.

Thus more than fifty years after the revolution the Soviet progressive intelligentsia are back at the positions adopted at the beginning of the nineteenth century by the liberals who opposed Tsarist absolutism. This would be less discouraging if in the meantime a Soviet vehicle had not landed on the moon, an achievement that the prophets of doom regard as a demonstration of the lack of any necessary connection between science and freedom and of the poor outlook of a struggle for rights that, in a world dominated by technology, may be no more than a formal tribute to an idea of man made obsolete by history.

CHAPTER TEN

Then came the Nobel Prize. It did not come as a surprise. It was the result of a long campaign, spread over at least three years, initiated by Russian exiles in the west with the support of the NTS (the popular labour union founded in Germany in the thirties) and soon taken up by admirers of Solzhenitsyn all over the world. They were certainly not insensitive to the political implications, but looked at the question in a wider and more complicated context than the crude anti-communism of the *émigrés*. This is shown by what happened between the spring and autumn of 1970, without there being any need to refer back to the steps taken in the west in 1968 and 1969, which came to nothing because of irresolution in Stockholm.

The first definite move was made in Paris by Art et Progrès, a cultural association that on 15th June wrote to the Swedish Academy proposing that the award be made to Solzhenitsyn; this had the backing of a number of French writers including Mauriac, Marcel, Aron, Clair, d'Ormesson, Simon and Châtenet (Mikhalkov, who was invited to support the proposal, promptly refused, indignantly denouncing it as a 'political provocation'). A similar proposal was made in July by the *Sentinel*, a Russian *émigré* journal published in Belgium. In August and September a number of journals, discussing the next Nobel award, pointed out that, the Pasternak case having been compensated for by the granting of the award to Sholokhov, the award should now be made to Solzhenitsyn as the greatest representative of a literature the merits of the anti-Stalinist side of which, being more fertile in human values, should now be acknowledged. If previously it had been possible to suspect that Solzhenitsyn's name was being put forward in circles in which critical objectivity was swayed by political passion, doubts were put at rest by a poll taken on 4th October by the Italian newspaper *Corriere della Sera*.

Literary critics of forty-seven countries, selected according to the political outlook of the journals for which they worked, were asked to state their choice, and there was a conclusive majority for Solzhenitsyn (and Borges). Since all those questioned had complete liberty of choice (critics of socialist countries such as Jugoslavia also picked Solzhenitsyn), provocative intentions could clearly be excluded; the critics chosen were closest to their reading public and the most direct interpreters of international taste, and their choice merely anticipated that made in Stockholm.

When the award was announced on the early afternoon of 8th October, the Norwegian journalist Hegge put through a telephone call to Solzhenitsyn, who said: 'I am grateful for the choice. I accept the award. I intend to go and receive it in person on the traditional day, if I am able to decide. My health is good. My physical condition puts no obstacle in the way of the journey.'

Meanwhile political undertones appeared in the citation ('for the ethical force with which he has pursued the indispensable traditions of Russian literature') and in the description of the author by Karl G. Gierow, the spokesman of the Swedish Academy, as 'a son of the Russian revolution, the revolution of Lenin, whose spiritual paternity Solzhenitsyn has never denied'.

The furious reaction of Moscow, which immediately accused Stockholm of having lent itself to the game of the 'White' *émigrés* in France and Germany, was above all due to this western presumption in declaring the heretic's work to be in the Lenin tradition. The neo-Stalinists, accustomed to issuing certificates of orthodoxy themselves, could not admit that any foreigner had the right to pronounce on the nature and limits of the Russian tradition. Awarding the Nobel Prize to a man expelled from the Writers' Union was not only a provocative affront to the Soviet authorities; it also sounded like indirect aid to those dissenters who appealed to the Lenin tradition and were thus, from their point of view, revisionists (it was not by chance that among the congratulatory messages to Solzhenitsyn there was one that reached him secretly from Yuri Galanskov in the camp at Potma).

For their part, the Stockholm committee were probably influenced more by the hostility of the left wing intellectuals to the Kremlin's authoritarian attitude to culture than by the sympathy that Solzhenitsyn enjoyed in anti-Soviet circles. No doubt they hoped, if all went well, to kill two birds with one stone, for their having previously awarded the prize to Sholokhov should have preserved them from Moscow's wrath. Instead both Moscow and those in the west who greeted the award to Solzhenitsyn as a challenge to the USSR by the free world should reflect on the use of it made by the communist parties no longer of strict Muscovite observance, who made it a symbol of the new Leninist international opposed to the bureaucratic centralism of the Kremlin. When *Izvestya* on 9th October said that the works of the *littérateur* Solzhenitsyn were being 'used by western reactionary circles for anti-Soviet purposes', claimed that the decision to expel him from the Writers' Union had been 'actively supported by Soviet public opinion', and deplored that the Nobel Prize committee 'had allowed itself to be involved in an ignominious game, not in the interests of the development of spiritual values and literary traditions, but dictated by reasons of political speculation', Moscow was chiefly addressing itself to communist parties in other countries (the French and Italian parties welcomed the award, and only the Bulgarians joined in the Moscow protest), in order to put them on their guard against one of the innumerable manoeuvres intended to free the left wing intelligentsia from its paternal tutelage.

Some western commentators noted with satisfaction that *Izvestya* adopted a much milder tone on this occasion than *Pravda* had twelve years before, when it denounced Pasternak for treachery to his country, and concluded that Solzhenitsyn would not have any difficulty in going to Stockholm to receive his prize on 10th December (in his telegram to the academy he said: 'I consider the decision . . . a tribute to Russian literature and our tormented history; I intend to come to Stockholm on the traditional day to accept the prize in person'). An ounce of realism would have made it evident that the *Izvestya* statement was merely the herald of another storm.

When four foreign journalists paid a surprise visit to the little house carved out of the garage of Rostropovich's *dacha* at Zhukovka, Solzhenitsyn refused to be interviewed. 'I can say nothing,' he said. 'I am a guest in this house, and I cannot ask you in. If it were my house, I should ask you in.' The situation was extremely delicate, and the slightest false move would have given the authorities an excuse to deny him the visa to travel to Sweden that he feared he would not be granted.

Similar cautiousness was not displayed by thirty-seven intellectuals, including Pyotr Yakir, who in a statement circulated on 10th October described the treatment of Solzhenitsyn by the authorities as a 'national disgrace' and said that they expected 'to see the Nobel Prize award transformed into another opportunity to continue the persecution of a writer who has always consistently and courageously defended his humanitarian principles'. This was a cheap prophecy. Sure enough, far from burying the matter in dignified silence, the whole press, beginning with *Izvestya* on 10th October, joined in denunciation of the Stockholm choice. Mikhalkov, speaking at a meeting of the Writers' Union at Archangelsk, declared the award to be 'the nth international act of an anti-Soviet nature'.

Literaturnaya Gazeta was ironic at the reference in the citation to Solzhenitsyn's 'ethical force' ('it is obvious that in this case the Stockholm committee by "ethical force" meant "anti-Soviet attitude" ', it said, and duly failed to publish the Swedish Academy's denial). Finally, on 17th October, having evidently failed to find writers willing to compromise themselves by putting their names to new slurs on Solzhenitsyn, a number of newspapers printed an article distributed by the Novosti agency that summed up the official position in the matter. After describing Solzhenitsyn as 'a man of morbid presumption, a slave to the adulation of those who denigrate the Soviet system irrespective of the means employed', it admitted that he had a certain talent, but denied that he was in any kind of dramatic situation. 'His real tragedy consists in his wearing dark glasses, thus depriving himself of the ability of seeing all the colours of Soviet life. He has made of his isolation, not a tragedy, but a commercial proposition; the literary elements in his work are very few in comparison with the political. Always in search of a scandalous glory, he has renounced the possession of a conscience, has lowered himself to the most shameful lie.' As for the continuity of Russian literary traditions, only experts in bad faith could compare him with the classics. 'It is clear that the determining factors in the Stockholm choice were not merit in relation to world literature, but the political aspects of Solzhenitsyn's activity.'

The statement suggested that his work might not even have been judged at first hand ('Solzhenitsyn's style makes the translated version of his works not very comprehensible to foreign readers'), reiterated the idea that he was incapable of rising above his own 'hypertrophied emotions', and ended with a combination of threats and a display of self-confidence.

On the one hand, by converting anti-Stalinism into anti-communism he had come out in open opposition to the very principles of socialism (hence he was an enemy of the people, and persecuting him was legitimate); on the other, his works were certainly not such as to present any sort of a threat to the powerful Soviet system (hence there was no reason to be afraid of him, it was sufficient to despise him).

If, as there is every reason to suppose, this is the definitive attitude of the Kremlin towards him, Solzhenitsyn has little reason to look forward to a quiet life. On 21st October the Moscow newspapers spoke of the Nobel Prize award as a return to the times of the cold war. On 28th October the East German writers' union called it 'an ill service to the relaxation of tension'. A vigorous *cri de coeur* by Rostropovich dated 31st October, denouncing the lack of qualifications of those who had the last word on literary and artistic matters in the USSR, was not published. On 18th November *Literaturnaya Gazeta* made a vigorous onslaught on Giancarlo Vigorelli, whom it called a 'miserable mercenary of anti-communism' and accused of having 'broken all records of buffoonery and presumption', merely because he had expressed pleasure at the award.

Thus Solzhenitsyn's decision, conveyed on 27th November, not to go to Stockholm to receive the prize was not merely the result of the failure of negotiations with the authorities to enable him to exercise the double privilege of expressing his feelings to the Swedish public and returning to his own country without fear of reprisals; it was also a result of the belief that it was not possible to obtain satisfactory guarantees from people who insisted on calling him an anti-communist and might thus from one day to the next feel themselves absolved from any obligation to respect an agreement with someone whom they regarded as a traitor. Rather than fall into the trap of being unable to return to his country (there have been rumours that he has been divorced from his wife and has married a young woman named Natalya Svetlova, the mother of a boy of ten), he preferred staying at home. Life in exile, with all its comforts (in 1970 the Nobel Prize was worth £32,000) would be too remote from the risks and harassments indispensable to a man of his temperament if he were to continue his mission as servant of the truth.

The letter he wrote to the Swedish Academy to explain his

absence from the ceremony was as follows:

'In a telegram addressed to the secretary of the academy I have already expressed and now repeat my gratitude at the honour conferred on me by the award of the Nobel Prize. In my heart I share it with those of my predecessors in Russian literature who, because of the difficult conditions of past decades, did not live long enough to win this prize, or while they were alive were little known to the world of readers of translations or even to their fellow-countrymen in the original. In the same telegram I stated my intention of coming to Stockholm, though aware that I should have had to submit to the humiliating procedures that apply in my country to everything having to do with foreign travel, which make it necessary to fill in special forms, get references from party organisations – even if one is not a member – and accept instructions on how to behave abroad. However, the hostile attitude towards the award made to me shown in recent weeks by the press of my country, and the unchanged state of persecution to which my books are subject (reading them involves dismissal from one's job and expulsion from institutions), have led me to believe that advantage would be taken of my trip to Stockholm to cut me off from my native country by simply preventing me from returning home. On the other hand, I conclude from the information you have sent me that the presentation ceremony is a very solemn affair. In view of my way of life and my character, that would be a great ordeal to me. As against that, the most important thing, the speech made by the winner of the award, does not form part of the ceremony proper. Later, both in your telegram and in your letter, you expressed fears similar to mine about the outcry that might accompany my stay in Stockholm.

'Considering all this, and on the basis of the information you have courteously given me, according to which the winner's personal presence at the ceremony is not absolutely essential, I have decided that for the time being it is not advisable to apply for authority to come to Stockholm. I could, if you have no objection, receive the diploma and medal of the Nobel Prize in Moscow from your representatives at a time most convenient to both. In any case, I am prepared, in accordance with the rules of the Nobel Foundation, to make the official speech or to send you the text of it within six months from the beginning of December 1970.

'This is an open letter and I have no objection to your publishing it.'

That is indeed the course that was adopted. On 10th December Solzhenitsyn sent another message to the Academy calling its attention to the 'notable coincidence' that the Nobel Prize ceremony was taking place on Human Rights Day. ('At this rich table let us not forget the political prisoners whose rights are limited or completely abolished,' said the message, which was not read aloud.) As if to underline the significance of his absence from Stockholm, two days later, when the news was circulated that he had joined Sakharov's civil rights movement, he did not deny it. Another wave of vituperation followed.

On 17th December *Pravda* attacked the whole 'gang' of dissidents and described Solzhenitsyn as 'spiritually an internal *émigré*, sunk in a swamp, alien and hostile to the cause of the people', and on 21st December Mikhail Alekseyev, one of the secretaries of the Writers' Union, described him on television as a 'fabricator of anti-Soviet slanders' and classified him with Sinyavsky, Daniel, Ginzburg and Galanskov as a writer who used his pen against his people and his country in the service of enemy propaganda. Barely five days later *Red Star* called him a renegade. While dramatic news started coming in from Poland and a new series of trials of Jews began in Leningrad, Rostropovich was refused a visa for a tour of Finland, and the Writers' Union called *Yunost* to order.

Thus at the beginning of 1971 the contradictions and fears of a régime that holds itself up as a model of a freer and more just society were more strident than ever. The award of the Nobel Prize to Solzhenitsyn was more than a literary fact. It was the reply of international culture and the international conscience to the world of the concentration camp. It might also have been the drop that caused the cup of hatred to overflow; the writers whose names were mentioned by Alekseyev together with that of Solzhenitsyn were all in labour camps; and on 27th January *Literaturnaya Gazeta* sowed the seed of vengeance when it printed a letter in which the American folk singer Dean Read accused Solzhenitsyn of making 'false accusations' against his country. The Twenty-Fourth Congress of the party was imminent, and the hard-liners wanted to attend it with their flanks and rear well covered. If Stalin's revenge were to be officially consecrated, the name of his most dreaded enemy must be trampled in the mud.

CHAPTER ELEVEN

And how did the west behave? In some instances little better than Solzhenitsyn's enemies at home who were waiting for him to make a false step in order to be able to silence him (in the summer of 1970 a copy of *The First Circle* in the possession of a Scandinavian professor who had been touring the Soviet Union was confiscated at the frontier, and he was forced to sign a document describing it as anti-Soviet literature). The west was unanimous in declaring the award to have been well deserved when such tributes cost nothing, and often used it as a political weapon against the Kremlin. But when called on to show solidarity with Solzhenitsyn in practice it was seized with trepidation.

The attitude of the Swedish Embassy in Moscow, for instance, was very ambiguous. If we are to believe the Norwegian Per Egil Hegge, correspondent of three Scandinavian newspapers in the Soviet capital, who by chance found himself called on to act as intermediary between Solzhenitsyn and the embassy before being expelled from Moscow on 9th February, 1971, the Swedish authorities showed little courage. Because of their reluctance to disturb their good relations with the Soviet Union (in February 1972 the film made of *One Day in the Life of Ivan Denisovich* was banned in Finland for the same reason), in September 1970 they declined Solzhenitsyn's suggestion that the presentation ceremony might take place at the embassy and also declined to forward his letter to the Swedish Academy.

In his book *Solzhenitsyn is Unwelcome*, published in Stockholm on 5th September, 1971, Hegge describes the various phases of the negotiations between Solzhenitsyn and the embassy about the possibility of the presentation being made in Moscow, and severely criticises Hr Jarring, the Swedish Ambassador. Hegge may well have been partly motivated by personal animosity in charging Hr Jarring and Hr Olof Palme, the Swedish Prime Minister, with 'diplomatic cowardice'; the fact remains that Sholokhov was much more cordially treated by the embassy at the time of his award, and that once again reasons of foreign politics took precedence over respect for the arts.

Meanwhile in the Soviet Union the situation became more and more oppressive. Always with the Twenty-Fourth Congress in mind, zealous police, obsequious judges and servile doctors conscientiously carried out political instructions intended to tighten the reins and remove 'subversive' elements from circulation. On 20th February, 1971 the Moscow public prosecutor's office sent for Chalidze, a member of Sakharov's committee for human rights, and called on him to cease activities that 'might be exploited for anti-Soviet purposes by the foreign press'. Arrests and interrogations of intellectuals suspected of belonging to the dissent movement were widespread. Those considered most dangerous were sent to mental hospitals (in the middle of March two such political prisoners, Feinburg and Borishov, went on hunger strike in Leningrad). Bukovsky, who in spite of his previous ordeals went on insisting on his right not to submit, suffered the same fate; he was arrested on 29th March and sent to the Serbsky Hospital in Moscow on the usual charge of anti-Soviet activity. The letter written next day by Sakharov to the Minister of the Interior calling for the immediate release of imprisoned intellectuals and protesting against the confiscation of the files of the committee for human rights availed nothing; delegates were already gathering for the Twenty-Fourth Congress of the party (held from 30th March to 10th April), the newspapers were exalting the country's unity, the big shots were polishing their medals, and triumphal choruses drowned the small but troublesome voice of protest.

This made what Brezhnev said in his introductory address to the congress sound almost derisory. 'We are in favour of an attentive and tolerant attitude towards artistic experiment,' he said, 'so that the gifts and talents of all may be manifested in all their plenitude for a variety and wealth of forms and styles worked out on the basis of the method of socialist realism.' He invited literary and artistic critics to apply 'the party line in a more active manner', combining 'exigent standards' with 'tolerance and balance', and thus sought to imply that some kind of dialectics between the conservatives and progressives still existed in the party.

In reality the bureaucratic restoration was now complete, all the levers of power were back in orthodox hands, and

clashes of opinion were so feeble, timid and su
to be unproductive in the face of the threat of
intervention and pressure imposed for 'the good
When Sholokhov addressed the congress, he ag
'ideological enemies and their revisionist aco...
that, 'in order not to dirty a clean room', he did not propose
to mention the internal problems of the Writers' Union, but
he called for 'still greater cohesion under the banners of the
party', and reiterated that Soviet literature 'was the voice that
awakened toiling humanity, summoning the spirits and heart
of every worker to the struggle for progress'. He also said that
'the world process of the development of literature is primarily
determined by its communist ideological charge and party
spirit', and renegades and revisionists must be met with 'our
most effective weapon, the eternal Leninist truth'. Alexander
Chakovsky called for the publication of books 'that will make
a vital contribution to literary Leninism; novels, stories and
poems that will show the popular roots of the great October
revolution'.

In contrast to this tedious reiteration of hackneyed phrases,
in which intransigence and tolerance seemed to have taken
each other's places, while dissenters were in hospital or prison
and large numbers of Jews were being put on trial, there was
a piece of news of great artistic importance; Solzhenitsyn had
finished *August 1914*, had offered it to a number of Soviet
publishing houses, which had declined it, and had therefore
been obliged to give it to the YMCA Press in Paris, which was
to publish the original Russian version in June, this time with
the author's explicit consent.

August 1914 is Solzhenitsyn's biggest and most ambitious
work; he has called it 'the central idea of my life'. It is the
first part, or instalment, of a trilogy that he proposes to continue up to the years of the revolution (the second part is to
be called *October 1916*) and the idea has been in his mind
since 1936. As a young witness of one of the blackest periods
of the Stalin era, it was then that he started thinking about
the causes of his country's tragedy and wondering whether
they should not be sought in the terrible years of the First
World War. Thus he has returned to the idea of a *roman-
fleuve* in which to paint a picture of that period, and he sets
about making a journey backwards in time, to the roots of
the collective and individual dramas that more urgent

of relief and perspective marked by a sense of composition and rhythm that has a classical touch. Revolutionary students who have broken with their families and, in spite of their confused ideas, have volunteered for the army, haughty aristocrats, members of the petty bourgeoisie and progressive or conservative wealthy merchants, technicians and clerks, and the great mass of illiterate soldiers and peasants dragged into war either by obligation or enthusiasm – there is hardly a single piece of the mosaic that is neglected by the historian Solzhenitsyn, who has scrupulously documented himself and says he will be grateful to all who supply him with fresh material for future volumes.

A skilful landscapist, an effective describer of religious ceremonies, popular festivals and military operations, and a portraitist with a powerful hand, he is never indifferent to his content. Whether he is presenting us with historical personalities or anonymous volunteers, he is always expressing his belief that life is an encounter between good and evil, so that it is senseless to mythicise ideologies that announce a golden age. No matter where man is, whatever skies he may live under, there is struggle and error. This does not of course imply absolution for the slothful and the cowardly, or accepting everything and condemning nothing; Solzhenitsyn's admiration always goes out to those who act or build, and pay for their good faith with suffering. Nor does he mourn for the Tsarist era. The picture of Russia that he presents is of a country slowly emerging from the feudal age suddenly thrown backwards by a war desired by an irresponsible General Staff. Military disaster was the spark that set off civil war, a catastrophe that should not for that reason be regarded as the dawn of a cleansing operation. 'Revolution does not rejuvenate a country; it ruins it for a long time.'

We shall have to await succeeding volumes for Solzhenitsyn's real view on the revolutionary period, but in *August 1914* he lays the foundations for an interpretation very different from the triumphalist version of Soviet official historiography. Nevertheless the permanent factor underlying everything remains the effort to discover the truth, independently of all rhetorical schemes and patterns, and to paint the sorrow of an epos that, wherever the action may be, from the Don to Moscow or Prussia, is imbued with profound spirituality, patriotism and religious faith. It was love of country that made Solzhenitsyn's father break off his studies to volunteer for the army, and religion that gave so many fighting soldiers the support of prayer and causes writers with strong Christian feelings such as Levitin-Krasnov to accept an extra four years of imprisonment.

The Solzhenitsyn of *August 1914* was immediately compared to Tolstoy (a meeting with Tolstoy actually occurs in the novel, just as there is an encounter with Stalin in *The First Circle*), and the book is certainly akin to *War and Peace*. It is not, however, sufficient to classify him among the great epigoni. In Solzhenitsyn there is a more modern style of narrative, and the polemics are more direct. The sincerity of his invention and description is not the fruit of the wisdom of a patriarch of the novel; it is a rejection of all dogmatic views of life such as are imposed by the preceptors of the present day, a re-affirmation of the metaphysical necessity of evil. 'Injustice did not begin with us, and it will not end with us.' Those are the concluding words of *August 1914*, and in that painful awareness of the human destiny there lies the primary reason for the hostility to Solzhenitsyn of the Soviet authorities, who are under the constraint of an obligatory optimism.

He continues to encourage this hostility by announcing his wish that the proceeds of the novel should be devoted to the building of a Russian Orthodox church 'anywhere in the west' and, in a postscript to the novel dated May 1970, denouncing the petty prohibition imposed by the Soviet authorities on printing God ('the supreme creative force of the universe') with a capital initial letter while capitals are used for terms such as Provincial Supply Headquarters and KGB. 'I cannot submit to this humiliation,' he says, and he adds that, if the book is published abroad, it is because of a censorship that is 'incomprehensible to any normal man'.

The publication in Paris of *August 1914* shortly preceded the fifth congress of the Writers' Union, held in Moscow from 29th June to 2nd July, 1971. The 500 delegates (the union now had 7,000 members) loyally abided by the instructions to ignore the existence of a Soviet writer named Solzhenitsyn, glossed over all that had happened in their organisation in the past four years, the consequences of Solzhenitsyn's letter to the fourth congress, and the fact that a colleague of theirs had won the Nobel Prize. The time passed quickly, but a dark curtain seemed to divide the past from the present, and even the voices that had been raised in defence of Solzhenitsyn in 1967 were silent.

The new secretary of the union, Georgy Markov, reiterated from the platform Brezhnev's recent declaration that 'the national and popular party spirit is the cornerstone of the fifty years of Soviet literature.' In vain attempts were made abroad 'to detach Soviet literature from the party, to spoil the relations between writers and the party, to destroy the writer's unlimited confidence in the party'. Though there were some who 'outrageously praised elements that had had to answer for their parasitism before the law, the provocative manoeuvres taken abroad would not deceive Soviet writers', who 'decide and will continue to decide for themselves who can be a member of the union and who cannot'.

The whole congress, one of the most obscurantist in the union's history, took place along these bogus lines. Only minor touches of colour were provided by the cautiously critical contributions of writers who are by now experts in the art of navigation, such as Simonov, who tried to issue a warning against the nationalist errors to which unbridled patriotism might lead, or Yevtushenko, who criticised his colleagues' contentment with the quiet life, the myth of Slav culture, bad taste, the now prevalent custom of giving control of literary reviews to old men, the obstacles put by the bureaucrats in the way of the free circulation of information ('an insufficiently informed or badly informed reader,' he said, 'is not a proper member of society'). As if to emphasise that every word spoken at the congress must pass through the party filter before reaching the country, *Literaturnaya Gazeta* changed one of Yevtushenko's sentences. 'We are the children of the Twentieth Congress, which condemned the personality cult,' he said, but the journal made it: 'We are the children of the party's decisions'.

In comparison with all this, it did not amount to very much that during these days Oleg Shestinsky, the secretary of the Leningrad branch of the Writers' Union, pointed out that, if the hero of a novel worked at a lathe for his living, that was no guarantee of anything from the aesthetic point of view. 'Judgment on a book must depend exclusively on its artistic merits,' he announced, with the air of one who has made a startling discovery. We know only too well that the yardstick by which art is measured in the Soviet Union is supplied by the party, and that the only writer who has rebelled against this, Solzhenitsyn, is also the only Soviet writer who has reached the top flight. After all this, even the most scrupulous observers of Soviet affairs ceased following the official literary life of Moscow with their previous curiosity. Up to a few years previously it had been possible to discern which way the struggle for power was going in the Kremlin from the polemics in the journals and certain forms of dissent, but now the situation was reversed; it was sufficient to follow the policy of the government to be able to guess what the repercussions in the field of culture were going to be. What this policy is has been demonstrated *ad nauseam* by the steps taken by the police and the sentences imposed by the courts, which continued to make use of Article 70 (at the end of July Valery Kukuy, a Jew, was given three years at Sverdlovsk 'for the dissemination of anti-Soviet information', and Sakharov sent his usual letter of protest).

Meanwhile the harassment of Solzhenitsyn continues. On 17th August a strange thing happened. He was ill, and asked his friend Alexander Gorlov to go to his *dacha* at Rozhdestvo (twenty-five miles from Moscow) to fetch a spare part for his car. Gorlov found that a number of men had broken into the house and were ransacking wardrobes and drawers. He shouted for help, believing them to be thieves, but they attacked, punched and kicked him, said they were 'on a mission', took him to the nearest police station, and told him that, unless he wanted his career to be ruined, he would be well advised not to say a word to anyone about what had happened. Next day Solzhenitsyn sent an indignant letter of protest to Yuri Andropov, the Minster for State Security, with a carbon copy to Kosygin, asking for 'identification of the thieves, their punishment as criminals, and a detailed explanation of the incident'. He said: 'For many years I have remained silent about the illegal behaviour of your subordinates, but after yesterday's raid I can no longer hold my peace.' In the absence of adequate explanation, he would hold Andropov responsible for the raid. In any case, he added in the copy to Kosygin, 'I hold him personally responsible for what happened.' Solzhenitsyn, so far as is known, received no official excuse or explanation, but on 9th September two policemen, who denied that they belonged to the KGB, explained to Gorlov that there had been a mistake; he had been attacked because he had been taken for a thief. Nor was any reply received to a letter sent to the Soviet Writers' Union on 23rd August by the National Union of Italian Writers pointing out that 'the indefinite and partial information' received from Moscow about Solzhenitsyn 'was likely to lead to further painful friction and reciprocal incomprehension' and asking for the union's version of the facts and an assurance that it would intervene 'to whatever extent may be necessary to assure respect for the rights and liberties, not only of Solzhenitsyn, but of all those writers who find themselves in similar conditions either of ideological conflict or politico-cultural isolation'.

Meanwhile Solzhenitsyn was also having trouble in the west, this time in connection with the translation rights of *August 1914*. Dr Heeb had been in contact with interested western publishers since March 1971, and had told them that Solzhenitsyn would decide to whom the rights should go when the Russian version of the novel was published in Paris. His decision was made known on 18th June, when Dr Heeb signed a contract in Zürich with Luchterhand, of Munich, for the German translation rights and the world rights. Meanwhile another German publisher, Langen-Müller, also of Munich, arranged for another German translation. This was published on 20th October, giving rise to a lawsuit between Luchterhand and Langen-Müller which will provide plenty of grist for the mill of the German courts. Luchterhand, relying on his contract with Dr Heeb, sold the American rights to Farrar, Strauss and Giroux, the British to The Bodley Head, the Italian to Mondadori, the French to Éditions du Seuil, etc. Luchterhand was given additional backing in a letter from Solzhenitsyn to Dr Heeb of 3rd September, confirming that he was the sole representative of his interests in the west. Langen-Müller claims that, as the Soviet Union is not a signatory of the International Copyright Convention, exploitation of the translation rights is open to anyone, and that its edition of the novel, 100,000 copies of which were launched on the German market, cannot therefore be described as 'piratical', any more than could the edition of *One Day in the Life of Ivan Denisovich* published in 1963 by the Herbig Verlag, which now belongs to the Langen-Müller group. 'To us,' Herbert Fleissner of the Langen-Müller group says, 'it is a literary duty to publish *August 1914*', the first copies of which were to be offered to Chancellor Brandt and the Soviet Ambassador in Bonn.

Meanwhile it was announced that a firm named Flegon in London was also about to publish a translation of the novel not authorised by Dr Heeb, and on 18th September Solzhenitsyn again protested in a letter to the journalist Hegge (he sent a still more indignant letter to Dr Heeb on 12th November in which he said: 'How many more times must I repeat before western publishers understand that you and you alone are entitled to handle all the foreign editions of my books?'). In his letter to Hegge he joined in the controversy roused by the Norwegian journalist's book which was reflected in the *New York Times* of 14th and 17th September in criticisms made by that newspaper of Ambassador Jarring and a reply by the Swedish Prime Minister. The latter confirmed that the Stockholm government did not want the Nobel Prize award to be made at the Swedish Embassy in Moscow for fear that the occasion might degenerate into an anti-Soviet political demonstration, but denied that Solzhenitsyn had ever asked that the award should be made there. If a personal request to that effect were made, Hr Palme said, the Swedish government would arrange for the handing over of the diploma and the medal to take place there. 'Is the Nobel Prize stolen property that it must be handed over behind closed doors without witnesses?'

Solzhenitsyn in turn replied on 18th September, and stated his conditions. 'I am ready to receive both medal and diploma at a ceremony in Moscow at any time, provided that it takes place in public and I am permitted to read a reply.' It was up to the Stockholm Academy to reach agreement with the Soviet authorities in the matter. 'I regard it as important that such an agreement be reached this year,' Solzhenitsyn said. However, though the Academy and the Nobel Foundation announced on 7th October that, so far as the Swedish Government is concerned, they were free to organise the ceremony, it did not take place on the lines that Solzhenitsyn suggested. On 13th January, 1972 he announced his agreement with Stockholm on a private ceremony to be held in Moscow in the spring of 1972, and on 28th January Mrs Furtseva indirectly confirmed this by stating that 'no-one has ever prevented Solzhenitsyn from receiving the Nobel Prize, because he has no need of any authorisation'.

Another factor explaining the delay was the impact made by further arrests and protests. On 30th September Sakharov appealed to the Supreme Soviet to grant freedom of emigration and a general amnesty for political prisoners; Nina Bukovskaya appealed that her son should not be declared insane; on 6th October the violinist Yehudi Menuhin made a speech at the International Music Congress in Moscow in which he referred to the 'force, depth and the significance of poetical expression' of artists such as Solzhenitsyn and Rostropovich (this was not reported by the Tass agency); and on 13th October police raided the house of Roy Medvedev and confiscated his manuscripts. In November a plenary meeting of the party central committee decided to intensify the ideological struggle in the party and the country to educate Soviet citizens 'in the spirit of Marxism-Leninism and proletarian internationalism'. This was a call for still greater efficiency on the part of the controllers and propagandists and, as we shall see, it was quickly taken up; in a way it can be said to have been justified by the small signs of autonomy in the juridical and bureaucratic apparatus that partly explains the elbowroom left to the *samizdat* and the spokesman of dissent.

The alarm felt by those Soviet citizens who are sensitive to the problem of individual liberty is implicit in Valery Chalidze's report of 10th December to the committee for human rights. This acknowledged that there had been an improvement in Soviet judicial practice since 1953, as the necessity of certain juridical guarantees was now admitted, but it complained that, though the masses were now assured of numerous economic and social rights, these did not include those relating to liberty of the person and liberty of culture. The still existing difficulties in the exchange of information and the circulation of books in libraries, the suppression of academic freedom in regard to problems that were assumed to have ideological aspects, the press censorship, the bans on leaving the country or choosing one's place of residence, the endless rules and regulations that were known only to the bureaucracy and were mistaken for laws, the lack of publicity for certain judicial proceedings, still provided too wide a field for arbitrary action by the state. The report concluded by saying that discussion of human rights should be a normal Soviet custom. Meanwhile it called for an amnesty for Amalrik, who was ill with meningitis. This was not granted. On the other hand, Larisa Bogoras Daniel was prematurely released in the middle of December.

On 18th December the death of Tvardovsky seemed to mark the end of an era. Solzhenitsyn for once appeared in public and attended the funeral in the Novodievechi cemetery of the man to whom he owed so much (he also took the opportunity of laying a rose on Khrushchev's grave). At the end of December a tribute to the former editor of *Novy Mir* was circulated, characterised by the touches of indignation and irony that are usual with him when he takes his enemies to task. 'There are various ways of killing a writer,' he said. 'That chosen for Tvardovsky was to deprive him of his favourite child, the journal for which he suffered so much.' He said of the 'fat and unhealthy' bureaucrats of the Writers' Union that, after persecuting Tvardovsky while he was alive, they mounted a guard of honour for him when he was dead. 'Since Pushkin that has always happened. . . . Even after his death the poet was an instrument in the hands of his enemies. Gathered in a close group around his catafalque, they said to themselves. "Now we have buried him", and thought they had won. . . . Idiots! When youth makes its voice heard, you will regret no longer having this patient critic, who was able to encourage all who would listen to him. Then you will want to dig up the earth with your bare hands to restore life to Tvardovsky. But it will be too late.'

It was not too late for everyone. At the end of the year a piece of news went round Moscow that showed that decent Soviet writers are capable of crises of conscience; it was the sort of thing that may persuade tomorrow's historians to refrain from wholesale condemnations. The news was of two expulsions from the Writers' Union, of Alexander Galich, the author of protest songs and a member of Sakharov's committee, and of Evgeny Markin, one of the five men who at Ryazan on 4th November, 1969, after putting up some feeble resistance, fell in with the majority and voted for Solzhenitsyn's expulsion. He promptly repented, and next day went to see a friend. 'Spit in my face,' he said, 'that is all I deserve. I did it because they promised to give me a bigger flat.' Two years later *Novy Mir* published two poems by him (and it is significant that they were accepted, just as it would be significant if that journal at last published Bek's novel, of which there is talk again). Between the lines of the two poems it was not difficult to discern remorse for his cowardice at Ryazan. Was it only for this that he was expelled from the

Writers' Union? If that was the case, this perverse act would seem to symbolise a year in which the great mass of Soviet intellectuals, so far from advancing along the road to liberation from fear, was subjected to fresh humiliations.

That 1972 had no consoling prospects to offer was shown by Bukovsky's fresh conviction on 5th January. His sanity was admitted, but the former editor of *Phoenix* was deprived of his liberty for twelve years (two in prison, five in a labour camp, five in banishment), a penalty inflicted at the end of a trial that took place in the absence of foreign journalists or witnesses for the defence. Bukovsky said: 'It is desired to intimidate all those who seek to tell the world the truth about the crimes of certain people. These gentry do not want dirty linen washed in public, so that they may go on presenting themselves to the world as irreproachable defenders of the oppressed. ... Our society is still sick, because of the fear that has come down to us from the Stalin era. But the process of awakening the conscience of public opinion has already begun and can no longer be stopped. Public opinion has already awoken to the fact that the real guilty persons are not those who wash dirty linen in public, but those who dirtied it.' In conclusion he appealed to Article 125 of the constitution. 'No matter how long I remain in prison, I shall never abandon my ideas, and I shall continue to express them to all those willing to listen.' His conviction was confirmed on appeal on 22nd February in spite of a letter to *The Times* signed by Harold Pinter, Arthur Koestler, Stephen Spender and Iris Murdoch. The speech he made in his defence is an important document, expressing the courage of an intellectual who insisted on acknowledgment of his sanity, and hence his sense of responsibility, rather than give any encouragement to suspicions about the significance of his politico-cultural stand. Cases such as his, though they are sporadic, have an echo in consciences that have not gone to sleep.

Comments that were not entirely favourable, though they were made surreptitiously, were provoked by statements such as that in *Literaturnaya Gazeta* on 12th January, when it mentioned *August 1914* for the first time, if only to observe that the publication of the novel in the west, after it had been sent there by the author together with the publication rights and detailed instructions about royalties, had turned out to be 'very useful to anti-Soviet elements of every type'.

Mentioning the novel was, of course, merely an excuse for fresh slurs on the author. *Literaturnaya Gazeta*'s chief concern was to quote an article in the German weekly *Stern* by Dieter Stener, who claimed to have interviewed in a village in the Caucasus an aged aunt of Solzhenitsyn's named Irene. She was said to have made a number of adverse remarks about his behaviour towards his relatives and his second wife. What chiefly interested *Literaturnaya Gazeta*, however, was the social origin of Solzhenitsyn's family, and the opportunity of being able to point to him as a descendant of enemies of the people. It therefore repeated with great satisfaction the information allegedly gathered by Stener to the effect that Solzhenitsyn's grandfather, Semion Isayevich, at the beginning of the century had owned more than 5,000 acres of land and 20,000 head of cattle in the village of Sablya; that his uncle had owned a Rolls-Royce; and that his cousin Xenia Vassilievna was now a war widow with a son on her hands, working in a kolkhoz, and that the writer neglected her. Thus Solzhenitsyn was exposed as the descendant of a feudal family, and his inhuman behaviour towards his less fortunate relatives served to corroborate these repulsive origins.

On 13th January Solzhenitsyn in a letter circulated in Moscow denied that his novel served any anti-Soviet purposes (his object being merely to describe the tragic situation out of which the revolution had developed). He said that the situation of his family in the old days had been 'comfortable' but not 'very wealthy', and he cast doubt on the genuineness of the interview with his aunt Irene, who lived in an area that was closed to foreigners. As a reporter of the Novosti agency had gone to see her in the previous August and presented himself to her as a Leningrad friend and an admirer of his work, Solzhenitsyn suggested that someone had gathered slanderous material in order to harm him and had offered it to *Stern*. What is the truth of the matter? This is not the first 'mystery' we have met in Solzhenitsyn's life, and it probably will not be the last.

For its part, *Pravda* sticks to its old refrain, and the police scrupulously carry out their orders. The dissidents and oppositional minorities, *Pravda* said on 13th January, were harmful to the security of the system; it was on them that the strategists of anti-communism relied. 'The perfection of socialism desired by ideologically unstable intellectuals, self-isolated from the people, would in practice result in a silent restoration of capitalism,' the newspaper said, and next day agents of the KGB raided the houses of suspected persons in Moscow (where, among other things, they confiscated documents about the Stalin camps gathered by Pyotr Yakir), Leningrad and Kiev, where they searched the house of Nekrasov. The Writers' Union of course refrained from protesting. Instead the secretariat, which met from 27th to 29th January, adopted as its own the condemnation of critics 'who indulge in subjectivism and aesthetic concessions irreconcilable with socialist reality' issued several days previously by the central committee, and expressed its gratification at this 'further evidence of the great attention paid to literature by the party'.

Against this background, news of a tour of the United States by Yevtushenko or of Natalya Gorbanevskaya's release could hardly be sufficient to lend serenity to a landscape that was sinister and funereal in spite of occasional and often well orchestrated gleams of light. Excuses for optimism were growing fewer and farther between, and the meeting between Nixon and Mao, with the stiffening of the Soviet position that it implied, did nothing to encourage it.

CHAPTER TWELVE

Seen through the Solzhenitsyn filter, the picture of the Soviet intelligentsia in the seventies presents the observer with two inter-related phenomena. The first is the hobbling of its critical maturation by a policy of repression dictated by the two spectres that haunted Stalin: military encirclement and ideological revisionism. (Less than ten years after Stalin's body was removed from Lenin's tomb his bust reappeared in Red Square; the treaty of friendship with Federal Germany and the deferment of the confrontation with China fit perfectly into the Stalinist tradition, the object being to secure the frontiers to enable efforts to be concentrated on the consolidation of orthodoxy within, which is regarded as the *sine qua non* of supervised development.)

The second is the extent and potential consolidation of a very diffuse opposition that, trusting in the people's capacity for independent judgement, sees in the revived use of those spectres, and in the institutionalisation of a state of emergency, mere excuses to perpetuate the tyranny of an authoritarian system. It regards these things as insuperable obstacles to a Soviet take-off, not only to levels of economic progress, moral consciousness and cultural productivity worthy of the country's political weight and its rôle as a great power but, above all, to the standards of humanity postulated by (a) respect for individual liberty and (b) Leninist theory. Dispute, whether open or subterranean, about Stalin's interpretation of Leninism and the police tactics of keeping minority groups divided without wiping them out completely (every totalitarian régime cultivates its rebels as a picturesque blot that breaks the monotony of the landscape) may be marked by alternating phases of increased severity and relative leniency towards the dissident intelligentsia, but cannot overcome the limitations imposed by the surprise actions taken every so often by the guardians of order.

In the second half of 1970 it seemed that the confirmation in power of the team of Brezhnev, Kosygin and Podgorny had re-established an equilibrium between the leading groups that left some freedom for manoeuvre for the elements that navigate in the opposing currents of the Kremlin and the Politburo and sometimes manage to secure some fragments of liberty for themselves and their friends. But at the end of the year *Pravda*, anticipating the basic theme of the Twenty-Fourth Congress, announced that the struggle against revisionists of right and left must be remorselessly continued, in order not to leave 'even a shadow of liberalism when the clarity of ideological positions is at stake'. Accelerations alternating with applications of the brake will remain inherent in the system, and there is no realistic hope of this rhythm being broken until the popular consciousness, led by a bold generation or as a result of unforeseeable outside intervention, becomes aware that it is manipulated by a bureaucratic apparatus that sacrifices the country's dignity and civilised development to the sectional interests of the 'new class' and states in concrete terms the necessity of an alternative to the regressive processes at work in the fields of doctrine and strategy. For this to happen much time and indomitable examples will be needed. To that distant goal Solzhenitsyn's personality and work are directed, with a consistency and pride that shorten the road in the minds of the just. But how long will his travelling companions be able to keep up the pace? Reasons for misgivings are not lacking.

In an age that everywhere offers examples of anti-authoritarian revolt, the Soviet intelligentsia, in relation to the size of a country of more than two hundred million inhabitants, does not represent soil as fertile as might be expected for dissent that is not content with passive resistance but actively claims the right of the individual to take part in the working out of a new system of social values. The severity of the Soviet courts, which put defamation or slander of the state on the same level as hooliganism, and thus put the undisciplined artist on the same level as the common criminal, makes the west tend to over-estimate the political significance of certain anti-conformist writers. It is not sufficiently appreciated that in the Soviet system literature is a collectively-owned product, and that its producers, who have grown up at the expense of the state and are well paid if they remain obedient to the party-made laws, risk at least unemployment and a charge of parasitism if they try to adulterate the product with additives harmful to the public health, which is what pessimism and irreverence towards structures and hierarchies which have the blessing of popular consent are judged to be.

The authorities' detestation of Solzhenitsyn derives from the mistrust that has always been felt of intellectuals suspected of trying to sabotage the creation of the new man by their absurd claim to the right to say whatever they wish. The most inflexible dogmatists are often honest in intention. Their revered masters taught them that goodness and beauty are identical, and they believe that the happiness of the masses and the triumph of the arts are measured by the index of industrial production. In the light of a doctrine that identifies economic prosperity with the peace of the human spirit, the writer who sows doubts or makes criticisms without putting forward acceptable alternatives is essentially a disturbing element in the country's development; he is playing the enemy's game, and is therefore an enemy of the people.

The abyss that separates the Soviet Union from the west, even from the socialist west, is represented by the impact made on moral values by a socio-economic doctrine based on materialism. The Soviet writer, within the limits in which he is allowed to make generalisations in the field of creative literature, sincerely believes in the necessity of disciplining his inspiration in order to produce a widely saleable product that meets the educational and recreational needs of the masses, increases their pleasure in life, and contributes to national pride. He does not ask himself whether the liberty of artistic creation, making possible deeper exploration of the great themes of life, might contribute more to moral and social progress than a merely consolatory mission; he was told many years ago of the dangers of plunging into deep waters that it is dangerous to stir, and since then he has contented himself with the surface of things, their decorative values, unaware that he is thus denying the very function of literature, the questioning of reality and history in the name of human truth.

Reiteration for half a century that culture, being the source of possible ideological contamination, must be supervised and protected, has been passed on from one generation of Soviet writers to the next without leading to any great dramas of conscience. The number of exiles is insignificant. The explanation is not only the circumstance that emigration to the west offers no real solution of the difficulties of those who wish to fill the spiritual void with art (the western equivalent of the alienation of Soviet man is an opposite kind of alienation that is just as devastating to the artist not satisfied with serving the market); it lies in the belief of the Russian intellectual that the exercise of his calling is not exportable, being tied to a socio-political context that is atypical with regard to the rest of the world. The belief that the true producer of culture is the people has persuaded the Soviet artist to accept a subordinate rôle, and often to aspire to it.

To those who have grown up in the liberal democratic tradition, the result is disconcerting; it is the lack of awareness, on the part of the Soviet intellectual base, of the imperfect integration of new social values with the traditional moral values that are still firmly anchored in their minds, however much they may declare them to be of bourgeois origin; in other words, their failure to appreciate at the level of artistic expression the price paid by Soviet man for pursuing the myth of a new order in which evil and pain have been eliminated. Opportunities of acquiring awareness and adjusting their sights accordingly have not been lacking in the past thirty years; the so-called thaw seemed in fact to set in train a process of reassessment which, if it had been consistently pursued, might well have strengthened the Soviet Union, saving it from being outflanked on the left, and spread in the world an idea of culture in which the debate on the relationship between art and the public might have received some fruitful stimulus from the Soviet experience (to the extent, that is, that destalinisation revealed its limitations). Instead, the thaw was stopped, and the way this happened confirmed that the intelligentsia, having shared passively rather than actively both in the flowering and the decline of new hopes, was unqualified to be the testing ground of the country's cultural and moral maturation. The Soviet writer, caught up in the conflict between reasons of state and an idea of liberty that seemed to be a carrier of the germs of anarchism and Trotskyism (though in reality the only aim was observance of the law enshrined in the Soviet constitution) took a few timid steps out of doors, but in most cases quickly dashed for shelter again, being incapable of finding models of dissident behaviour in the western intellectual left wing, which was reshuffling all the cards in the Marxist-Leninist pack in accordance with Lukács's saying that the way to fight revisionism was to get rid of dogmatism.

Some were shocked at the spirit of resignation with which

the intelligentsia, concealing its timidity behind a proud sense of security, refused to adopt the role of director of conscience at a time when the man in the street, the non-party member, was trying to understand what had happened in Russia between Stalin's death and Khrushchev's fall. All things considered, however, in the light of the foundations laid in the years of blood and iron, it could hardly have been otherwise; all the dialectical qualities of the Soviet writer, to which he should have had recourse in order to explain this crucial moment in history to himself, had been used up in the debate on socialist realism. Well protected by his privileged position, isolated from the developments in social life, he had no answer to the questions raised by the battle over the personality cult. Only Solzhenitsyn had the strength to offer an interpretation and a way of salvation.

If the subjects discussed at the first writer's congress in 1934 are compared with the doctrine preached nearly forty years later in the tedious articles of *Literaturnaya Gazeta*, it is astonishing and dismaying to note the monotonous insistence in stereotyped terminology on exactly the same themes, re-masticated by the grandsons of Zhdanov without any serious attempt to adapt them to a social, economic and spiritual reality in which vast changes have taken place. References to power stations on the Dniepr and steelworks in the Urals have given way to the sputnik and the Lunakhod, but no-one points out that, bearing in mind the sacred principle of interpreting the present on the basis of the future, the question that now arises is how the future postulated in 1934 is being realised today, and hence whether it may not be necessary to subject the interpretation of the present to modifications. Zhdanov, let us recall, said that the truth and historical concreteness of artistic representation must be accompanied by the ideological transformation and education of the workers in the spirit of socialism.

The room for manoeuvre offered by this principle has not been exploited; Soviet writers, far from reflecting the vital process at work in the social context during all these years, have continued to behave like dusty engineers of musty minds. The country has passed them by, and the party has had no serious difficulty in using their subservient organisation as a pawn in the struggle for power. In view of the fact that the constitution of the Writers' Union stated from the outset that writers' participation in the construction of socialism must take the form of 'careful and deep' study of concrete reality, the quality of the output is the more disappointing.

If we now refer once more to what we said at the beginning of the book about the party's aims in setting up the Writers' Union, and the apotheosis of the utilitarian theory of art in the Stalin era, we can see the havoc wrought by an intelligentsia that lacks independence and the spirit of initiative and believes it deserves the gratitude of the state for carrying out its daily task of edification. Even while Stalin was the absolute master of the country, to say nothing of after his death, the writer could to some extent have contributed to a maturation of taste and given his public some knowledge of the drama of the realisation, or attempted realisation, of the Soviet ideal. Sometimes the way to the obligatory smile was necessarily by way of tears; and there were some who achieved notable results in trying to reproduce an exciting and stormy reality. But they were exceptions. Whatever mitigating circumstances can be pleaded, the majority of writers and poets, those who give colour and personality to a literary period, cannot be absolved of responsibility for hampering the development of a socialist idea that, even within the limits of a utilitarian theory of art, would have had very effective support in them, at any rate to the extent that Soviet man might have been spared the duty of blessing his own sufferings.

All this causes one to follow the dissident movement with a degree of apprehension. Its minute dimensions, we repeat, constitute a warning against over-estimation of its detonatory potential (which the relative freedom of movement left it by the KGB tends to confirm). But in a context in which the intelligentsia have always played an educational role it is impossible to ignore the significance of a trend in which men of letters and scientists stand side by side. Our misgivings derive from the suspicion that this movement, led by ambitious young men and disillusioned older men, is forming at the level of the superstructures, remaining essentially alien from the dialectic between the various social strata, and that its primary though unconscious motive may therefore be the struggle of a new caste, theoretically to gain more opportunity for the voice of the base to be heard, but in reality to assume the heritage of a highly politicised generation and pass it on to a more efficient generation of sociologists and technocrats. In that event the change would be fruitful only in appearance. The crude bureaucrat of the repressive apparatus, whose intellectual void is nevertheless in many cases filled with the ideal tension surviving from the revolutionary impetus, would in the long run be replaced by a manipulator of the cultural industry, who would probably rationalise criticism of the system to the point of emptying dissent of the whole of its subversive charge.

Nevertheless no criticism of its intentions can diminish the significance of a phenomenon that threatens to break up the enforced idyll between politics and culture and is taking shape among a group of people who are slowly acquiring the courage publicly to dispute the principle of authority and build up throughout the country a secret network of solidarity with the persecuted. Dissent, whether rooted in mysticism or the Enlightenment movement, expresses a combativeness at the personal level that is unusual in the relations between the base and the hierarchy; we have seen evidence of this in the large number of letters and public statements that form the foundations of the world of the Soviet new intellectual. If the atmosphere that prevailed at the time of the Sinyavsky-Daniel and Ginzburg trials is compared with the much milder atmosphere that followed the broadside of threats directed at Solzhenitsyn when he was awarded the Nobel Prize, one cannot help noting a diminution of tension, though that is partly a consequence of the leaders of dissent being in prison or mental hospital.

A certain stagnation in the field of literary dissent has been compensated for by its spread to much wider fields, the absorption of all the tedious controversies about the relationship between style and content, tradition and experimentalism, mass culture and experimental literature, into the big stream of the movement for civil rights. We are not referring only to Sakharov's movement, but to the vigour with which a growing number of ordinary people, without being members of organised groups, appeal for respect for the law, and in particular for a liberal democratic interpretation of the Penal Code, for greater liberty of movement inside the country, the absolute right to emigrate, and fewer administrative controls. These demands puncture the ancient myth according to which all the country's tensions reach equilibrium in the party, and for the time being they absorb the sectional claims of men of letters and scientists into a vision of reforms that will guarantee the

rights of the individual. The object is to replace th
inherited from the Tsars and the heirs of Stalin
organism based on a genuine socialist spirit
opposed to autocracy.

The extent to which the protest movement
demands made by the Russian liberals from the beginning of
the nineteenth century onwards is familiar. But vigorous rejection of the reign of dogmatism, seeing the latter as a stupid
obstacle in the path of continual ideological renewal, is a
product of new times, of a crisis in the growth of international
communism. When *Pravda* announces yet another campaign
against the revisionists of right and left, the Soviet dissident
knows that new turns of the screw are on the way, because
at the centre dogma prevails, and only those with the levers
of power in their hands are able to say what is required in
order not to depart from it. The apparatus, forced to accen-
tuate the régime's authoritarian characteristics, detaches itself
from the base, grows atrophied, becomes the party's grave-
digger.

In the prospect opened up by a writer such as Solzhenitsyn,
who cannot dissociate economic and social progress from the
exercise of the critical spirit and respect for the individual,
lucid artistic and civil expression is given to the urgent task of
restoring to all men the hope of being able to participate, each
in the light of his own experience, in the construction of a
socialism remodelled by the knowledge that the cementing
factor is the individual's sense of responsibility towards life
rather than to ideas. When Solzhenitsyn claims the right to
discover the historical reasons for the sufferings of the Russian
people, he is not moving towards an anti-communist position;
he is simply restoring currency to a coinage that was arbitrarily
removed from circulation but remained stored up in men's
minds and in the back-rooms behind the official culture, buried
under piles of paper ideologies. Looking at the country's
history, laying bare the roots of the evil, identifying the factors
that made its growth different though not less troubled than
that of other countries, means restarting the motor of redemption that first began to work with the dawn of socialism and
examining it in the light of the Christian hope.

Solzhenitsyn does not put forward alternatives to the Soviet
system, but to its administration. He knows that an absolutist
system cannot be liberally administered, but he does not for

reason abandon the ultimate ideal of a movement of generation. Marked by his experiences of labour camps and excommunication, the whole of his talent is devoted to the service of the Russian people (a Solzhenitsyn in exile is unthinkable) and of the literature of his country, in order to awaken it from its torpor and stimulate the qualities on which the thaw opened a ray of light.

Ten years have not yet passed since the publication of *One Day in the Life of Ivan Denisovich*, but that short period has nevertheless yielded fruit. Humanity, assessing the tragedy of a part of itself with the aid of Solzhenitsyn's art, has grown. The wish for knowledge has taken the place of complaint. And in Russia, though confusedly, a form of resistance is crystallising out that prevents tyranny from camouflaging itself as a prophylactic. We are not of course attributing to Solzhenitsyn all the credit for the ferment at work among the Soviet intelligentsia. But it cannot be denied that it is only thanks to him that the most sensitive and intelligent of those involved have come to appreciate the true place of culture in society and have seen the basis on which a spontaneous relationship between author and public is realisable in the Soviet Union. The difficult conditions in which this relationship is developing feed the intolerance of the base of the repressive methods of the hierarchy and justify Solzhenitsyn's struggle to free men from the cancer of indifference, fatalism and cowardice.

The Soviet Union, now on the threshold of the consumer society, threatens to compete with the west in the most unbridled hedonism; the process of de-ideologisation has gone a long way, and there is a danger that the best antidote to dogmatism may seem to be a generalised and alienating mistrust. Thus Solzhenitsyn is moving along a razor's edge. On one side is the abyss of total scepticism (how many of his Soviet readers, comparing his moral standards with the malevolent obtuseness of those who should abide by them, may not give in to it?); on the other is the rugged landscape of a life of daily struggle, involving personal risk and a multitude of scars. The optimists are right in believing that Solzhenitsyn's work, escaping from the abysss, will continue to act as the leaven for a virile and austere vision of human life. Soviet man, brought up in the worship of an ideal, no matter that it has been largely betrayed, at bottom preserves a moral tension, an honesty of feeling, a visionary *élan*, that are likely to make him put up a stronger fight against resignation than in the past.

Gobetti said that 'the Russians have more than other people a shining audacity to make new beginnings'. They may detest the verbal edifices that masquerade as ideologies, but they believe in the life of the heart. They mistrust rational mechanisms, because they have burned their fingers on them, but they have a rich and vibrant imagination. The melancholy vein that runs through their nature does not diminish their keen interest in tomorrow. Not only Solzhenitsyn's work, but his personal example also, his combination of contemptuous pride and paternal understanding, warm their spirit and give them hope. He responds to the radical changes taking place in social life and in the individual by presenting to the consciousness of his readers at home and abroad a whole cluster of questions that cannot be avoided, because they are the key questions of the age: whether man, if he is to keep the forces of nature and the new technologies under control, must not first and foremost preserve a sense of justice; whether civilisation is not to be measured by the respect it shows for the liberty of each and every individual; whether the inspiration of social life must not be a spirit of harmony between all created things.

It is no chance that in the limited living-space to which Solzhenitsyn is now restricted there is an open piano with the études of Liszt on the stand, that he enjoys the close friendship of Rostropovich, and that there is a symphonic touch about all his works. Once more music, literature and mathematics show their kinship as the vehicle for an ideal that links the ancient pain of Russia with the cares of the masses as they approach the year 2000, countering revulsion from life with an art built to man's measure as a fragment of eternity.

INDEX

Three Superb Titles by Alexander Solzhenitsyn from Sphere

ONE DAY IN THE LIFE OF IVAN DENISOVICH   30p
WE NEVER MAKE MISTAKES   30p
FOR THE GOOD OF THE CAUSE   30p

The world famous *One Day in the Life of Ivan Denisovich* is the devastating story of twenty-four hours inside a Stalinist prison camp in Siberia. Based on his own experiences, this masterpiece has become a classic indictment of Stalinist brutality.

Two novels make up *We Never Make Mistakes* – two stories of the terror of the secret police and the relentless breakdown of human dignity caused by the dreaded system. This book contains an introduction and glossary by Paul Blackstock, the translator.

How ordinary people fall victim to ambitious and ruthless bureaucrats is the theme of *For the Good of the Cause* – a novel that created much trouble for Solzhenitsyn with the Soviet authorities and marked him for future harassment.

Inside The Third Reich

ALBERT SPEER

Here is the definitive account of Nazi Germany by Hitler's Armaments Minister. By far the most revealing and interesting book to come from the Nazi side about World War Two, Speer's apologia gives new insight into the most significant and dramatic episode in twentieth century history – the rise and fall of Nazi Germany.

75p   Illustrated

A Selection of Warfare Titles from Sphere

THE DOUBLE CROSS SYSTEM IN THE WAR 1939–1945
John Masterman   35p
A thrilling and fascinating study of wartime intelligence.

PATHFINDER   Air Vice-Marshal D. C. T. Bennett   35p
The story of the famous elite air crews of World War Two.

THE MAKING OF ISRAEL'S ARMY   Yigal Allon   40p
A superb history of one of the world's most highly-rated
fighting forces.

BORODINO   Christopher Duffy   60p
An exciting account of the famous battle between the
Russian army and the forces of Napoleon. In enlarged
format; illustrated.

HITLER'S LAST DAYS   Gerhard Boldt   35p
The amazing story of the last days of the Third Reich by a
man who lived in the famous Berlin bunker at Hitler's H.Q.

HITLER AS MILITARY COMMANDER   John Strawson   60p
WELLINGTON AS MILITARY COMMANDER
Michael Glover   75p
Two highly praised books assessing the military strategy
of the two famous leaders – in enlarged paperback format.

HOSTAGES AT COLDITZ
Giles Romilly and Michael Alexander   35p
Two former inmates of Colditz have written the classic
story of this notorious prisoner-of-war camp.

A Selection of General Fiction from Sphere

A Selection of Gift Packs from Sphere

The Golden Sovereigns   £2.40
A marvellous series of historical romances. Six books that
cover the lives and reigns of England's monarchs from
Edward IV (1442–1483) to Elizabeth 1 (1533–1603)

The Six Wives of Henry VIII   £1.80
Six historical novels by accomplished writers in this field,
each one about one of Henry VIII's wives

Upstairs Downstairs   £1.20
Four novels based on the characters of the enormously
popular television series which give a fascinating insight into
life above and below stairs

Farmhouse Cooking   £2
Two books full of English country cooking recipes. This
superb collection will enable all lovers of good food to redis-
cover the real, traditional culinary arts

Opera and Concert Guides   £1.80
Two recommended reference books that give a complete
guide to more than one thousand operas and the entire field
of orchestral and choral music

The Connoisseurs Concise Encyclopaedia of Antiques £1.50
Two handsome volumes which survey more than 500 years
of skilled craftsmanship

All Sphere Books are available at your bookshop or
newsagent, or can be ordered from the following address:

Sphere Books, Cash Sales Department,
P.O. Box 11, Falmouth, Cornwall.

Please send cheque or postal order (no currency), and allow
7p per copy to cover the cost of postage and packing
in U.K. or overseas.